# Ethnic Diversity, National Unity

"This timely text critically probes ethnic diversity and national unity in Ethiopia, one of Africa's oldest nation-states, by critically analyzing political crises, explores the idea of unity in diversity, and invites readers to think about the self and the other in a common national space in light of a moral vision that promotes coexistence. This interdisciplinary text draws insights from history, law, ethics, scriptural studies, moral and political theology. I highly recommend this because it offers excellent perspectives on the quest for harmony."

—**Elias Kifon Bongmba**, Rice University

"Recent global political events have once again highlighted the importance of critical academic studies at the intersections of ethnicity and nationhood. This volume of essays is a very timely and important contribution to the field. It presents an important series of interdisciplinary, and transdisciplinary, reflections on the moral pedagogies of belonging and identity among Ethiopians. Each of the texts left me with new insights, answers to important questions, and a deeper understanding."

—**Dion A. Forster**, University of Stellenbosch

"Ethiopia has always been able to construct a story that it could tell to the outside world. However, internally negotiating a story that does justice to its ethnic and religious plurality remained its Achilles' heel. Even when political architecture was not strong enough, it was the moral arc that held the nation together. That, however, is now being eroded by the social media-driven grievances and a sharp rise of ethno-nationalist politics. As a result, the discursive space has significantly shrank and Ethiopia's long-held national unity has been increasingly threatened. Therefore, sober and skilful reflections on the moral foundations of living in a shared space vis-à-vis ethnic plurality was long overdue. Theodros A. Teklu's *Ethnic Diversity, National Unity* is a stunning achievement not only in addressing this very timely issue in Ethiopia, but also in bringing together young and bright Ethiopian scholars into the conversation."

—**Mohammed Girma**, author of *Understanding Religion and Social Change in Ethiopia*

"This is a thoughtful and fascinating book which addresses a question academically relevant as well as foremost in the minds of many Ethiopians today: how to reconcile the facts and feelings of ethnic diversity and its discursive representations with sources of moral thinking and action in shared spaces. . . . The various contributions break new ground and suggest that religious thinking can provide rich and unifying elements for sociopolitical discourse not only geared towards toleration but also towards acceptance of the 'Other' in an overarching framework of symbiosis and understanding that the country needs. . . . When ethnicity or, in some cases, religion are used for developing antagonism or 'enemy images,' that is a *choice*; it is never a necessity or destiny. In this vein, the book offers very interesting reflections and case studies that will interest a broad readership, with crucial elements for developing a new ethical discourse of interaction, acceptance, and unity in diversity, and with the underlying view that humans are all one under the eye of the eternal and can work to realize that vision."

—**Jon Abbink**, Leiden University

"*Ethnic Diversity, National Unity* is a rare jewel of masterful insights on ethnopolitical cohesion for the Ethiopian context and elsewhere. The contributors creatively handle the various aspects of ethnicity, politics, and identity issues that have often been causes of hostility, prejudice, and rivalry among the various ethnic communities not only in Ethiopia but also throughout the world. The writers see the antidote of ethnopolitical violence in morality, religion, and justice. Thus, this book is relevant beyond Ethiopia. I, therefore, recommend it to those keen on understanding the aforesaid issues and finding a solution to them."

—**David Tarus**, Association for Christian Theological Education in Africa

# Ethnic Diversity, National Unity

Moral Pedagogies of Togetherness for Ethiopians

EDITED BY
Theodros A. Teklu

WIPF & STOCK · Eugene, Oregon

ETHNIC DIVERSITY, NATIONAL UNITY
Moral Pedagogies of Togetherness for Ethiopians

Copyright © 2021 Wipf and Stock Publisher. All rights reserved. Except for brief quotations in critical publications or reviews, no part of this book may be reproduced in any manner without prior written permission from the publisher. Write: Permissions, Wipf and Stock Publishers, 199 W. 8th Ave., Suite 3, Eugene, OR 97401.

Wipf & Stock
An Imprint of Wipf and Stock Publishers
199 W. 8th Ave., Suite 3
Eugene, OR 97401

www.wipfandstock.com

PAPERBACK ISBN: 978-1-7252-8635-1
HARDCOVER ISBN: 978-1-7252-8634-4
EBOOK ISBN: 978-1-7252-8636-8

Scripture quotations are from the New Revised Standard Version Bible, copyright © 1989 the Division of Christian Education of the National Council of the Churches of Christ in the United States of America. Used by permission. All rights reserved.

Scripture quotations marked NASB are from New American Standard Bible®, Copyright © 1960, 1971, 1977, 1995, 2020 by The Lockman Foundation. All rights reserved.

01/27/21

# Contents

Introduction | 1
—Theodros A. Teklu

## Part I—Interpreting the Signs of the Times

1 Politics as the Hatred of the Ethnic Other | 9
—Theodros A. Teklu

## Part II—Ethno-Political Crisis and Resolutions: Past and Present

2 Reflections on Conundrums and Prospects of Writing Ethiopian History | 31
—Afework Hailu

3 Ethnic Diversity and Legal Responsibility in Ethiopia | 60
—Fasil Nahum

4 "Deeply Mediatized" and "Deeply Ethnicized" Politics in Ethiopia (2014–19): Signposts toward Moral Articulation for a Digital Space | 72
—Sara Abdella Kedir

## Part III—Unity and Diversity: Moral Visions of Togetherness

5 Identity in the Light of Unity-in-Diversity | 101
—Daniel Assefa Kassaye (Abba)

6 "Ethnic" and "Christian" Identity: Ethiopian Reflections from the Epistle to the Galatians | 113
—Nebeyou Alemu

## Part IV: Self and Other: Moral Visions of Togetherness

7 The "Ethnic Other" as the "Neighbour": A *Perichoretic* Imagination of Moral Responsibility | 137
—Youdit Tariku Feyessa

8 After Self Assertion: On a *Paraclesis* of a Political Theology of *Kenosis* | 157
—Samson Tadelle Demo

9 The Rite of "Footwashing" at *Abinet* Schools and Its Ethics of Humility | 182
—Setargew Kenaw

10 The Christian Moral Responsibility of Embracing the Ethnic Other | 201
—Nishan Cheru Degaga

List of Contributors | 221

# Introduction

———— Theodros A. Teklu ————

Embarking on any study related to the "nation" places one at the crossroads of various theoretical routes leading to divergent interpretations of this entity that Tom Nairn calls "the modern Janus."[1] No less ambivalent is the subject of "ethnicity" with a "chameleon-like capacity,"[2] as Katsuyoshi Fukui and John Markakis have rightly described it. Issues of nationality and ethnicity are contested both theoretically and practically, posing serious moral–religious challenges. Hence, the title of the first volume of the Centre for Christianity and Society (CCS):[3] *Ethnic Diversity, National Unity: Moral Pedagogies of Togetherness for Ethiopians*. Admittedly, the equilibrium between "ethnic diversity" and "national unity" is rarely mere fact on the ground, and never a conclusive achievement. Instead, it is a political, legal, social, and moral project that demands considerable effort to realize.

Although asserting one's ethnic identity is not morally wrong, the manner in which one ethnic group construes or relates to the ethnic other(s) obliterates the bond of togetherness and creates the insecurity of life. Ethiopia, which is home to ethno-linguistically diverse groups, exhibits a proclivity to ethnic-based hostilities and conflicts. As a result of such hostilities, Ethiopia has suffered recurrent small and large scale deaths, and in the last half decade millions have been internally displaced and live in dire conditions. This book aims at generating Christian moral resources which can

1. Nairn, *Faces of Nationalism*, 71.
2. Fukui and Markakis, *Ethnicity and Conflict*, 3.
3. The Centre for Christianity and Society (CCS) is a research hub of the Ethiopian Graduate School of Theology (EGST) established to serve as a platform for dialogue on social issues within a multiethnic/national Ethiopian society.

respond to this and other similar situations by drawing on a wide range of disciplines. This interdisciplinary engagement is meant to buttress the task of interpreting ethnic diversity and ethnic relations within both contemporary and historical Ethiopia. Most of the chapters also draw on biblical, theological, philosophical, and cultural resources for moral articulation as a response to ethnic hostilities and the ensuing humanitarian crisis.

Underlying all the chapter contributions of this interdisciplinary volume is a set of issues about Christian moral responsibility within the sociopolitical milieu of ethnic-based hostility in Ethiopia. Written by authors of diverse gender, ethnic, and ecclesiastical affiliations, this book is premised on an understanding that Christian moral responsibility is first and foremost about peaceful togetherness, and survival. "To be good is first to be."[4] The book has ten chapters. Theodros A. Teklu's chapter, "Politics as the Hatred of the Ethnic Other," begins the dialogue by interpreting the contemporary political situation in Ethiopia as a crisis of political culture that obliterates the bond of togetherness. For such an interpretation Theodros[5] employs the concept of the political as the hatred of the enemy (à la Carl Schmitt) and the present epoch as the epoch of fighting enemies (à la Achile Mbembe). As an antidote to the mindset of distrust and the fantasy of extermination that underpin this culture, he proposes a critical revision of three most important themes: self-writing/narrating, self-determination, and the will-to-political-power in order to suggest that the future of multiethnic togetherness depends on developing and enacting a philosophy of togetherness and civility as a philosophy for "the self" and "the other." This chapter is paradigmatic in articulating two needs: the need to interpret past and present ethnic hostilities in Ethiopia, and the need for moral visions that respond to these hostilities. The consequent chapters, categorized in three parts, can be framed according to these two niches.

Part I, titled "Ethno-political Crisis and Resolutions: Past and Present," meets the first need, presenting descriptions and interpretations of the historical and contemporary realities of ethnic relations in Ethiopia. In Chapter 2, "Reflections on Conundrums and Prospects of Writing Ethiopian History," Afework Hailu articulates the crisis in historiography, and accentuates the need to go beyond the prejudiced historical narratives of "the assimilationist, Ethio-nationalist" thesis and "the exclusivist, Ethno-nationalist" antithesis. To this end, he makes a summons for

---

4. Verharen et al., "Introducing Survival Ethics." The practical exigency of survival preceeds any kind of thought or deliberation regarding what is deemed as the "good" in terms of human flourishing.

5. According to the Ethiopian convention, the first name—rather than the family name—is considered as the principal designation of a person.

implementing a synthesis—a viable and inclusive approach—in writing Ethiopian history, forwarding some comments on how writers of both sides handle the available historical sources for a more constructive approach in writing Ethiopian history.

While Afework engages Ethiopia's sociopolitical history, in chapter 3, a chapter titled "Ethnic Diversity and Legal Responsibility in Ethiopia," Fasil Nahum engages the Ethiopian constitution to interpret the contemporary ethnic hostilities. He argues that the Ethiopian constitution is based on natural law jurisprudence that affirms equality of all human beings before the law and celebrates ethnic (and other forms of) diversity. Therefore, he argues, the ethnic hostilities exhibited in contemporary Ethiopia are the results of failures of state organs to fulfill their legal responsibilities: understanding and implementing the constitution and safeguarding the rule of law.

The law does not, however, exhaust the notion of responsibility, and hence in the fourth chapter titled "'Deeply Mediatized' and 'Deeply Ethnicized' Politics in Ethiopia (2014–19): Signposts toward Moral Articulation for a Digital Space," Sara Abdella Kedir engages digital spaces as moral crossroads that stand at the limit of rule-based approaches. Such a limit, she argues, begs for a fostering of a practically wise self for a digital space, a self who is aware that responsible action includes seeking to understand the nature of new media as the digital expands the impact of the self's communicative action. To foster such understanding by making the abstracted power of new media perceptible, Sara engages new-media research which discusses the ubiquity of new media in everyday life and its capacity to alter the nature of social interaction (i.e., "deep mediatization"), with practical examples of how "deeply mediatized" communication is currently constructing ethnicity and ethnic relations in Ethiopia. She then maps out a number of observations about such construction to reinforce thoughtfulness about the digital as the sphere of one's action.

Such movement from historical and legal inquiry into sociological and moral inquiry brings the book to the next two parts, Parts III and IV, which draw on Christian moral resources to curate "Moral Visions of Togetherness" in contemporary Ethiopia. These visions respond to two types of problems: the problem of simultaneous unity and diversity, and that of self–other relations. Part III, "Unity and Diversity: Moral Visions of Togetherness," includes chapters 5 and 6. In "Identity in the Light of Unity-in-Diversity," the fifth chapter, Daniel Assefa Kassaye (*Abba*) engages the Christian message that is permeated with the creational mystery of the one and the many. Drawing on Paul Ricoeur's notion of narrative identity, he argues that what comes out of it is the noncontradictory, yet mysterious relationship between unity and diversity, which can foster a healthy understanding of identity.

Nebeyou Alemu, in the sixth chapter titled "'Ethnic' and 'Christian' Identity: Ethiopian Reflections from the Epistle to the Galatians," takes a distinctively biblical task by closely examining the Pauline treatment of ethnic diversity and the particularity of the Christian identity within the Epistle to the Galatians. He argues that Paul abrogates ethnocentrism by rendering Christ both the center and the boundary of Christian identity, offering a vision of a community that is both radically united in Christ and radically inclusive of diverse (ethnic) groups. Following this, Nebeyou draws out a number of implications for Christian identity in contemporary Ethiopia.

Part IV, "Self and Other: Moral Visions of Togetherness," spanning chapters 7–10, touches upon the problems of ethnic diversity from the perspective of self–other relation, where the other is the ethnic other. In chapter 7, "The 'Ethnic Other' as the 'Neighbor': A *Perichoretic* Imagination of Moral Responsibility," Youdit Tariku Feyessa construes the ethnic other as "the neighbor," and attempts to curate a political theology of the neighbor. She argues that the paradigmatic treatment of the political other as "enemy" and the curtailing of "the neighbor" to the private renders politics and ethics mutually exclusive (à la Carl Schmitt), obliterating the space of their overlap and rendering the political violent. As an antidote, Youdit draws on the Christian theological concept of "perichoresis" as a mode of relation between self and other to render the other as neighbor and hence an object of the imperative of neighbor-love.

While Youdit emphasizes the imperative of neighbor-love, Samson Tadelle Demo, in chapter 8, "After Self Assertion: On a *Paraclesis* of a Political Theology of *Kenosis*," takes a kenotic turn to the politics of self–other relations. He looks at the assertion of ethnicity as the center of identity and the resulting anthropology of *homo ethnicus* in Ethiopia as an excess that lends itself to nihilistic tendencies in relation to the ethnic other. To challenge these tendencies, Samson introduces the anthropological concept of *homo kenosus* to the political by tapping into the theology of Hans Urs von Balthasar. This anthropology, he argues, fosters a fluid identity that embraces difference, and wills neither complete assimilation through domination nor annihilation of the other, but rather flows out to the other in service and mission.

In the ninth chapter titled "The rite of 'footwashing' at *Abinet* schools and its ethics of humility," Setargew Kenaw emphasizes service as a paradigm of self–other relation, with an emphasis on the "the ethics of humility" in the practice of footwashing as a symbol of humble service. His aim is to counter the inclination to obliterate the ethnic other exhibited in Ethiopia. He does this by drawing on both the biblical story of Jesus's feet-washing practice and its ritualization in the Abinet Schools, traditional schools of the Ethiopian Orthodox *Tewahido* Church. In these schools, senior students wash the feet of new students who arrive at the schools after tiresome journeys from different parts of Ethiopia. This practice, Setargew argues, provides a paradigmatic example for the capacity of the tradition rooted in Jesus's ethic of humility to overcome exclusion and conflict-ridden self–other relation through inclusion and service-orientation, and thus provides moral vision to turn around the hostilities in Ethiopian institutions of higher education.

The book concludes with chapter 10, "The Christian Moral Responsibility of Embracing the Ethnic Other," in which Nishan Cheru Degaga addresses the challenge of ethnic exclusion. For the development of her argument and recommendations, she takes Miroslav Volf as her primary dialogue partner and Emmanuel Katongole as a secondary one. Nishan draws on the theological insights of both dialogue partners to develop a theological account of moral responsibility of the self in the embrace of the ethnic other. To this end, she points out significant provisions of the Christian faith in countering ethnic exclusion for the ultimate realization of the kingdom of God as the community of all believers from every nation, tribe, people, and language as proclaimed by the apostle John in Revelation 7:9.

We are grateful to each author for their academically rigorous and contextually relevant chapter contributions on the theme of ethnic diversity and national unity, focusing on moral pedagogies of togetherness. We are particularly grateful to Nathaniel Veltman for proofreading the manuscript and Sara A. Kedir for her assistance in the initial stage of drafting the proposal for this book. Many thanks to those academics who offered valuable comments and feedback on the different parts of this collection: Andrew DeCort, Frederike van Oorschot, Jörg Haustein, Kyle Gingerich Hiebert, and Meron Tekleberhan. The publication of this interdisciplinary volume was made possible by the financial support of the Centre for Christianity and Society (CCS). We believe the scholarship contained in this book will invite and deepen the conversation on the theme, and contribute towards our understanding of Christian moral responsibility within a multiethnic context. We are extremely delighted not only because this is the inaugural publication of CCS, but also because it showcases the contributions from our former and current students: Nebeyou, Nishan, Sara, Samson, and Youdit. Finally, in line with Ethiopian tradition, which considers the first name as the principal designation of a person, all the chapters in this collection list Ethiopian authors (in their bibliographies) by their first name, rather than their family name.

## Bibliography

Fukui, Katsuyoshi, and John Markakis, eds. *Ethnicity and Conflict in the Horn of Africa.* Athens: Ohio University Press, 1994.

Nairn, Tom. *Faces of Nationalism: Janus Revisited.* London: Verso, 1997.

Verharen, Charles, et al. "Introducing Survival Ethics into Engineering Education and Practice." *Science and Engineering Ethics* 19 (2011) 599–623. DOI: 10.1007/s11948-011-9332-9.

# Part I

# Interpreting the Signs of the Times

# 1

## Politics as the Hatred of the Ethnic Other

#### Theodros A. Teklu

Discerning the "signs of the times" is a prerequisite to any moral-philosophical/theological engagement that aspires to be contextually relevant. Consequently, one should ask, "What is the time?"[1] The question of time produces a descriptive account of our past and present, paving the way for reflection on what ought to be done. In this light, I would like to pose the following critical question: Where are we today in Ethiopia, sociopolitically? To anticipate my answer: we are in a milieu of ethnic enmity. Burdened by its political history, Ethiopia, which is home to anthropologically diverse ethno-linguistic groups, manifests a distinctive vulnerability to ethnic-based conflicts. The construal of the ethnic other as a threat and an enemy, which is not necessarily synonymous with the political and legal recognition afforded to ethnic identity in the current Constitution, obliterates the bond of togetherness between people. At present, ethnic-based violence is on the rise, causing security and humanitarian crises. Arguably, such crises are causally related to the crisis in political culture. By "political culture," I refer to "the values and political conduct of individual or collective agents"[2]—including the participation of the citizenry and not necessarily confined to formal political figures and institutions.

---

1. Ward, *Cities of God*, 1–5. Ward's focus on the relevance of posing the question of time is congruent with Edward Schillebeeckx's negative dialectics or contrast-experience, which is a criterion of correlation (between human question and religious answer). Hermeneutically, one proceeds from negative experiences of life to the Christian horizon of hope; Schillebeeckx, *Understanding of Faith*, 78–101.

2. For the older and newer definitions of political culture, see, for example, Silva et

The purpose of this chapter is to articulate the crisis in political culture in terms of politics as the hatred of an ethnic enemy while arguing that the assertion of ethnic identity or diversity needs to be conjoined to the moral responsibility of multiethnic togetherness. To this end, drawing on Carl Schmitt[3] and the contemporary African philosopher and postcolonial theorist, Achille Mbembe, I will start by articulating the concept of the political as the hatred of an enemy. In this light, I will then interpret the contemporary political situation in Ethiopia primarily as a crisis of political culture, in two stages. First, I will offer a cursory review of Ethiopia's longstanding political culture of alliance/enemy-making, which showcases politics as the hatred of an enemy. Second, I will focus on the current psychic regime of ethnic hatred, which results in ethnic-based hostilities. Admittedly, there are certain coherences and divergences between the traditional form of alliance/enemy-making and its modern appropriation. In the case of the latter, relationships of enmity assume a total feature leading to the extermination of the political enemy while in the traditional system subduing or subordinating enemies was the end goal. Finally, this chapter will draw certain protocols for the future of responsible multiethnic togetherness. Taken together, the introduction of this book and this particular chapter set the agenda for subsequent chapters, which will focus on bringing together ethnic diversity and moral responsibility to contribute towards developing moral pedagogies of togetherness for Ethiopians.

## Conceptualizing the Political as the Hatred of an Enemy

Humans are social creatures capable of speech and moral-political reasoning, which distinguishes them from the rest of the animal kingdom. For this reason, political thinkers—ancient and modern alike—consider humans as political animals (*politikon zôon*).[4] Doing politics involves a rationalization of one's view(s) about *the good* of a given group (association) or the *common good* of society at large. In the process of dialogue, inevitably, there will be differences and contradictions that need to be resolved,

---

al., "Political Culture," 1.

3. Carl Schmitt was a controversial German jurist who served the Nazi party. He is the first modern thinker who articulated the so-called political theology. After decades of obscurity, Schmitt's work is now gaining a new recognition in the scholarly domain. Partly, this is inspired by the discontents of liberalism in the West, after the global collapse of socialism (à la Francis Fukuyama's cliché "the end of history"). Hoelzl and Ward have translated Carl Schmitt's *Political Theology II*.

4. See Mulgan, "Aristotle's Doctrine," 438–45.

affirming the notion that there is no politics without a difference. Defining what constitutes the difference that makes politics possible is, nonetheless, subject to divergent and contending interpretations.

In his book titled *The Concept of the Political*, Carl Schmitt claims that "the specific political distinction . . . is that between friend and enemy."[5] A caveat: the political enemy must be a public enemy, not a personal one. For the political to be effective, there must be mutually exclusive hostile people groups, which are ready to enter into war against each other, rendering the distinction between war and politics fluid. Such friend–enemy distinction must result in "association" (among in-groups) and "dissociation" (from people of another group).[6] Willingness to die *with* and *for* other members of one's group is a sign of the utmost degree of association. In contrast, the desire to kill others who belong to the hostile group shows the maximum degree of dissociation.[7] Associations and dissociations may require identity markers based on language, ethnicity, culture, or religion, which instill collective identity that differentiates people groups.[8] Such markers of collective identity and difference become decisive because of their instrumental, not intrinsic, value.[9] Thus, the distinctions are not necessarily essential or substantial, but merely political.

For Schmitt, the political requires ensuring that the boundary of the nation-state clearly defines the distinction between friend and enemy. Who ensures that? For Schmitt, the sovereign dictator or the populist sovereign is the one who—by an appeal to the friend–enemy distinction—homogenizes the community of collective identity and exterminates the enemy both internal and external.[10] The sovereign dictator has the authority to suspend (and even manipulate) law in the name of the state of emergency or the state of exception. Such a suspension of law is analogically likened to the miracle in theology. In *Political Theology*, Schmitt argues that all theories of the state are secularized theological concepts and that political theorists (Thomas Hobbes and Machiavelli seem to be in view, here) found their approaches in negative or pessimistic political anthropology.[11]

   5. Schmitt, *Concept*, 26.
   6. Schmitt, *Concept*, 26, 38.
   7. Schmitt, *Concept*, 32–33.
   8. Schmitt, *Concept*, 25–27.
   9. Schmitt, *Concept*, 37–38.
   10. Schmitt, *Concept*, 46–48.
   11. Schmitt, *Political Theology*, 36–52. Schmitt, *Concept*, 58–68. Jürgen Habermas warns readers that dealing with Schmitt's work demands great care; Habermas, "Political," 23. Underlying political authority based on friend–enemy distinction is the theological view of the Original Sin. Still, by contrast, liberal orders, according to Schmitt,

Alluding to Carl Schmitt on friend–enemy distinction and the contemporary Italian philologist and philosopher Giorgio Agamben on sovereignty and the state of exception, Mbembe articulates his version of the political as the hatred of an enemy. In his articles titled "African Modes of Self Writing" and "Necropolitics," Mbembe refers to sovereignty as the capacity to decide over life and death. Here, Mbembe refers to Agamben who, in his book titled *Homo Sacer: Sovereignty and Bare Life,* interprets sovereignty in terms of the state of exception, which justifies the authority of the sovereign to decide over life and death. *Homo sacer* is an ancient Roman figure who cannot be sacrificed to the gods, and if killed by someone, the killer would not be charged with homicide. According to Agamben, the *homo sacer* or bare life and sovereignty are like two faces of a coin. Although sovereign dictatorship has become outdated in post-World War II Europe, Agamben argues that the refugee camps that are included by the mere fact of their exclusion are illustrative examples of the interplay between sovereignty and bare life today. His main argument is that Western democracies are based on the politics of exclusion. Nonetheless, the exclusion of groups by their inclusion in society is also a characteristic feature of many nations globally. We find bare life wherever there is the sovereign who takes the opportunity of the state of exception, or any "war machine"[12] that exercises sovereignty as a decision over life and death.

Sovereignty understood in terms of the capacity to decide over life and death should not necessarily imply struggling groups and war machines can exercise a supreme state authority for it. In this regard, Mbembe describes the states of war as that which involves sacrifice (the willingness to be killed) and massacre (the will to exterminate the enemy).[13] His article "The Society of Enmity," Mbembe defines the contemporary global milieu as characterized "by forms of exclusion, hostility, hate movements, and, above all, by the

---

wrongly assume optimistic political anthropology that fails to distinguish between the friend and the enemy in their cosmopolitanism. Consequently, liberalism must be rejected because it has a depoliticizing tendency.

12. The term was first coined and used by Deleuze and Guattari; see Mbembe, "Necropolitics," 32: "War machines are made up of segments of armed men that split up or merge with one another depending on the tasks to be carried out and the circumstances. Polymorphous and diffuse organizations, war machines are characterized by their capacity for metamorphosis. Their relation to space is mobile. Sometimes, they enjoy complex links with state forms (from autonomy to incorporation). The state may, of its own doing, transform itself into a war machine. It may moreover appropriate to itself an existing war machine or help to create one. War machines function by borrowing from regular armies while incorporating new elements well adapted to the principle of segmentation and deterritorialization. Regular armies, in turn, may readily appropriate some of the characteristics of war machines."

13. Mbembe, "African Modes," 266–71.

struggle against an enemy."[14] For him, underlying the struggle against an enemy is a master desire for an enemy:

> Once uprooted from its structure, desire then sets out to capture the disturbing object. But since in reality this object has never existed—does not and will never exist—desire must continually invent it. An invented object, however, is still not a real object. It marks an empty yet bewitching space, a hallucinatory zone, at once enchanted and evil, an empty abode haunted by the object as if by a spell.[15]

In the footsteps of Gilles Deleuze and Félix Guattari, Mbembe refrains from defining desire in the conventional sense of lack; but, he offers an understanding of desire as a productive force inventing its object. While to be human is both to desire and to be desired, desire for an enemy is a peculiar political phenomenon connected to the will-to-power: "Yesterday, as today, the political as conceived by Schmitt owes its volcanic charge to the fact that it is closely connected to an existential will to power."[16] Above all, such desire for an enemy works with the prevailing "logic of suspicion where everything must be seen as secret or as belonging to a plot or conspiracy."[17] This desire implies that epistemic certainty in identifying the enemy, and whether the perceived enemy is a real enemy has little place. Consequently, according to Mbembe, the "desire for an enemy" and "the phantasy of extermination" are diffusing "psychic structures and generic passionate forces" that "are responsible for the dominant affective tonality of our times" and sharpening "many contemporary struggles and mobilizations."[18] In this context, politics ceases to be the "forward dialectical movement of reason"; instead, it becomes "death that lives a human life."[19]

In general, what we understand from the contemporary era that reveals the exigency characterized by the desire for an enemy is that political reasoning based on deliberations has little space in the political domain. As long as there is popular (mass or mob) support, any political agenda could become dominant. When it insinuates itself in a multiethnic context, the desire for an enemy assumes the form of ethnic strife. Bonds of togetherness will be highly compromised, paving the way for a Hobbesian war of all against all. In this light, in what follows, I wish to examine the psychic regime of ethnic enmity

14. Mbembe, "Society," 23–34.
15. Mbembe, "Society," 23.
16. Mbembe, "Society," 26.
17. Mbembe, "Society," 26.
18. Mbembe, "Society," 26.
19. Mbembe, "Necropolitics," 15–16.

in Ethiopia briefly. Before that, however, I will briefly discuss the political culture of alliance/enemy-making in Ethiopia.

## The Political Culture of Alliance/Enemy-making

> [I]f representative A from region X wants to dominate representative B from region Y, he will enter into an alliance with representative C from region Z and maybe even representative D from region Y itself, in order to conquer B. The sub-partners of the alliance (C and D) will gain authority as a reward when A has installed himself in a dominant position, as in a patron–client relationship.[20]

Taking a cue from this passage drawn from Kjetil Tronvoll, we recognize that alliance/enemy-making is intricately related to power struggles in Ethiopia. In the traditional system of politics in Ethiopia, which Tronvoll refers to, contesting parties engage in warfare that culminates in one coming out as the victor. Nonetheless, the defeated enemy is not exterminated but would be allowed to hold a vassal or subordinate position. Margery Perham best describes such system as a strong man rule: "The Ethiopian system . . . was a tough–man system . . . There was one order to which all Ethiopians responded at once; that of *tillik saw*, the great man."[21]

Such system indicates that power in traditional Ethiopia was never a possession of a hereditary monarchy, but a relatively open field of competition. The position of authority was not fated, and defeat was never final, suggesting that there could be reversals of positions.[22] Besides, the authority of the conqueror was accepted by both the nobilities or regional lords and the ordinary people. They will then act not as representatives of their respective regions or peoples, but as appointees of the victor (or, *mislené* in local parlance). An old Tigrigna proverb, which captures the fact about the people's shifting allegiances from one ruler to another, states: "Any sun that rises to the east—is our sun. Any king that sits on our throne—is our king."[23]

Although the above remark is based on the assessment of the traditional political system, the technique of alliance/enemy-making is still relevant to understand the contemporary political culture of Ethiopia. However, the modern appropriation of this technique suggests that it has transformed under the milieu of radical politics and competing ideologies

20. Tronvoll, *War*, 33.
21. Perham, *Government*, 164.
22. See Messay, *Survival*, 158.
23. Tronvoll, *War*, 55.

in Ethiopia, distinguishing it from the traditional.[24] For two reasons, the interlude of the Ethiopian Student Movement of the 1960s and 1970s, which adopted Marxism-Leninism as its guiding ideology, is of particular interest, here. First, the rise of messianic politics, which was a new development in the history of modern Ethiopia, accentuated the idea of sacrifice. Politics was understood as a sacrificial process, involving the will to kill (massacre) and to be sacrificed (martyred).[25] Such sacrificial politics demanded friend–enemy distinction and mechanisms of association and dissociation. Second, the student movement gradually differentiated itself into various movements, which aspired to form vanguard parties, claiming to represent the interests of a class or a group (e.g., the proletarian or an ethnic community) to act on their behalf.[26] By default, competing movements or parties rival to the vanguard party are labeled as enemies of the people that should be eliminated. The legacies of these two developments (messianism and vanguardism) are still felt in contemporary politics.[27]

In the wake of the 1974 Ethiopian revolution, a military junta, the Därg controlled power and co-opted the socialist movements by stealing their ideology.[28] Two socialist parties, which were identical in ideology, the Ethiopian People's Revolutionary Party (EPRP) and All Ethiopian Socialist Movement (*Ma'ison*), entered into conflict because the latter opted to ally with the Därg while the former rejected the alliance.[29] The discursive disrespect and the distrust and the intolerance between them grew to the point where they engaged in assassinating each other's members, culminating in the so-called Red Terror.[30] As the well-known Ethiopian historian Bahru Zewde comments, "Politics, the art of compromise, was reduced to a zero-sum game. You destroy or you are destroyed. The verbal violence that characterized the student debates of the early seventies prepared the way for the physical violence of the late 1970s."[31] Because of this, within two years, between 1976 and 1978, Ethiopia turned into a necropolis with thousands of atrocious

24. Teshale, "Modernity," 345–371.

25. "If religious orthodoxy was a prime occupation in former times, political rectitude has been the essence of Ethiopian political life in more recent times"; see Bahru, *Society*, 331.

26. The tripartite constellation of state, people, and in between these two the Ethiopian Student Movement, see Theodros, *Politics of Metanoia*, 104.

27. Theodros, "Mirror," 85–87.

28. See Donham, *Marxist Modern*, 21–27.

29. Some several groups and parties were struggling for power; see Interview with Andreas, *Documenting*, 106.

30. Bahru, *Society*, 428–444.

31. Bahru, *Society*, 433.

killings: "The State, which thus [began] to exercise ever tighter control over its subjects assumed leviathan proportions."[32] During the military-socialist regime (1974–91), decisions over the life and death of citizens were carried out without any moral restraint. In comparing Mangestu Haile-Mariam and Yohannes IV, Bahru Zewde writes the following:

> Nothing expresses . . . more dramatically than Emperor Yohannes's words of remorse at the end of one of his devastating campaigns in Gojjam: "I do not know whether it is through my sin or that of the peasant, but I went on devastating the country" . . . Yet, these words of remorse are indicative of the moral restraint that permeated the actions of even the most ruthless rulers. Alas, one seeks in vain for even a faint echo of such remorse in the recent "memoirs" of Lt. Colonel Mangestu Haile Mariam![33]

In a nutshell, the political culture of alliance/enemy-making implemented in its modernized form transformed the friend–enemy distinction in politics, not merely dominating but exterminating the perceived enemy. The final fate of the Därg regime was defeat by rebel groups such as the Tigray People's Liberation Front (TPLF) and the Eritrean People's Liberation Front (EPLF), which it had labelled as enemies of Ethiopia. The subsequent political dispensation inaugurated by the formation of the coalition known as the EPRDF (Ethiopian People's Revolutionary Democratic Front), aimed to create "an all-inclusive state-nation: a new unity in diversity" beyond the "psychology of distrust" among political elites.[34] In terms of multi-party politics, EPRDF's commitment to broadening the political matrix was impressive, especially during the 2005 elections. Soon, however, the matrix started to narrow, as the rhetoric shifted from democracy to an alarmist discourse—the danger of "disintegration" and "fragmentation" (*yemebetaten adega*), and the condemnation of political elites as chauvinists, narrow nationalists, and terrorists.[35]

Although the government insisted on having no enemies except poverty and that all other political entities, including foreign countries, can be allies in the fight against poverty, the specter of hostility insinuated itself forcefully. The crisis that ensued is attributable to both the government that

---

32. Bahru, *Society* 329.
33. Bahru, *Society*, 431.
34. Adhana, "Mutation," 28.

35. Adhana pointed out EPRDF sought to strike a balance between these duos as they are construed as two extremes, see Adhana, "Mutation," 28; Assefa, "Theory," 147; Tronvoll, *War*, 213.

tended towards authoritarianism and the opposition that had an all-or-none approach, perceiving the ruling party as an enemy to be eradicated. In subsequent years, TPLF was accused of dominating the EPRDF; the OPDO (Oromo People's Democratic Organization) was indicted for "anti-Tigrayan" sentiment and "narrow nationalist" inclinations.[36] Gradually, the EPRDF failed in maintaining the strength of its internal dynamics through the usual mechanisms of "democratic centralization" and *gemgema* (an Amharic term for evaluation that involves both self-criticism and critique of others within the Party/coalition) due to an internal caesura that later led to a splinter.[37] The psychology of distrust and intolerance infiltrated into the parties making it difficult to continue as a coalition, leading to a transfer of the government from the hands of Former Prime Minister Haile-Mariam Dessalegn to Current Prime Minister Abiy Ahmed for the remaining two years of the former's term:

> Following the opening up of political space, new alliances and coalitions emerged in the run up to the next election including the ruling party coalition which dissolved itself and merged its constituent parties, except the Tigray People's Liberation Front party (TPLF), to form the Prosperity Party.[38]

Both in the process that led to the government change and after, we have witnessed the mobilization of ethnic sentience and resentment that became the basis on which alliances and enemies are constructed. With the forging of the Oromara alliance (between Oromo and Amhara elites), and the formation of the new Prosperity Party, one may recognize the concurrent

36. Asnake, *Federalism*, 42.

37. By democratic centralization, I refer to a mechanism of controlled decontrolling deployed through discussions and consensus formation: "It is the task of the Party, the vanguard of the working class, to direct the economic, administrative, etc. activities of the state. . . . elaborates the main course of the development of the society and struggles for the realization of its plans. The resultant system of democratic centralism is the system of proletarian dictatorship. In it leadership and consensus are inseparably one" (Asnake, *Federalism*, 35–36).

38. "Ethiopia: 'Beyond Law Enforcement,'" 12. See also the mutual accusations between Amhara and Tigrean elites: "Open Letter to Ethiopians"; "To the Global Community." Based on the rhetoric by the prime minister in Afan Oromo, some question the way that member parties of EPRDF evolved into a new unified party called the Prosperity Party by extricating itself from its shell (the EPRDF) is said to be a political intrigue to dislodge the TPLF, perpetuating the political culture of alliance/enemy-making; PM Abiy's speech in Bale: "GMN Ethiopia–You Tube." Cf. also the speech by the deputy president of the Oromia regional state, Shimelis Abdissa, who articulates political act as gambling full of tactics and calculations on how to mischievously convince some and confuse others to strategically include allies and exclude enemies: Borkena, "Shimelis Abdisa's Leaked Audio, Prosperity Party Political Agenda."

construction of Tigrean-otherness and relationships of enmity that tend "to assume a total character"[39] endangering multiethnic togetherness.[40] Politics is not known as an art of compromise, and such failure keeps Ethiopia in the cyclical pattern of regime changes through the instrumentality of coup d'état or states of war without building a meaningful democracy. Currently, the initial euphoria of reform seems to have faded away, and contradictory interpretations are being given to the anticipated change.[41] Generally, looking at the patterns of Ethiopian politics through this cursory view, we deduce that the political culture of alliance/enemy-making continues to be the dominant mode (modus operandi) in which political elites operate.

## The Psychic Regime of Ethnic Enmity

In multiethnic societies such as Ethiopia where ethnic-based mobilization is common, a crisis in political culture highly intensifies ethnic-based hostilities. There are already indications that there is a consolidation of friend–enemy distinction based on ethnic identity, solidifying the psychic regime of ethnic hatred. A plethora of information, disinformation, and fake news coming from political elites, digital activists, and bloggers are tributaries to this growing ethnic-based hostility. It is becoming commonplace to disseminate hate speech without being held responsible. The country is demonstrating some traits of a failed-state such as the compromise of the rule of law, anarchy, and irresponsible rhetoric ("talk is on the loose"[42]). Such things continue to happen in the milieu of this conjectured change.[43]

---

39. Bahru, *Society*, 433.

40. The construction of otherness and hostility against the TPLF and Tigreans reveals a Girardian mimetic desire and sacrificial victim. For a Girardian interpretation of the situation proves to be plausible, the chaotic situation should have been supplanted with a peaceful order following the slandering, the accusation, the denouncing, and marginalization of the scapegoat. See Girard, *Scapegoat*; Tronvoll, "Tigray."

41. Those who oppose the incumbent government interpret the "reforms" as the consolidation of power to prepare the political arena for a dictatorial rule with a vision of establishing a unitary state while those who support it envision a new democratic Ethiopia and that the current turmoil is just natural in the path of change. Some consider the change essential but criticize the way the change is handled; see Ezekiel, "Commentary."

42. "Failed States."

43. "The period after the government of Prime Minister Abiy Ahmed instituted human rights reforms was interspersed with political and ethnic tensions that prompted military insurgencies and inter-communal violence in Amhara, Oromia, Harar, Dire Dawa, Benishangul, and the Southern Nations Nationalities and Peoples (SNNP) regions." *Amnesty International* (May 2020), 5.

Quibbles aside, the report by Amnesty International (May 2020) demonstrates the fact that political advantages overweigh human rights in Ethiopia.[44] Overall, the report unveils truths of bodies abducted, bodies disappearing, bodies mutilated, bodies dismembered, bodies butchered, bodies slaughtered, bodies in mass graves, bodies thrown on the streets and in bushes.[45] The displacement of hundreds of thousands whose unwilled adjacency with the ethnic other resulting in conflicts involving the massacre of people and all kinds of atrocities are becoming quite common.[46] The sacrificed bodies mentioned above are mirrors of our society suffering from a psychic regime of enmity facilitated by the enactment of sovereignty as the decision over life and death. From a human rights point of view, what is disturbing is the effect of the psychic regime of ethnic hatred on the social body. Many alarming developments already confront us, but we should be reminded of the fact that numbers should not necessarily measure human rights, as even a single life matters.

Let me evoke the figure of the person lynched by a mob in 2018, and which is not included in Amnesty International's report, as illustrative of the psychic regime of ethnic enmity. As reported by Reuters: "a man was lynched and left hanging upside down in a public square in the Oromia town of Shashemene by a mob who wrongly suspected he was carrying a bomb. Police stood by idly, according to an eyewitness."[47] The body of

---

44. The charge that the report is biased is somehow resonating around the question of magnitude based on numbers such as whose death is included and who is not. Admittedly, the report is not exhaustive as explicitly spelt out in the document itself: "It is not a complete documentation of all human rights violations and abuses committed during the period under review in the two regions," *Amnesty International* (May 2020), 8. The complaints on the magnitude of the human rights abuses could be a fig leaf to cover up and blame-shift to proclaim one's political righteousness. The report holds various agents responsible for the crisis: government soldiers, military splinters from the Oromo Liberation Front (OLF) such as *Shane* (Oromo Liberation Army) and informal youth associations.

45. The report demonstrates in regions where the command post operates such as Oromia and Amhara regional states, there have been extrajudicial executions, arbitrary arrest and detention under miserable conditions, torture and ill-treatment, rape and gender-based violence, forced indoctrination, forced evictions, and the destruction of civilian properties.

46. Around 2.35 million people have been displaced according to Directorate General for European Civil Protection and Humanitarian Aid Operations (DG–ECHO) report on Ethiopia for the year 2018; DG–ECHO, *Ethiopia Internal Displacement*.

47. The mob killing happened during a public gathering organized to welcome the well-known Oromo activist, Jawar Mohammed. The incident has been reported by several news agencies including Reuters and African News: Aaron, "Ethnic unrest"; Abdur Rahman Alfa Shaban, "Ethiopian Activists"; the photo of the lynched person is available at Engidu Woldie, "Ethiopia."

that person is a mirror to the political body that is immersed in politics as the hatred of an ethnic enemy, which is indicated by the police who were either indifferent spectators or (passive) collaborators with the mob. Actually, the death of the victim is incomprehensible if we do not inquire about his ethnic identity and what that identity represents to the crowd. By ethnicity, he represents an ethnic other, an enemy, representing the image of an "illegitimate" outsider who does not belong to the region. This person did not die as a messiah for his death cannot bring about the expiation or atonement of sins like that of Christ the crucified. Nor did he die as someone who struggled for freedom/liberation so that we consider him as a martyr. Instead, echoing Giorgio Agamben, he died just like a *homo sacer*. In brief, he symbolizes a bare life (a subhuman category far removed from his human and political rights).

For Agamben, as for Mbembe, sovereign power and bare life are like two faces of a coin. Of course, the sovereign should not necessarily be the highest authority of the state, and the sovereign could be a mob, as in the case of the lynched person. In Ethiopia today, sovereignty seems to be parcelized with anarchic groups as functionaries of sporadic violence. What I am trying to say here is that the death of the lynched person like all the others who have been massacred did not have any meaning at all—they are not martyrs, but sacrifices, utterly meaningless expenditures. What we witness in this real scenario is the extermination of ethnic others as cathartic objects of hate (cathartic objects of hatred stricken to dissipate one's anger, sometimes as a substitute in the absence of the real object of hate). Nonetheless, such deaths cannot produce meaningful therapeutic catharsis for the murderers, dissipating or diffusing and expressing their corked emotions. Nor should they be taken as expressions of a euphoric sense of freedom, or triumphalist bravado.

The reason I rehearse the horrible death of the lynched person is not to make a critique of a particular ethnic group that committed such an abomination; ethnic Oromos are themselves being killed brutally over the past two years, as recorded in several human rights violation reports such as Amnesty International reports. Instead, I wish to highlight the fact that— whoever does it—the death of the lynched person symbolically defines the hate of ethnic others and could be paradigmatic for all ethnic-based killings (ethnic cleansing or genocide). What happened to him could potentially happen to anyone of us at any time and at any place, as his death cannot be taken as an isolated incident. Unless they derive moral and political lessons from such scenarios, Ethiopians will continue to obliterate the bond of their togetherness. In general, the crisis of political culture is affecting the social body at large. In light of what we discussed under the previous sub-chapters, sovereign power (whether in the form of formal government authority and its military and security apparatuses, or war machines) is exerting its power on bare life. The situation can be interpreted as the crisis of the political, which has degenerated into the political as the desire for and hatred of an enemy. The friend–enemy distinction is solidifying, and there are ample indications of associations and dissociations that are proliferating.

If we look at the syntax of the public, it is saturated with discursive disrespect. Virtual and real interpersonal communications are becoming tenser. One is labeled quickly as an enemy and a threat to one's ethnic community or national unity. The public spaces display a contradictory mélange of sacred words such as love, forgiveness, and unity on the one hand and derogatory labels such as *yeqen Jib* (daylight hyenas), *banda* (a villain-citizen who works/spies for other states or foreign enemies), *neft-egna* (gun-holder; symbolic of unitarist politician or the ethnic other—ethnic and cultural Amhara—living outside of his/her region), *zeregna* (divisive racist/ethnicist), and *zerafi* (robber, corrupt). With the changing of political alliances and the making of enemies, there seems to be a propensity towards a civil war (Hobbesian war of all against all) as the International Crisis Group has warned.[48]

Such a tendency is introducing an internal societal caesura that divides people as friends and enemies. There are already constructions of otherness and the movement of images of hostility that pit one group against the other. Even among those who condemn ethnic hostility, there is a misconception that political elites of one ethnic group are responsible for the ills of the country, consequently believing that their extermination will automatically alleviate the ethnic tensions. This is not a different standpoint from the scapegoating of alliance/enemy-making. In this psychic regime, everyone appears to be a threat and an enemy to everyone, appearing that there is no escape from relationships of ethnic hostility. The freely floating images of enmity continuously construct ethnic others as either friends or enemies. With the continuous shifts in alliance/enemy-making among political agents, one places and is placed by others in positions of a friend and an enemy to others even without being intentional about it.

Consequently, since you represent an ethnic group that may be considered an enemy by others; you are a potential enemy and threat to your ethnic other(s) despite the fact that you do not want to be an enemy to anyone. In other words, I can legitimately claim that I am not an enemy to anyone; however, I cannot claim that I do not have enemies. Who am I then? Borrowing the words of Mbembe, I am "The enemy, that other that

---

48. International Crisis Group, "Crisis Group Africa Report No. 283," 14.

I am."⁴⁹ Implied in this expression is that associations and dissociations are becoming decisive in contemporary politics. The requirement for preserving oneself from a possible threat has become participation in an economy of hatred. Here and there, the desire for an enemy hunts for its objects of hate. This desire is not a real therapeutic catharsis as commented above, but a master desire for an enemy—a fantasy of extermination. In this situation, one legitimately fears that such a growing hatred will eventually develop into tragic episodes of an apocalyptic doom unless people change their evil ways. The more Ethiopians gaze into the abyss, the abyss will look back at them (à la Frederick Nietzsche). The consequence of this would be a total degeneration of politics into necropolitics in which killing an ethnic enemy becomes a moral good and an end in itself.

## The Future of Multiethnic Togetherness

Is there a horizon of hope beyond the current crisis? There is hope insofar as political elites and citizens are determined to affirm ethnic diversity and galvanize national unity. Failing to manage diversity and unity, and perpetuating the political culture of alliance/enemy-making, will only obliterate the bond of togetherness between people. Reinstituting the country as a unitary state and introducing majoritarian democracy will be simplistic and reductive solutions, as Ethiopia has already passed a certain irreversible threshold after the federal experiment. Since the burden of this book is on the issue of moral responsibility, I would prefer to revisit some notions that are pertinent to the political (political culture) and moral wellbeing of Ethiopians. In this light, I propose that multiethnic togetherness will have a future insofar as there is a renewed commitment to human values that promote cohabitation, which implies the unchosen character of inhabiting the land. Cohabitation is the primordial (ontological) condition before (and after) any social contract, and ethical and political existence, and as "cohabitants on earth"⁵⁰ "We are given to each other. We can't choose."⁵¹ To promote multiethnic togetherness, and peaceful and reconciled cohabitation as an antidote to the desire of the enemy, I wish to make the following three considerations or protocols as a preferred mode of multiethnic togetherness.

First, revisiting *self-writing/narrating*: Self-writing is writing or narrating about oneself or one's history by oneself. While self-writing or

---

49. Mbembe, "Society," 26.

50. Butler, "Is Judaism Zionism?," 84.

51. See, the words of the well-known philosopher, Taylor et al., "Concluding Discussion," 111.

self-narrating is not morally wrong in itself, a narcissistic obsession with the self—often strengthened by biases in historiography—may result in the hatred of the ethnic other. Self-writing is vital to understand the dynamics of ethnic politics because how the ethnic other is portrayed reveals and determines the real-life relations with the other. If we look at history writing in Ethiopia, there is a considerable contestation.[52] Instead of maximizing objectivity by adopting a critical approach, historians and politicians opt to prioritize advancing their political agendas and advantages. Even though looking to the past to take the present to the future is essential, it is equally crucial that political elites ensure that they do not unnecessarily burden citizens with the factual or perceived unsettled debts of their ancestors. As long as the current modes of self-writing/narrating, which are often conveyed through the media, are not tuned constructively, they will continue to endanger peaceful cohabitation. Insofar as the "self" of self-writing/narrating cannot be morally responsible in history writing and take the moral responsibility of embracing the ethnic other(s), friend–enemy distinctions will consolidate, exacerbating internal divisions.

The second consideration is related to enacting *self-determination*, which implies the practice of self-rule. In the current global milieu, in which freedom is one of the foremost political agendas, nobody opts to be determined by another (external) will. To exercise freedom is to enact one's right to self-determination. In principle, self-determination is both necessary and desirable to actualize one's freedom to administer one's locality. Pragmatically, this is both a concrete way of enacting a direct form of democracy and governance with organic or natural representatives from one's own locality and by one's own people.[53] However, if we inquire about how it is being practiced in Ethiopia, empirical evidence may prove otherwise. If it replicates local tyranny against ethnic others co-inhabiting a particular locality, then self-determination is implemented contrary to its intended purposes, against its practical cogency. But, the existence of malpractices does not mean that self-determination is intrinsically evil. Sometimes, good systems may result in undesirable consequences like what the Harvard-based philosopher Martha Nussbaum describes as the "fragilities of the good."[54] Such fragilities remind us that human goodness

---

52. See Crummey, "Ethiopian Historiography," 7; Bahru, *Society*, 15–43.

53. Given that rebellion during Haile Selassie's regime assumed not only ethnic but also a regional form erupting even in so-called Amhara region such as Gojjam, it was inevitable that decentralization (self-determination) was the only antidote to the maladies of centralization (Clapham, "Centralization," 81).

54. Nussbaum, *Fragility*. For Zär'a Ya'ǝqob, "all is good if we are good" (Dawit, *Ethics*, 267).

can make sound systems work while human malevolence corrupts good systems. Insofar as the "self" of self-determination entertains a mad dream of living without ethnic others, the positive reciprocity between the self and its ethnic other will be damaged, promoting the friend–enemy distinction and endangering cohabitation.

The third consideration relates to the *will to political power*. The dominating "self" takes a center position relegating others to the periphery. Who would accept being dominated? Be it in the name of a majoritarian democracy or an imposed unity (a hegemonic Unitarian state), nobody sees the necessity and desirability of being dominated and hence peripheral. Given the insufficient distinction between the state and government, which are conflated by one Amharic word, "mengist," any endeavor to re-institute the state and restructure the regional states could be destabilizing. Besides this, alliance-making between "A" and "B" to scapegoat (exterminate) a perceived enemy "C" will not solve the quandary of cohabitation, and cannot even endure long. Alliance-making could only fulfill tactical purposes (co-belligerence), but will not be sustainable insofar as it promotes enemy-making. If Ethiopia should move forward with its citizens feeling a sense of belongingness, political agents need to keep power in balance. Besides systems of checks-and-balances and transparency, there should also be what Hannah Arendt calls "power-in-common" and "action in concert."[55] Thus far, Ethiopia's political challenges are related to maintaining equilibrium of power through the federal structure which one expects to institute power-in-common, and this problem will continue insofar as a single group seeks to manipulate that common in-between space or the federal-between. For genuine reform that empowers citizens to move from a divisive understanding of the political as the hatred of an enemy to embracing the ethnic other it is mandatory to uphold shared power. Thus, the future of multiethnic togetherness is guaranteed and fostered by enacting respect and social esteem towards all citizens of diverse ethnic backgrounds who willingly cohabit with ethnic others.

## Conclusion

In this chapter, we have looked at how the political could be conceived as the hatred of an enemy. The chapter started by briefly describing how Carl Schmitt and Achille Mbembe conceptualize the political as the hatred of an

---

55. *"Power* corresponds to the human ability not just to act but to act in concert. Power is never the property of an individual; it belongs to a group and remains in existence only so long as the group keeps together" (Arendt, *Crisis*, 143).

enemy. In this light, the chapter then examined the Ethiopian case by looking at the political culture of alliance/enemy-making, and the psychic regime of ethnic hostility. According to the discussion, ethnic-based violence is a characteristic feature of the political enacted as the hatred of an ethnic enemy. Political mobilizations, including reform movements, have not been able to extricate themselves from ethnic sentience and resentment. In a nutshell, there is a crisis of political culture that is spilling out to the social body, and going beyond such toxic relations requires a genuine transformation. While reform is somehow a social or institutional change from above that may trickle down to the bottom (baseline communities), it is vital to recognize the exigency for a bottom-up approach. Since religiosity is a characteristic feature of Ethiopians, this bottom-up approach should be encouraged by religious institutions. If there is hope for Ethiopia, the last resort could be the moral-religious reserve. The subsequent chapters will articulate this, aiming at examining the ethno-political crisis and resolutions in Ethiopia's past and present (Part II) before addressing the problem of unity-in-diversity (Part III) and the ethnic "self" and its "other" (Part IV).

## Bibliography

Aaron Maasho. "Ethnic Unrest Tarnishes New Ethiopian Leader's Reforms." Reuters, August 24, 2018. https://www.reuters.com/article/us-ethiopia-violence idUSKCN1L914V.

Abebe Zegeye and Siegfried Pausewang, eds. *Ethiopia In Change: Peasantry, Nationalism and Democracy*. London: British Academy Press, 1994.

Arendt, Hannah. *Crisis of the Republic*. New York: Harcourt Brace Jovanovich, 1972.

Asnake Kefale. *Federalism and Ethnic Conflict in Ethiopia: A Comparative Regional Study*. London: Routledge, 2013.

Bahru Zewde. *Documenting the Ethiopian Student Movement: An Exercise in Oral History*. Forum for Social Studies. Addis Ababa: Eclipse, 2010.

———. *Society, State and History*. Addis Ababa: Addis Ababa University Press, 2008.

Borkena. "Shimelis Abdisa's Leaked Audio, Prosperity Party Political Agenda." https://borkena.com/2020/08/10/shimelis-abdisa-s-leaked-audio-prosperity-party-political-agenda/.

Butler, Judith. "Is Judaism Zionism?" In *The Power of Religion in the Public Sphere*, edited by Eduardo Mendieta and Jonathan Van Antwerpen, 70–91. New York: Columbia University Press, 2011.

Clapham, Christopher. "Centralization and Local Response in Southern Ethiopia." *African Affairs* 74.294 (1975) 72–81.

Crummey, Donald. "Ethiopian Historiography in the Latter Half of the Twentieth Century: A North American Perspective." *Journal of Ethiopian Studies* 34 (2001) 7–24.

Dawit Worku. *The Ethics of Zär'a Ya'əqob: A Reply to the Historical and Religious Violence in the Seventeenth Century Ethiopia*. Rome: Editrice Pontificia Universita Gregoriana, 2012.

DG–ECHO. "Ethiopia | Internal Displacement (December 2018)." https://reliefweb.int/map/ethiopia/ethiopia-internal-displacement-december-2018-dg-echo-daily-map-22012019.

Donham, Donald. *Marxist Modern: An Ethnographic History of the Ethiopian Revolution*. Berkeley: University of California Press, 1999.

Engidu Woldie. "Ethiopia: Arrest in Mob Killing of Innocent Man in Shashemene." *ESAT News*, August 13, 2018. https://ethsat.com/2018/08/ethiopia-arrest-in-mob-killing-of-innocent-man-in-shashemene/.

"Ethiopia: Beyond Law Enforcement: Human Rights Violations by Ethiopian Security Forces in Amhara and Oromia." Amnesty International Report, Issued on 29 May 2020. https://www.amnesty.org/en/documents/afr25/2358/2020/en/.

Ezekiel Gebissa. "Commentary: Dangerous Interregnum: The Anatomy of Ethiopia's Mismanaged Transition." *Addis Standard*, December 5, 2019. https://addisstandard.com/commentary-dangerous-interregnum-the-anatomy-of-ethiopias-mismanaged-transition/.

"Failed States: Where Life Is Cheap and Talk Is Loose." https://www.globalpolicy.org/nations-a-states/failed-states/49966-failed-states-where—is-cheap-and-talk-is-loose.html.

Girard, René. *The Scapegoat*. Baltimore: The Johns Hopkins University Press, 1986.

GMN Ethiopia. "GMN: Abiy Ahmed Speech in Bale 2020." *YouTube*, February 12, 2020. https://www.youtube.com/watch?v=2CzEZtozsxE.

Habermas, Jürgen. "'The Political': The Rational Meaning of a Questionable Inheritance of Political Theology." In *The Power of Religion in the Public Sphere*, edited by Judith Butler et al., 15–33. New York: Columbia University Press, 2011.

International Crisis Group. "Crisis Group Africa Report No. 283: Keeping Ethiopia's Transition on the Rails." https://www.crisisgroup.org/africa/horn-africa/ethiopia/283-keeping-ethiopias-transition-rails.

Kiss, Arthur. *Marxism and Democracy: A Contribution to the Problems of the Marxist Interpretation of Democracy*. Budapest: Akademia Kiado, 1982.

Mbembe, Achille. "African Modes of Self-Writing." *Public Culture* 14.1 (2002) 239–73.

———. "Necropolitics." *Public Culture* 15.1 (2003) 1–40.

———. "The Society of Enmity." *Radical Philosophy* 200 (Nov/Dec 2016) 23–34. https://www.radicalphilosophy.com/article/the-society-of-enmity.

Mendieta, Eduardo, and Jonathan Van Antwerpen, eds. *The Power of Religion in the Public Sphere*. New York: Columbia University Press, 2011.

Messay Kebede. *Survival and Modernization: Ethiopia's Enigmatic Present: A Philosophical Discourse*. Lawrenceville, NJ: Red Sea, 1999.

Mulgan, Richard Grant. "Aristotle's Doctrine that Man Is a Political Animal." *Hermes* 104 (1974) 438–45.

Nussbaum, Martha. *The Fragility of Goodness: Luck and Ethics in Greek Tragedy and Philosophy*. 2nd ed. Cambridge: Cambridge University Press, 2001.

"Open Letter to Ethiopians and to the International Community RE: Communique of 'Concerned Ethiopians.'" *Satenaw News*, July 28, 2019. https://www.satenaw.com/open-letter-to-ethiopians-and-to-the-international-community-re-communique-of-concerned-ethiopians/.

Perham, Margery. *The Government of Ethiopia*. London: Faber & Faber, 1947.
Schillebeeckx, Edward. *The Understanding of Faith: Interpretation and Criticism*. London: Sheed & Ward, 1974.
Schmitt, Carl. *The Concept of the Political*. Expanded Edition. Translated by George Schwab. Chicago: University of Chicago Press, 2007.
———. *Political Theology: Four Chapters on the Concept of Sovereignty*. Translated by George Schwab. Chicago: University of Chicago Press, 2005.
———. *Political Theology II: The Myth of the Closure of any Political Theology*. Translated by Michael Hoelzl and Graham Ward. Cambridge: Polity, 2008.
Shaban Abdur Rahman Alfa. "Ethiopian Activists Condemn Mob Action, Violence during Rally in Oromia." https://www.africanews.com/2018/08/14/ethiopian-activists-condemn-mob-action-violence-during-rally-in-oromia/.
Silva, Filipe Carreira da, et al. "Political Culture." *The International Encyclopedia of Political Communication* 1 (2015) 1–10. DOI:10.1002/9781118541555.wbiepc161.
Taylor, Charles, et al. "Concluding Discussion." In *The Power of Religion in the Public Sphere*, edited by Judith Butler et al., 109–17. New York: Columbia University Press, 2011.
Teshale Tibebu. "Modernity, Eurocentricity, and Radical Politics in Ethiopia, 1961–1991." *African Identities* 6.4 (November 2008) 345–71.
Theodros A. Teklu. "Mirror of Memory: Some Thoughts on the Ethiopian Red Terror." In *The Healing of Memories: African Christian Responses to Politically Induced Trauma*, edited by Mohammed Girma, 77–94. Lanham: Lexington, 2018.
———. *The Politics of Metanoia: Towards a Post–Nationalistic Political Theology in Ethiopia*. Frankfurt: Peter Lang, 2014.
"To the Global Community, Prime Minister Dr. Abiy Ahmed, Ethiopian Embassy From Concerned Ethiopians Across the Globe." http://aigaforum.com/documents/Open-Letter-to-International-Community-Concerned-Amhara.pdf.
Tronvoll, Kjetil. "Tigray: Towards a De-facto State?" *Ethiopian Observer*, May 14, 2020. http://www.ethioobserver.net/Tigray_defacto_state.htm.
———. *War & the Politics of Identity in Ethiopia: Making Enemies & Allies in the Horn of Africa*. Cumbria, UK: Currey, 2009.
Turton, David, ed. *Ethnic Federalism: The Ethiopian Experience in Comparative Perspective*. Athens, OH: Ohio University Press, 2006.
Ward, Graham. *Cities of God*. London: Routledge, 2000.

# Part II

# Ethno-Political Crisis and Resolutions: Past and Present

# 2

# Reflections on Conundrums and Prospect of Writing Ethiopian History

## Afework Hailu

ETHIOPIA IS A DIVERSE country with complex layers of history. As one of Africa's most populous countries and as a home of multiethnic people, Ethiopia is characterized as a "museum of peoples"[1] that displays a copious diversified culture. In this regard, much has been written to broaden our understanding of Ethiopia's cultural diversity, peoples' interaction, and means and methods of empire/state formation within its long history.[2] Admittedly, however, the occurrence and maintenance of such "mosaic" display in the country has led to contradictory and often conflicting theses. This in turn became the reason for a production of divergent historical narratives: on the one hand, we encounter what can be referred to as "the assimilationist, Ethio-nationalist" thesis[3] which some would character-

---

1. Conti-Rossini's description of Ethiopia as *un museo di popoli*. On the one hand, note that Donald N. Levine assumes that there are many common traits shared among Ethiopians, and "[t]o see Ethiopia of a mosaic of distinct peoples is to overlook to many features they have in common . . . and to ignore the numerous relationships these people groups have had with one another" (Levine, *Greater Ethiopia*, 21); thus, the country must be regarded as "a single cultural region" even though it is politically, religiously, and linguistically diverse.

2. Among many others, see Taddesse, "Process of Ethnic Interaction," 5–18; Merid, "Southern Ethiopia"; Merid, "Population Movement," 266–281; Pankhurst, *Social History*; Pankhurst, *Ethiopia*.

3. In some cases, this can be referred as *ahadawi* ("Unionist"). Below is discussed how twentieth-century political formation of the center is important in the categorization of the "north-south" divide; in this perspective, the understanding of the "northern" thesis, I argue, emanates from the opposition to the center-politics of the ruling

ize as a "northern" thesis, and on the other, we come across narratives of Ethiopian history as a "southern" approach which could be referred as an "exclusivist, ethno-nationalist anti-thesis."[4]

The current dominant historical narrative entangled between the Ethio-nationalist narrative and its anti-thesis (Ethno-nationalist) discourses almost successfully control the imagination of many Ethiopians actively involved in the nation's socio-political engagement. In such a perspective, I see my reflection as a rejoinder to voice a call for implementing a viable and inclusive approach in writing Ethiopian history. By discussing some brief historical excerpts from the long history of Ethiopia, I will show that there are many additional and complex trends in Ethiopian history beyond the discussion of mere "north-south divide" and the interpretive mode that has long focused on class struggle between the *ruling center* and the *dominated periphery*. In light of this, as a way forward towards a better construction and reconstruction of Ethiopian history, I further offer necessary comments on how writers of both sides handle the available historical sources.

## Ethiopian Historiographies

Writing history in general is not merely an interpretation of historical event and data but highly involves imagination that is shaped by memory, knowledge, and even an art of communication,[5] which we also see in the writing of Ethiopian history. This is well captured by Ethiopian thinker Geubre Heywet Baykedagn, who states:

> የታሪክ ትምርት ... የሚጠቅም የውነተኛ ታሪክ ትምርት ሲሆን ነው ። እውነተኛንም ታሪክ ለመጻፍ ቀላል ነገር አይደለም። የሚከተሉት ሦስት የእግዚአብሔር ስጦታዎች ያስፈልጉታሉ ፦ መጀመሪያ ፦ ተመልካች ልቦና የተደረገውን ለማስተዋል ፤ ኹለተኛ ፦ የማያዳላ አእምሮ በተደረገው ለመመርምር ፤ ሦስተኛ የጠራ ፡ የቋንቋ አገባብ— የተመለከቱትንና የፈረዱትን ፡ ለማስታወቅ ።[6]

---

class of twentieth-century Ethiopia (that aligned itself with the Orthodox Church's "Amhara" dominant culture). "North" in this case then is area dominated by the Orthodox Christianity, from Debra Bizen in Eretria to Dabra Libanos in Shoa.

4. This is designated by some as *zewugeyawi* ("of Ethnicity"); note that the "southern" could be misleading since the view concerned for the "oppressed" people groups in Ethiopia, whether from the northern or southern part of the country.

5. In historical discussion, note that not only the data and evidence used but its narratives are important, and thus in historical writing, there must be a critical engagement with all such aspects; for a good discussion, see White, *Content of the Form*, 1987.

6. Geubre Heywet, "አጤ ምኒልክና ኢትዮጵያ" ["Aṭe Menelik enna Iythopiya," Amharic]; see also Bahru, *Pioneers*, 49–52; most importantly 141–42.

> To be useful, study of history . . . must be authentic study of history. It is not easy to write authentic history for it requires three God-given gifts. The first, thoughtful observation to understand what happened [in the past]; the second, impartial mentality when passing judgement on the events; the third, flawless use of language in order to communicate one's own observations and judgement.

These important history-writing principles, according to the writer, were not strictly followed, which in turn led the traditional history writers to commit three "crimes"—literally sins: "በትልቁ ነገር ፈንታ ትኒሹን ይመለከታሉ ፤ ለእውነት መፍረድንም ትተው በአድልዖ ልባቸውን ያጠባሉ ፤ አጻጻፋቸውም ድብቅልቅ እየኾነ ላንባቢው አይገባም።"[7] According to Geubre Heywet, these mistakes were committed by both writers of the chroniclers of the royal court and those of the monastery, the clerical historians: the former's writings cannot be regarded as history for they are intended to get favor and honor from the king in exchange for the praises they pour to him, while the latter devoted in the praises of the kings those who were supporting them and vilify those who benefit the people.[8]

Other writings also offered critical discussion on Ethiopian historiography, among others,[9] Bahru Zewde's meticulous discussion has widened our understanding of Ethiopian historiography.[10] In this part of the chapter, I further expand the discussion and highlight the basis for two

---

7. "They focus on the minor more than the major. They did not truthfully pass judgment but rather confine their thinking [lit.: 'hearts' to impartiality. Their writing being confused, it confounds the reader." Geubre Heywet Baykedagn, aṭe Menelik.

8. "እንዱ ዓይነት የቤተ መንግሥት ሊቃውንት ይባላሉ ፤ ማለት እንጆራን ሲፈልጉ ከቤተመንግሥት ተጠግተው ንጉሡ ያዘዛቸውን የራሱን ውዳሴ ታሪክ ብለው ጽፈው ለኋላው ትውልድ የሚያስቀሩ አቄላማጭቾች ። ኹለተኛው ዓይነት ግን መነኮሳት ናቸው። እሱም የሚጻፉት ታሪክ አድልዖ ይበዛበታል የሳቸውን እንጀ የሕዝቡን ጥቅምና ጉዳት ከፉ አያቅሥሩምና ስለዚህ የለባቸውን የማፈጽምላቸውን ንጉሥ ቅዱስ ቅዱስ ይሉታል። ከድንቅርናቸው ወጥቶ ከፉ ባለ ግሊና ተመርቶ ስለዚኞቹ ልማት የሚጥር ግን ርኩስ።" Geubre Heywet Baykedagn, aṭe Menelik; see, Shiferaw, "Gäbrä-Heywät Baykädañ," 106–20; a short but good summary on the life of Geubre Heywet, in Bahru, *Pioneers*, 49–52.

9. For example, somehow in line with the critique offered by Geubre Heywet, an important observation was also made in the early nineteenth century by Tamrat Ammanuel; for him the church scholars (whom he refers to as *däbtära*) wrote Ethiopian history (mainly as in the form of chronicle), the main problem in their writing being full of adoration for the king who sponsored their work. Note that, in addition to his criticism against the traditional scholars of the church, Tamrat also has shown reservation regarding Western writers whom he however admires; only a few of them "know perfectly the languages, the character of the people and the customs of the country and they sway between the two extremes of adulation and viruperation" (Bahru, *Pioneers*, 144).

10. Among many other aspects of Ethiopian historiography he has ably analyzed, his critical discussion on the ethno-nationalistic discourses is very important for our discussion here.

trends (ethno and Ethio-nationalist) that highly shaped the contemporary Ethiopian historiography.

## Ethio-nationalist Narrative

The task of writing Ethiopian history started at least in the fourteenth century AD in the form of writing of the history of kings (*Tarikä Nägäśt*)[11] and narratives that endeavored to cover "the whole gamut of social justice, administrative reform and economic analysis as well as historical reconstruction."[12] As related to the former, we also observe other accounts that tangentially discuss the history of the land that gives attention not only to the story of the "northern" parts of Ethiopia but with some vigorous impressions of biases against the rest.[13] It is obvious that emphasis is given to Orthodox Christianity, extending from the narrative that Ethiopia is the land favored by the Divine and destined to play a central role in salvation history, as evident in *Kəbrä Nägäśt,* which serves as a kind of Ethiopian national epic that entangles the religious with the political affairs of empire.

Originally produced among the Tigre in a bid to establish a strong legitimacy to rule and establish Əndärta's dynasty—in the midst of Zagʷe and Shoan conflict—*Kəbrä Nägäśt* can rightly be regarded as the most important book that shaped the Christian religious and political ethos of post-fourteenth-century Ethiopia.[14] Two very important but interrelated themes dominate the *Kəbrä Nägäśt*. It asserts that the glory of God departed from Israel as the ark of the covenant was taken to Ethiopia, and as a consequence of this, the divine will sealed the supremacy of the Ethiopian "Solomonic" kings. Ensuing to this grant, other nations in the land are destined to be the fortunate subjects, as highlighted in the book:

> And DĔMÂTĔYÔS (the Patriarch TIMOTHEUS (?) who sat from 511 to 517), the Archbishop of RÔM (i.e.,

---

11. According to Professor Bahru Zewde, "on the positive side, one can cite their factual detail and their strong chronological framework, even if it would require considerable labor to convert their relative chronology to an absolute one. On the negative side are their decidedly political and religious bias, their predilection for supernatural explanation of historical phenomena, and their aversion to quantification" (Bahru, "Century of Historiography," 20).

12. Bahru, "Century of Historiography," 20.

13. In many cases, the romanticizing of northern Ethiopia's past as some historical books and notes clearly follows the notes on "vulgar," "savage," "pagan" culture of the non-Orthodox Amhara-Tigray culture.

14. *Kəbrä Nägäśt* has received enormous attention by many Ethiopists hailing from a wide range of disciplines.

CONSTANTINOPLE, BYZANTIUM), said, "I have found in the Church of [Saint] SOPHIA among the books and the royal treasures a manuscript [which stated] that the whole kingdom of the world [belonged] to the Emperor of RÔM and the Emperor of ETHIOPIA." . . . From the middle of JERUSALEM, and from the north thereof to the south-east is the portion of the Emperor of RÔM; and from the middle of JERUSALEM from the north thereof to the south and to WESTERN INDIA is the portion of the Emperor of ETHIOPIA.[15]

The divine will attested in the *Kəbrä Nägäśt* served as the most important aspect of identity formation in Ethiopia by promoting God's choice of this holy nation as the favored new "Solomonic Israelite" kingdom, blended with notes from memory of the glorious days of the Aksumite Kingdom.[16]

Historical sources reveal that more than his predecessors of the Amhara "Solomonic" Dynasty that has been established in 1270, the successive victories of Amdä Ṣəyon (1314–44) and stories of conquest taken to resemble what the *Kəbrä Nägäśt* promises: he conquered the "pagan" lands, he subjugated the Jews (in Ethiopia, the Fälasha), and Muslim territories were put under his dominion by military might. At the dawn of the fourteenth century, it is clear that the *military and political power* of the "Semitic" south of the Amhara propitiously blended with the northern *myth* of the *Kəbrä Nägäśt*. The Ethiopian king was now of Israelite heritage. Aksum was the New Jerusalem. The Ethiopian temporal kingdom was garbed in an eternal divine agenda.

> From . . . cultural realities a 'national' destiny was derived and formalized into a literary epic, known as the *Kebrä Nägäst* which claimed for Christians, Semitic-speaking Ethiopians the patrimony of biblical Israel. Ethiopia was, quite simply, the New Israel. Its rulers took their regnal names seriously: Amdä S'eyon 'Pilar of Zion', Newayä Krestos 'Possession of Christ', Zär'a Ya'qob 'Seed of Jacob', Bäe'dä Maryam 'By the Hand of Mary'. Christianity gave Ethiopia's rulers access to a tradition of social thought, running back to the teachings of St. Paul, which enjoyed submissive behaviour to the powers that be.[17]

---

15. Budge, *Sheba*, 14–15. We now know that the *Kəbrä Nägäśt* is produced and financed by an Əndärta nobility.

16. The book mentions kings of Aksumite Kingdom, which lasted from about the first century BC until about the seventh century AD.

17. Crummey, *Land*, 21.

It has long been assumed that Ethiopia is a Christian island encircled by Muslims and pagans, but all divinely destined to subjugation. The theme of the book—the blessed rightful and legitimate rule due to the direct connection of the bloodline of Ethiopian kings to that of Solomon of Israel—has clearly dominated the Ethiopian religio-political life until the second half of the twentieth century, shaping some aspects of the historical reconstruction of Ethiopia.

This claim to legitimacy and the propaganda it inculcates on the faithful can also rightly be seen in non-religious works; the history writers from this wider camp depend on the writings produced from the Christian dominated northern part of the country, which is a literate society, almost annulling the history of the "south."[18]

We note similar "north"-centric historical accounts delivered not only from church-affiliated chroniclers but also from pages of the writings produced by the elites of the society who produced volumes of books, particularly in nineteenth and twentieth centuries. This group unsurprisingly has mainly been dominated by the "Solomonic"-centric writers, with greater emphasis given to the "north" (from Tigray to Shoa) and its Orthodox Christianity, developing a trend that seems to be the rule of its writing: an "unintentional" forgetfulness of the rest. Differences emerge, however, when it comes to alliance, as evident in discussions of the place of the kings originating from a particular place in the "north."[19] At this junction, it is right to assume that all the weaknesses from this side remain the stronghold from which the criticisms of Ethno-nationalist writers emanate.

18. When the "rest" is remembered, it is to narrate the challenge it posed to the Christian empire; see, for example, the writings of *Abba* Baherey (in 1593) and Tekle Tsadiq (1990); regarding *Abba* Baherey's Oromo history, see the translation from Ge'ez to Amharic: Getatchew, የአባ ባሕርይ ድርሰቶች ኦሮሞችን ከሚመለከቱ ሌሎች ድርሰቶች ጋር; see Maimire, "Abba Bahrey's Zenahu LeGalla," 1–28. And Tekle Tsadiq Mekuria, አጼ ዮሐንስ (*Atse Yohanes*, in Amharic).

19. This is an underlying problem of chronicle writers, the bias was shared by this well learnt writer of the time; for example, although Heruy Walda-Selassie, one of the twentieth-century historian of this bloc and who aimed to present a more objective history of the land which he achieved in some degree, can rightly be criticised for undermining the place of Emperor Theodros II in the expense of praises to emperors Yohannes IV and Menelik II (probably for the reason noted below), while Afawarq Gabra-Iyyasus, who also wrote a historical account of Menelik II, undermined Emperor Yohannes IV favouring Menelik II, for which Geubre Heywet critiques him: "ዳግማዊ ምኒልክንም ለማመስገን ዳግማዊ ዮሐንስን መስደብ የሚያስፈልግ ያስመስላል።"/"he tries to depict that it is proper to vilify Yohannes [IV] in order to praise Menelik II" (Geubre Heywet, "አጤ ምኒልክና ኢትዮጵያ," 6).

## Ethno-nationalist Narratives

On the ethno-nationalist side, as Bahru notes, important successes have been made particularly following the historical pivots of 1974 and 1991. Some historical ethno-nationalist narratives have shown us that there is more in Ethiopia than the usual praise offered for the legitimacy of the imperial era's restrictive Solomonic–centred political culture. Relevant to the time after the 1990s, we also see the ultimate challenge posed against the hegemony of the centre, which in turn extends our understanding of the contribution of multiethnic peoples towards the Ethiopian state-building processes. This means that the attempt to delineate the divide between north and south in Ethiopia narrowed not only politically but also in its focus of social studies: the change affirmed once again that the Ethiopian history could not be the story of the so-called "Semitic" north only; and furthermore, the southerners are successfully taken as subjects more than objects of history.[20] With all its weaknesses and its reactionary approaches, and its problem of dwelling in the past's injustice, the attempts in the production of historical materials regarding numerous people groups by the Ethno-nationalists could rightly be taken as a decent start in our aspirations of writing of a more inclusive Ethiopian history. Publications and academic discussions from this perspective no doubt highlight "the other side" of history of Ethiopia, stories of injustices purported by the ruling class against the non-Orthodox faith communities and the southerners. They lament that the power used in empire building processes have been brutal and dehumanizing, even considered parallel to the European scramble for Africa, but posited by "black colonisers."[21] The attempt to annul the nations in the empire is the culprit for the diminishing of peoples' culture,[22] which they believe caused unending colonization not only of the land but also the minds and souls of the "non-northerners." This is well articulated by the infamous article presented by the 1960s Ethiopian revolutionary Walleligh Mekonen:

---

20. This does not mean that there were no attempt to write history of the "southerners" by those from the north, with its weaknesses and often unfounded claims (the highly criticized book by Baherey on the history of Oromo people is the earliest, written in 1593 EC and mentioned above; other "controversial" books are, Atsme-Giorgis Gebre-Mesih (Allaqa) ፤ የ [ኦሮም] ታሪክ /History of [the Oromo] 1; Taye Gebre-Maryam (Allaqa), የኢትዮጵያ ህዝብ ታሪክ / History of the People of Ethiopia. Note that for this paper, I take liberty to put "Semitic" and "Cushitic" in quotation marks to affirm my stance that the "Semitic"–"Cushitic" difference is linguistic than racial.

21. See Asafa, "Two National Liberation Movements," 152–74; such an argument is already outlined in Holcomb and Sisai, *Invention of Ethiopia*; also, Baxter, "Ethiopia's Unacknowledged Problem," 283–96; a general discussion from periphery's point of view is presented by Bereket (see Selassie, *Conflict*).

22. See Bahru, "Century of Historiography," 34–35.

Is it not simply Amhara and to a certain extent Amhara–Tigre supremacy? Ask anybody what Ethiopian culture is? Ask anybody what Ethiopian language is? Ask anybody what Ethiopian music is? Ask anybody what the "national dress" is? It is either Amhara or Amhara–Tigre!! To be a "genuine Ethiopian" one has to speak Amharic, to listen to Amharic music, to accept the Amhara–Tigre religion, Orthodox Christianity and to wear the Amhara–Tigre Shamma in international conferences. In some cases to be an "Ethiopian", you will even have to change your name. In short to be an Ethiopian, you will have to wear an Amhara mask (to use Fanon's expression).[23]

In such an approach, one can easily understand that stories of injustice purported by the ruling class against the non-Orthodox communities and the "southerners" are realized; the empire-building process is considered as a dehumanizing process that used a cultural monopoly as a brutal machinery that aimed to annul the identity of the subjugated nations,[24] a process that some even considered as "black colonizing black people."[25] A strong refutation against the hegemony of the "north" (Amahara–Tigre) Orthodox Christian culture, the view can be seen as deconstruction of the Ethio-nationalist view discussed above. However, for our discussion here, one may choose to see it as a complimentary input for the further development of common history of Ethiopia, for such struggle aspires to see "a state in which all nationalities participate equally in state affairs, it is a state where every nationality is given equal opportunity to preserve and develop its language, its music and its history. It is a state where Amharas, Tigres, Oromos, Aderes [Harari], Somalis, Wollamos [Wolaytas], Gurages, etc. are treated equally."[26]

It is important to note that both *Ethio-nationalist* and *Ethno-nationalist* historiographers have so far exhibited some achievements for the development of writing of Ethiopian history. It is indeed through the numerous

23. Wallelign, "Nationalities," 4–7.

24. For example, regarding Oromo, a historian laments that "It is not an exaggeration to say that no people have had their history so distorted or ignored and their achievements and human qualities undervalued as the Oromo have in the Ethiopian historiography . . . Until very recently, Oromo history has been either neglected, as M. Abir admits, or it has been totally ignored, or it has been distorted by prejudice" (Mohammed, *Oromo of Ethiopia*, 2); however, this is compensated by the numerous twenty- to twenty-first-century writings, thus calling for a more synthesis approach to the writing of Ethiopian history.

25. Asafa, "Liberation Movements," 152; see below (related to, footnote 54) Merera Gudina's critique offered against "colonial thesis."

26. Wallelign, "Nationalities," 5.

Ethio-nationalist historical writings that we have a broader understanding of aspects of Ethiopian political history (even though, in this category, we find hagiographers, popular writers, and also professionals, etc.) in shedding light on the sacrifice paid (in blood and sweat) in the process of Ethiopia's empire/state-formation. In such a narrative, admittedly, it is the center, not the periphery, which is painted as more important; but seen positively, it is through such narratives that the wide gap evident in writing Ethiopian history has significantly narrowed. It is an approach with more attention to the stories of the elites, not the commoners. Nonetheless, it is through such an adventure of writing of history that we learn the main ideologies and perceptions implemented in the formation of the Ethiopian empire and state. The main problem with this approach, as has been noted by many scholars, is mainly that it is burdened with the denial of existence of diversity in Ethiopia and if it encounters such, the aim is to assimilate it to the dominant "melting-pot" culture.

What then can we conclude? It is apparent that both the Ethio- and Ethno-nationalist discourses tend to be a rejection of the other, each building itself at the expense of the other. Moreover, both views exhibit weakness in handling historical accounts of the complex dynamic routes in the formation of the Ethiopian empire/state as I have shown below. Thus, one should not only adopt better methodology but must also consider different and complex layers of writing Ethiopian history to avoid credulous conclusions.

## Toward a Viable Historiography

The claim that the blood and sweat poured into Ethiopian empire-building (or even the process of state formation) only belongs to one stock of a particular people group in Ethiopia is equally guilty of the claim that there has never been a political space for the northerners (non-Orthodox and Amhara/Tigrians). Despite the fact that some writings (which are written by unprofessional historians) are identified as "objective" history of Ethiopia, when closely examined it becomes evident that the art of writing history in Ethiopia is mainly shaped by the understanding of the authors' lack of ability to handle complex narratives, which destined their writings to repeat the same predicament observed throughout time, that is, the guilt of omission, and/or selection, and/or deletion, and/or overgeneralization of one aspect of past event from the other, and this only to produce ill-informed narratives.

I assume that all self-respecting historians would give due attention to proper historical methodology, currently recognized as a *critical philosophy of history.*[27] It is believed that the work of a historian is an attempt to articulate presentations of historical data, which further needs an appropriate level of interpretation; the interpretation is a process in finding that best explanation of the facts:

> *There are always alternative ways to interpret . . . our evidence,* so that an essential part of our task, as historians, is to figure out *which among these alternative interpretations is best,* which involves, among other things, determining which among them is *most likely to be true.* Yes, *true.* For the fundamental point of the historical quest, from the start, has been to discover the truth. And *discovering* that—as opposed merely to *inventing* it—means deciding among competing interpretations on the basis of whatever *reasons* seem relevant and whatever *evidence* is available. Thus, in philosophy of history, getting back to the basics, whatever else it might mean, centrally involves figuring out how we can discover what really happened in the past and what it means that it happened.[28]

This interpretation, we are told, should be aimed at some degree of objectivity. What is this "degree of objectivity" then? We know that, as all well-trained historians affirm, interpretation is a mental process—perhaps imagination—that no doubt is subjective. As Bahru Zewde rightly said in agreement with the world-leading historian Burke, "in as much the *total* historical truth cannot be known, historians . . . could profitably employ some literary techniques to fill the gap between their research findings and to what could have actually happened. After all, the best literary historians had always combined factual investigation and creative imagination."[29]

I do believe that we aim to present an "objective" history within a reasonable subjective interpretation but this can only be achieved when guided by some principles. At this junction, I advocate the necessity of adopting critical philosophy of writing history. We ask:

- who writes history, with what agenda in mind, and towards what end?

---

27. This chapter is not intended to discuss the genesis, progress, and pros and cons of different historical methods and historiographies—from Ranke in nineteenth century to Hayden White and Raymond Martin in the twentieth century—however aspires to present the main emphasis of the debate on critical philosophy of history, which is considered as a more inclusive method in ways to implement it in interpreting history, and this is well presented by Martin, "Objectivity," 25–50.

28. Martin, "Objectivity," 29.

29. Bahru, "Century of Historiography," 16.

- how accurate can a historian ever hope to be, analyzing past events from the vantage point of the historian's present?
- does the historian's *own* perspective, impacted as it undoubtedly is by gender, age, national and ideological affiliation, etc., contribute to an "agenda" that the historian's work is playing into, unwittingly or consciously?
- what about the types of sources, both primary and secondary an historian chooses to base his or her work upon? Do *they* too contribute to the above-mentioned "agenda?"
- does the very selection of sources (and, by extension, the decision to exclude certain other sources) prejudice the outcome of the historian's work in certain ways? *et cetera*.[30]

I presume that all these questions can guide and help writers to be thoughtful when embarking on the task of writing history in general and that of Ethiopia in particular. And, perhaps, it offers some protection from creating a narrative in our own image (and worse, shaping the past events within our own perception) at the expense of what we could have known, and this in turn advances a better understanding in the writing of Ethiopian history—as I briefly attempt to apply them below.

## Handling Multi-faceted Stories from Ethiopia's Past: *towards an Understanding of Ethiopian History*

### Dynamics in the Ethiopian Empire(s): *Empire Built by Blood-and-Sweat*

For one, we must admit that war has been the main machine that shaped the political map of a country and built its central power, and this fact generally remains true for almost all of history of any imperial state formation in the world from time immemorial to the modern era. Meaning, numerous empires/states have been built by blood and sweat and evidence from Ethiopian history should not—by any means—be expected to affirm the contrary. Historical sources at least from the Aksumite era (first century BC to seventh century AD) show that there had been countless wars recorded in inscriptions on the pages of the chronicles of the conquering kings, and in the oral traditions and memories of those defeated and subjugated peoples. For example, the so-called "Adulis Inscription" gives a vivid testimony to what

---

30. Bahru, "Century of Historiography."

happened in about 150 AD.[31] The inscription on the throne addresses the tribes and people groups ruled by an unnamed king who ruled over many nations including Aksum and its surroundings.[32]

The monarch[33] is reported to have ruled over the Aksumite kingdom and lands in South Arabia, as well as the eastern parts of Africa, including Barbaria (Somalia) and Sasu, a country located far south of Barbaria.[34] In addition to the many "tribes" submitting to him willingly and "became likewise tributary," the king tells of his success in bringing numerous "nations" under his rule. He further declares:

> I sent a fleet and land forces against the Arabites and Cianaedocolpitae[35] who dwelt on the other side of the Red Sea, and having the sovereigns of both, I imposed on them a land tribute and charged them to make travelling safe both by sea and land. I thus subdued the whole coast from Luencê Cômê to the country of the Sabaeans. I first and alone of the kings of my race made these conquests. For this success I now offer my thanks to my mighty God, Arês, who begate me, and by whose aid I reduced all the nations bordering on my own country, on the East to the country of frankincense, and on the West to Ethiopia[36] and

---

31. See Indicopleustes, *Christian Topography*, 54–67. Written in Greek characters on the back of an ancient throne the "Adulis Inscription" is one of the earliest inscriptions discovered at Aksum (see comments by McCrindle on 54n2).

32. Views on the date of the inscription are discussed (Indicopleustes, *Christian Topography*, 59n59). The Adulis Inscription is important since it details the imperial formation under the (pre?) Aksumite Kingdom which took place not later than the second century AD. It is both a triumphal as well as a dedicatory inscription in which not only the names of the "tribes" and "nations" conquered by the king are listed, but also the religious conviction of the king is recounted.

33. The unnamed king perhaps was ruling from coastal region of Adulis (see Phillipson, *African Civilisation*, 64.

34. Quoting V. de Saint-Martin, McCrindle gives us a summary of the vast area ruled by the monarch: "at least of the districts and tribes mentioned in the inscription shows us his first conquest in the neighbourhood itself Aksum, and at a little distance from that city, which was evidently the seat of his native principality. Then we see his arms carried successively into . . . Tana . . . the kingdom of Adel, into the country of Harrar and the Somalis . . . Finally crossing over the narrow basin of the Arabian Gulf" (Indicopleustes, *Christian Topography*, 59–60, n3).

35. Possibly mean "a branch of the great tribe of Kinda, to which the tribe of Kelb united itself. They occupied Hedjaz, which is now the Holy Land of Arabia, containing as it does the sacred cities of Mecca and Medina" (Indicopleustes, *Christian Topography*, 64n1).

36. Indicopleustes, *Christian Topography*, 65n1. Here Ethiopia might have been a reference to Nubia (Sudan), or possibly, to the territories in the interiors of the kingdom.

Sasu.³⁷ Of these expeditions, some were conducted by myself in person, and ended in victory, and the others I entrusted to my officers. Having thus brought all the world under my authority to peace, I came down to Aduli and offered sacrifice to Zeus, and to Arês and Poseidôn, whom I entered to befriend all who go down to the sea in ships. Here also I reunited all my forces, and setting down this Chair in this place, I consecrated it to Ares in the twenty-seventh year of my reign.³⁸

The "Adulis Inscription" mentions the names of the "nations" subjected, made tributary-paying nations within the territory of the king, and tells how he managed to bring many tribes under his kingdom, securing peace and ensuring safe travel routes. From northeast Africa, the area that includes environs of the town of Aksum, he waged war against "nations" and brought them all under his rule.³⁹ The king also adds that in addition to those submitted to him "of their own accord" those who ferociously resisted soon submitted to his military force when overwhelmed by his war strategy: though they were protected "by mountains all but impregnable, I conquered, after engagements in which I myself present. Upon their submission I restored their territories to them, subject to the payment of tribute."⁴⁰ Interestingly, the king offers praise to the gods for availing their powers in the raid (in this

---

37. The whereabouts of Sasu (rightly, Kasu) is debated: while Kaffa, the southern part of proper Ethiopia, is suggested as an option, scholars like Dillmann, Glaser, and McCrindle assume that it is "located only in or near Meroe [ . . . thus] The king penetrated westward to Ethiopia and Kasu, that is, into the region of Khartoum" (Indicopleustes, *Christian Topography*, 63–64, n1).

38. Indicopleustes, *Christian Topography*, 64–66.

39. He also conquered many other "tribes," named Gaze, Agame, Sigye, Aua, Tiamo, Gambela, "and tribes near them" such as Zingabane, Angabe, Tiama, Athagus and Semenoi—"a people who lived beyond the Nile on the mountains difficult of access and covered with snow, where the year is all winter with hailstorms, frosts and snow into which a man sinks knee-deep Lazine; other "tribes" are also named: Zaa, Gabala, Atalamo, Bega. Indicopleustes, *Christian Topography*, 59–62. See footnotes on these pages regarding the geographical locations for all these "nations." Many of the places and "nations" mentioned can be traced to these days, and for example, on Semenoi. On the borders of Egypt, he went against Tangaitae and "made a footpath giving access by land into Egypt from the part of" his dominions; from the coasts of the Red Sea area, "tribes" like Annine and Metine as well as Sesea became his subjects, and the king tells that it was the "Rhausi I next brought to submission: a barbarous race spread over wide waterless plains in the interior of the frankincense country. [And then advancing towards the sea] I encountered the Solate whom I subdued and left instructions to guard the coast"; the "tribes" mentioned seems to be in areas that stretch from borders of Egypt to south of Somalia (see Indicopleustes, *Christian Topography*, 59–64).

40. Indicopleustes, *Christian Topography*, 63–64.

case, Mahrem).⁴¹ Here, readers of Ethiopian history should brace themselves to read how the kings boastfully count their booty, using their success stories as propaganda that probably would again trigger invasion of new territories that have never been occupied by their predecessors.

I discuss this inscription at some depth to present evidence from the long history of the land that could possibly exemplify the main trend that the empire is built (or, in many instances, resisted) at the point of the sword[42] rather than peace treaties and negotiations (particularly when the defeated ruler shows willingness to take a status of a dignified local leader).[43] And in this particular case, incorporated under the empire with payment of tribute on their head, the subjugated kings and rulers of the nations were left to rule their territory, which, with a few exceptions, was the case in most centuries of Ethiopian history.[44]

## Ethiopia's "Center–Periphery" Dynamics:
*Multi-colored Events in Ethiopian History*

The above-mentioned "Adulis Inscription" well portrays the power of the established center of Aksumite Dynasty. Furthermore, evidence from available historical data and other inscriptions also provides us some relevant clues as to how a once subjugated nation would become the powerhouse of the Ethiopian empire/state within a few centuries. Interestingly, for example, in one case the "Cushitic" Agaw is mentioned as one of subjugated peoples of the Aksumites.[45] As we learn from another inscription, which claimed to be a production of *Ḥaṣani* Daniel (probably a new king from the "Cushitic" Zagʷe), that the Aksumite king has been reduced to a vassal to the new king and kingdom, and made a tributary-paying ruler with a very small territory:

ወመፅ: ንጉሥ: ወፈተወ[:] ይንግሰኒ: እንዘ: ሀሎኩ[:] በአክሱም: ዘከመ: ግአዜ: አበዊሁ: በነደየ፤ ጸዋዖኒ[:] ጸዋ መፅ አክሱም ወገዐየ[ሰ] [ወአፍሪሀየ:] ዘዕዉየ

41. In other inscriptions the "Lord of Heaven" is mentioned, and another produced in the first decades of the fourth century, the Christian God—Trinity—also mentioned; for important discussion regarding inscriptions from Aksum and its environs, see Sergew Hable Selassie, *Ancient and Medieval History*, 89–113.

42. See Taddesse, *Church and State*; mainly chapter 5 "Territorial Expansion", 119–155.

43. For which, as mentioned below, we also have some historical evidence.

44. Mentioned below is the case of King Ṭona of Wolaita, who was removed from his territory and imprisoned by Emperor Menelik II.

45. The Aksumites and the Agaw are designated as "Semitic" and "Cushitic" respectively because of affinity of their languages in classification of Afro-Asiatic language groups.

> [ጼ]ወዉኩ[:] ዘመጽአ፤ እምቅድመ: [ይት]ከወ.[:] ደም ቀ[ነ]ይኩ: ንጉሰ:
> አከሱም: ወፈነዉክዎ:ይነጽር: አከሱም: ብሐረ: መንግስትየ[:] [ወተረ]ነወ[ξ]ወ ..
> [አዉ]ፈርኩ[:]

> And there came the King while I was in Aksum and [he] wanted also to rule after the way of his fathers, as a poor man (?); he came to Aksum also looting and catching. But when I moved out and [startled] my enemy (?), I imprisoned the newcomer without bloodshed; I subjugated the King of Aksum and I released him in order to govern Aksum, as a land under my dominion; [and he] was released (?) And I sent into the battlefield.[46]

The once glorious king of Aksum and the empire that subjugated numerous nations in Africa (south to Egypt) and across the Red Sea (South Arabia) is now defeated and remained under the mercy of the new Christian king who allowed him to govern the town of Aksum. This trend is not an isolated incident in Ethiopian history, since the fluidity of the center had been highly marked by power struggle which would leave the winners to seal their destiny as new rulers, and then leaving its mark regarding the inter-ethnic conflicts and tensions that existed for centuries.

Again, it was none other but the Amhara who once had been civil servants in the Zag<sup>w</sup>e Royal court that later established the so-called Solomonic Dynasty, reducing their former lords to (dignified) subjects of their empire. The empire was established by Yekunno Amlak (1270–85) whose family root was not from the royal court, the same story shared by some kings of the same dynasty, like "Tewodiros (1855–1868), Yohannes (1872–89), and Menelik (1889–1913), none of whom may have had any royal blood, were successful in founding their 'Solomonic' dynasties."[47]

The Ethiopian Jews, the Betä Ǝsraʾel (known as "Fälasha"), who once established their kingdom, expanding their dominance by successfully converting Christians to Judaism, finally lost their dominance in the fourteenth century. As reported in many sources, strong animosity between them and the Christian power of the center developed. After successive revolts upon losing control over their territories, their defeat led them to be subjugated and ostracized, and then coerced to adopt Christianity.

Sources on events before the sixteenth century also testify that some of the Islamic sultanates in the south and eastern part of the country were left as tax-paying nations to the Christian kingdom originated in Shoan

---

46. Littmann et al., *Deutsche Aksum-Expedition*, 46. Inscription 14.
47. Getatchew, "Unity," 484.

plateau, which probably led to establishment of dominant "Semitic" Christian culture in those subjugate areas.⁴⁸

It has to be noted by writers of Ethiopian history that even when territories are put under the rule of the empire, the relationship between the political elites of the center and the subjugated "periphery" was never a mere "rigid"/"sharp" dichotomy. Even after a war that has caused bloodshed, political negotiation was often made smoother through different means, like political marriage (as it was evidently seen from the story of *ətege* (Queen) Əleni, from Hadiya),⁴⁹ which aimed to seal a close relationship between the sole-ruler and the regional leaders, the list is long:

> Indeed, the mother of the founder of the dynasty, Yekunno Amlak, was a slave of unknown origin, while many queens, including the consort of Dawit (1344–88), mother of Zer'a Ya'iqob (1434–68), were Tigreans. Zer'a Ya'iqob's wife, the mother of Be'ide Maryam (1468–78), was a [Wolaita] (from Hadiyya. The queen of the great King Serze Dingil (1563–97), the mother of Ya'iqob (1597–1603), was a Felasha; her sister was the mother of Susiniyos (1607–32); his son, Fasil (1632–67), was married to a European; while the wife of Iyyasu II (1730–55), the mother of Iyyo'as (1755–69), was an Oromo . . . Ar'aya, whom Yohannes IV's "groomed to be his successor"], was born of an Afar from the Tiltal of the lowlands. Menelik II (1889–1913) of Shoa was born of a woman who was in the service of the parents of his father. Haile Sellasie (1930–74) . . . his queen, Menen, was an Oromo from Wallo.⁵⁰

Similar trends are also true for the successive events following the sixteenth century Ethiopia, the era in which the once dominant "center" (which was the "Christian north") was nearly reduced to the periphery due to successive military aggressions of the peoples from the south—of the former periphery. First, the Islamic power personified by the successes of *Amir* Aḥmed ibn Ibrahim al-Ġāzī dominated the center for more than thirteen years, after a war that put the Christian empire on its knees. We are told that the only

---

48. Linguists classify Amharic as a "Semitic" language which adopted "Cushitic" sentence structures with numerous loanwords (thus is "Semitic-Cushitic").

49. She was the wife of Emperor Zarayacob (r. 1434–68), regent during the early reign of *aṣe* Ləbnä Dəngəl. Originally from Muslim background, from Hadiya which is from the southern part of the country, some would give her a credit for the diplomacy between Ethiopia and Portugal against *Amir* Ahmed Ibn-Ibrahim, also known as *Gragn*, "the left-handed" (who waged war against the Christian north for economic independence with religious fervency); see Ayele et al., "Catholicism," 699.

50. Getatchew, "Unity," 465–87.

choice being given to the survivors of war was none other than conversion to Islam. Secondly, the rule of *Amir* Aḥmed, brief but of major significance for the coming centuries in the history of the land, was followed by the ascension to power of the Oromos, who successfully eradicated (or assimilated or accommodated) many of the nations into their newly conquered land.[51] Hardly homogenous in their polity, the "integration" of the Oromos in the empire historically noted, in and after the seventeenth century, they became the powerhouse during the so-called Zämänä-Mäsafənt (or, rather the era of Wärä-Šeh Mäsafənt—often known as Yäju Dynasty), ruling Ethiopia "in the name of the Solomonic dynasty."[52] It is in relation to this fact that historians noticed that the Oromo language, even replacing Amharic, became the language of Gondar's Royal court in eighteenth century,[53] which no doubt negates the "colonial thesis." Historical notes are then often quoted to denounce the assertion that the "north" colonized the rest, as in the case for the Oromo; for example, Merera Gudina emphatically argues that

> The difficulty with advancing a colonial thesis for the Oromo, then, is that they do not fit neatly into a historically recorded colonial system. Moreover, there are some other awkward historical facts which Oromo nationalists have to contend with. Queen Victoria, for example, did not marry a Ghanian, a Nigerian or a Kenyan but Ethiopian kings frequently married Oromos—Tewodros, Menilek, and Haile Selassie being the best examples. By the same token, Ghanaians, Nigerians or Kenyans never dreamt of becoming kings or queens of the British empire, under whatever conditions of assimilation, but Oromo were able to become

---

51. Hence, what currently known as the Oromia Regional State. The cultural methods made available by the Oromo for the non-Oromo (to spare one's own life during the expansion) were *Moggassa* ("naming")/ *medhica* or *Gudiffacha* ("adoption"). The expansion changed the geography and demography of Abyssinia (see Levine's "Oromo Anti-thesis" in his *Greater Ethiopia*, 76–79); the effect of Oromo expanssion and aggression on other ethnic groups, see Haile, "የብሔር ጥያቄ? [Yebeher chiqona]," 21–22.

52. See Shiferaw, "Reflections," 157–79. Since there was still a puppet Solomonic king put on the throne, while exercising "absolute authority over their provinces," rulers in other part of the country were made pay regular tributes (Shiferaw, "Reflections," 158–59).

53. Pankhurst, *Ethiopian Royal*, 139–43. Gondar, established by Amaharic speaking kings made the capital of the empire by the time, became bilingual: "Furthermore, the Regents in Gonder/Debre Tabor who governed in the name of the nominal monarchs, following the iron-handed rule of Mika'el Sihul of Tigray, were Oromo from Yejju. From the time of Iyyo'as (1755–69) to the rise of Tewodiros (1855–68), the members of the palace, as well as the city of Gonder, were bilingual, using [Affan Oromo], the language of the Oromo, and Amharic (Getatchew, "Unity," 487); particularly, Iyyo'as was remembered for his eloquence in Affan Oromo (a language of his preference over Amharic); the same was said of Sahelle-Sellasie, the grandfather of Menelik II.

kings and queens of imperial Ethiopia— the best examples being Iyyassu, Hailesellassie, King Michael of Wollo and King Takle—Haymanot of Gojjam."[54]

The historical evidences no doubt would put the narrative of Ethiopian history in a better perspective. Indeed, we know that the place of the Oromos in shaping the center politics took its summit in the twentieth-century with *Lij* Eyasu and Ras Teferi's political influence. It is known that *Lij* Eyasu was the grandson of Ras (later King) Mikael of Wollo,[55] and who remained the choice of the powerful monarch to succeed him—although this failed disastrously due to opposition sparked within his extended family, one accusation was his alleged conversion to Islam, a "charge of apostasy [which] was therefore the most handy to disqualify a competitor who had to be eliminated for many other reasons including personal humiliations and diverging political views";[56] interestingly, this opposition was led by Ras Teferi (later Emperor Haile Selassie I), who also believed to be of Oromo origin through his grandfather,[57] the demise of the heir was but finally sealed by a General from the same ethnic group, Habte-Giorgis Dinegede.[58]

These and similar factors show that not only the periphery replaces the center through power play, but Ethiopian history evidences that the dynamics of center-periphery is more than what has been articulated; we see that the expansion of the periphery through war to finally become the center plays a critical role in the process of Ethiopian empire/state building. We also see that power and dominance is of greater consequence than religion, politics, and ethnicity, etc., as discussed below.

54. Merera, "Contradictory Interpretations," 125.

55. Formerly Ras Mohammed Ali, he was converted to Christianity and took the name Mikael.

56. Ficquet, "Lij Iyasu," 6; see that the book edited by Éloi and Wolbert presents excellent academic works on the life and times of *Lij Iyasu*; among the writers, except for Erlich Haggai who seem to trust the claims of his antagonists (when referring to the autobiography of Haile Sellasie I), all scholars who have closely studied the life of *Lij* Iyasu claim that he retained his Christian faith and lived as Christian (see, the papers by Aramis Houmed Soulé, Richard Pankhurst, and Zuzanna Augustyniak, Estelle Sohier); but this was undermined by the popular view shaped by his "political enemies."

57. Ras Teferi Mekonen is believed to be of Oromo descent through his grand-father Wolde-Mikael (who married the daughter of King Sahele Sellasie of Shoa). Levine's argument that there had been peoples' interactions in Ethiopia even before Menelik II must be recognized (Levine, *Greater Ethiopia*, 21, 27); the book shows that there was a high degree of interaction among Ethiopians, through different means (whether trade, warfare, peoples movement, intermarriage, common religions, and languages—as the factor of Amharic and Affan Oromo shows).

58. Merera, "Elite," 146.

The establishment and reestablishment of the Ethiopian empire in nineteenth and twentieth centuries, through different ways and means, thus cannot be seen as an isolated story in light of the history of the land for at least two millennia. As the center expands and subjugates, those in the periphery either submit or resist. This then is also true for the accounts relating to the eras of at least three King of Kings Tewodros II, Yohannes IV, and Menelik II as presented from both Ethio- and Ethno-nationalists perspectives. Taken seriously and critically analyzed, one would testify this: the rulers/kings of any targeted nations were forced to submit to the empire (and then survive), or perish if they resist.[59]

What then can we conclude? There have been numerous wars (instigated both from the powerhouse of the center and/or the periphery) in which uncountable lives must have been lost from both sides that finally led to the formation of the Ethiopian empire/state. It was the custom of the day then that the winner registers its heroes while the losers count their dead, a harsh reminder that military might—surely no other means—remained the source of power in Ethiopian past. We must then allow that stories of victims and heroes should be told and retold from the accounts of archives (literary and oral) of both parties. In this regard, however, even from the accounts of history which we may claim to *understand*, we may need to advise ourselves the need to keep some amount of sanity in presentation of such facts since, probably, discoverable sources from the other side would testify to the contrary. Since what happened in the Ethiopian past has proved to be something that is not only destined to be forgotten but also to be celebrated and lamented on, we need to learn to look at the past events from different vantage points and angles, assessing from different narratives, entertaining all while being critical of them, so that we may *better understand* our time here and now and project the future that would help the state to serve a common good.

The problem with some aspect of the continuation of the ill-informed interpretation of Ethiopian history as exhibited in the writings of both assimilationists and ethno-nationalists, I think, is their fixation on the twentieth-century history of Ethiopia, an era which was dominated by the highly

59. When finally defeated or having surrendered, the fate of the regional king was either to be spared to rule over his land, or face the ultimatum of banishing from the land (to be replaced by a favorite of the emperor; compare Ṭona of Wolaita with Abba Jiffar of Jimma—the latter retained not only his territory as king but also his Islamic conviction); as compared to the highly centralized government of Haile Sellasie I (1930–74 AD), one would rightly claim that a "federal" type of imperial government was practiced by Meneilik II and, when comes to the Christian kings of territories in the empire, even more plausible in this aspect is the rule of Yohannes IV (who however criticized for being intolerant to his Muslim subjects of Wollo); Caulk, "Religion," 23–41.

centralized government of Emperor Haile Selassie I, to which an in-depth study has already been offered by scholars across the stream.[60] We know that Haile Selassie attempted to create a highly centralized government (some even consider to an extent of establishing a nation-state).[61] It is within the understanding of the above point that we learn how reading and writing Ethiopian history requires a closer look at the long history of the country, advisably as an art of zooming out to go beyond the twentieth century, a quest for striking the balance in our understanding of nineteenth- and twentieth-century history of the nation. A better understanding of Ethiopian history comes when we compare and contrast the earliest developments to that of the reality of pre-Emperor Haile Selassie I's rule, to see that even within the empire which was "built"/"re-built" by Emperor Menelik II,[62] self-rule had been a possibility, particularly at the regional level. Historical sources clearly show that regional lords were kings, and the emperor was the King of Kings. Even in this case, it is not difficult to admit the existence of coercion-in-another-form, whereby strong pressure exerted from the dominant central culture that would (wittingly or unintentionally) create a cultural hegemony; for example, the expansion and privilege of Orthodox Christianity alongside the State and the Amharic language as lingua-Franca of the land, affecting the growth of the culture of "others," if not completely diminishing it.[63]

## Diversity within Nations, Multi-faceted Ethnicity

(1) As shown above, Ethiopian political history reveals that the route to attain emperorship and control of the throne is dynamic. This shows how ascension to the throne was not entirely a matter of ethnicity but also ideology based on the myth of Sheba–Solomon, as throne transfer from the eras of Aksumite to Zag$^{we}$'s to "Solomonic" shows. Even though rulers of Ethiopia in the Modern Era (for example from Theodros II, Teklegiorgis II, Yohannes

60. For example see Clapham, *Haile-Selassie's Government*.

61. One can argue that the attempt is an extreme corrective measure against the earlier policy of Italian rule that attempted to divide the country into four "autonomous" regions, alongside language divides (Tigrigna, Amharic, Oromo, and Arabic); for Italian invasion of Ethiopia and its policy, see Sbacchi, *Ethiopia Under Mussolini*.

62. Actually, the "unification" of southern regions in Ethiopian empire was started and partly accomplished earlier than the era of Emperor Menelik II, during Yohannes IV; see, Zewde Gabre-Sellassie, *Yohannes IV*, 1.

63. Two facts remain challenging for us: the advancement of Amharic, and the survival of the cultures of numerous nations in Ethiopia (even in some cases, remained intact); those who are more able than me could offer a better theory how two completing and opposing factors remain strong at once.

IV, Menelik II, *Lij* Eyasu, to Haile-Selassie I) belong to the same religious confession, all were from different ethnic groups.[64]

Even among these "northerners," ascension to the throne and the method of keeping power was through much bloodshed, demonstrating that religious and ethnic affinity would do little when it comes to establishing one's own dynasty. Against any simplistic north-south dichotomy of conflict and division in the land, it seems important to broaden our focus when dealing with the issue of "dominance of Christian north." We already have discussed the dynamics of center–periphery above. In relation to the event that changed the political sphere of the land from an Aksumite to that of the Zagʷe's rule, we also should note from the source how a king affiliated with a particular religion would humiliate another king of the same religious affinity, the Agaw against the Aksumites, tension between Meneilik II (of Shoa) and Yohannes IV (Tigray). The following story from *Gädlä* Iyasus Mo'a relates how the last Zagʷe king, despite his plea for help from Saint Cirycus (Qirqos), was killed in the church's yard by another Christian king of the same religion:

> Then King Yekʷenno Amläk proceeded towards the country of Bagē Medr. He found there his Zagʷē enemy in the land of Ansatā, which is part of the land of Gāyent. And he killed him in the courtyard of the church of Qirqos. Actually the Zagʷē king entered the church of Saint Qirqos and said: "I place myself under your protection, o Qirqos," while King Yekʷenno Amläk said: "Do not put [him] under protection, against me o Qirqos because Zagʷē has reigned without his father [i.e. he reigned while his father was not king]." He was killed by the hands of Yekʷenno Amläk.[65]

Here, contests of power rather than religion would leave a resilient mark in shaping some of the historical events in Ethiopia. As it is true that there were some religious-oriented wars in Ethiopia, Ethiopian history also witnessed ferocious wars between elites of the same religion, as was between Tekle-Giorgis II and Yohannes IV in 1871.

Honest treatment of the time of *Lij* Eyasu against the conspiracies that shaped the first two decades of twentieth-century Ethiopian politics, Ras Teferi at its center, shows that the young prince's main weakness were rooted not in his change of religious confession from Christianity to Islam—which is unfounded—but simply in his mishandling of a contest between his own

---

64. Tekle-Giorgis of Gojjamm can be categorized as Amhara ethnically alongside Menelik II, though both were usually identified regionally than ethnicity.

65. Bausi, "Kings and Saints," 174.

royal circle, conspiracies from his own family of the same stock.[66] This shows that among the house of the kings "legitimacy" matters over imperial ideology, ethnicity, and even religious affinity. Considering this would help us reanalyze the ideology behind the power, power struggle, and complex and diverse ways regarding ascension to the empire's throne, and this furthermore would no doubt deconstruct the tales that takes one people group as "a ruling class," and the other as a subjugated "other."

(2) If we surely want to be true to our conscience when writing Ethiopian history in order to create a better understanding of the factors that shaped Ethiopian history, there must be room for us to nuance not only the place of inter-ethnic tensions but also aspects of intra-ethnic tensions in Ethiopia, which actually has been the cause for a long-lasting conflict within major ethnic groups. The dominance of strong *regionalism*, as practiced before the time of Emperor Haile Selassie I, mentioned above, may open another interesting step towards our understanding of the history of the land, how it became a setback in the establishment of hegemony within a specific ethnic group.

We know that it was regionalism, not intrinsically a mere ethnic affiliation, which was an overriding aspect of identifying oneself in the empire for a long time. This intra-ethnic tension should be also noted, which highlights the fact that there had hardly been unified ethnic-shaped states (as currently known) as "Amhara," "Tigray," or "Oromia," etc., in the previous eras of the empire.[67] In light of strong special regionalism, we may know little of why the Shoan Amharas were not considered pure Amhara but "Oromos" by Amharas of the same ethnic affiliation (in light of this, one wonders why such a tension (or prejudice) existed among the Amharas of Gojjam and Gondar). Again, what can be referred to as the Shoa's Amhara could be hardly applied to the way of life of the Amharas located in another part of the country.[68] True, there have been times the Shoan Oromo (and probably all Christian Oromos) were considered as Amharas[69] as compared to the non-Christian Oromos.[70]

66. See Pankhurst, "Reign of Lij Iyasu," 91–100.

67. This take may not concern the numerous hegemony of smaller ethnic groups mainly located in the Southern part of the country, though the case of a few nations in the area, like the Kembatta, should be treated differently.

68. This could be one criticism that possibly leveled against Levine's *Wax and Gold*; see Taddesse, "Amhara," 352–54.

69. See Shiferaw, "Reflections," 166. It is also true that Oromos of a particular region would also consider themselves as pure Oromos as compared to the others.

70. As it was true for almost all ethnic groups in Ethiopia, the diversity among the Oromo is obvious (Levine, *Greater Ethiopia*, 135), for a general note: "Oromo-speaking peoples of Ethiopia were always diverse and were not aiming to consolidate into a unified larger state nor to establish political hegemony or permanent dominance over

These highlight that surely there had been a complex conundrum of Ethiopian center–periphery dynamics that should be considered in understanding the multi-layers of historical epochs of the land.

What this intra-ethnic "diversity" can surely reveal is the depth of diversity within an ethnic group in particular and the nation in general. This sheds important light on the fact of diversified ethnicity in an already diversified country. Simply put then, any attempt of generalization in presenting Ethiopian history even in the "micro level" should be cautious. An attempt to use Ethiopian historical notes as subservient to the creation of story of hegemony of a specific ethnic group may not be easy as much as attempting a political project aimed at creating hegemony of ethnic identities and, I argue, this is a lesson from history that all interested groups should consider wisely.

## The "Already But Not-yet" of Ethiopian History: *A Long Way to the Future*

We have to simply admit that due to the country's "natural" diversity we find ourselves unable to fully understand the history of its people *in toto*. Towards a better future of writing Ethiopian history, as a passing remark, let me also emphasize that we should consider current global developments in historical writings. We observe that the focus and scope of historical investigation has been broadened in recent times: from political history to sociocultural, from metahistory ("the grand historical narrative, or even philosophy of history") to microhistory ("the lives of commoners in localized setting").[71] This is an important and worthy consideration since sociocultural and micro-history helps to fill in the gap in light of what is lacking in the already-developed Ethiopian general historiography. In light of what some countries achieved so far, the interaction of most people groups in Ethiopia's long years of history, given its diverse community (literate–oral, center–periphery, etc.), the writing of Ethiopian history has proved to be in an indistinct stage. We have to admit that we only know what can be known but not what we could have known. In general, however, we have to surely

---

parts of Ethiopia before the last quarter of the twentieth century, despite their ability to conquer and control most parts of the country in the sixteenth century. There was never an historic Oromo nation-state" (Abreham, "Ethnicity," 56; see also pp. 22–24; 41–42.

71. This is different from the micro-history I mentioned above when discussing differences within a single ethnicity. For further discussion, see, Bahru, "Century of Historiography."

admit that the writing of Ethiopian history is in its infancy, which needs a scholarly rethinking regarding a way forward.

This means we have to humbly admit our limitations when it comes to the micro-socio-political history of the Ethiopian people. We still have to ask ourselves: what is Ethiopian history without the discussion of the place of the numerous Ethiopian people groups missing from pages of Ethiopian history?

One should simply admit that, despite how much historians and anthropologists have tried so far, the knowledge we have regarding Ethiopian history is still far from a complete history of Ethiopia. It is true that there is no historian who, or single book which, ably discusses the interaction of all ethnic groups within the central state power. In light of the span from Kushitic, Omotic, and Nilo-Saharan language-speaking groups, we must humbly admit that discussion of the place of the Kebena, Gumer, Gora, Ari, Mao, Oyida, Chari, Gebato, Opo, Surma, Woito, and many others have been simply missing from many of historical discussions and Ethiopian history books. Yes, we have to admit that even if there are many books that have been published with a title of *Ethiopian History*, we all understand that a presentation of Ethiopian history in a single book is not possible. We have come to a reality that writers of Ethiopian history have attempted something they could never achieve in order to meet the existing knowledge gap regarding the history of the land.

A mention is necessary for one of the main problems that stands against our understanding and presentation of Ethiopian history: the predicament of a claim for ownership of a sole "objective" history of the nation and the tales of a particular ethnic group. We know that the duty of a historian to present his/her account of history by identifying the limit of the study. One particular aspect of such a weakness in Ethiopian history writing is exhibited when we compare the dearth of social and cultural history of the nation to that of the highly entertained political history of Ethiopia. I also insist that we have to give attention to sources that would highlight particular dynamics of inter- and intra-ethnic conflicts and the place of religion so that we may equivocally deal with the trends in Ethiopian history. In our attention to the trends in Ethiopian history, there remain a huge number of Ethiopic literatures at our disposal to be analyzed and discussed. In connection to this, it seems also important to note that Ethiopia's comprehensive history is yet to be rediscovered, and this is possible only when we are willing to adopt a multidisciplinary approach in writing history. The lacuna in our understanding of Ethiopian history will be addressed when we consider oral history of the "non-literate" societies of Ethiopia for which the lessons from anthropological studies in the appropriation of historical reconstruction remains mandatory.[72] As such, in writing a history of Ethiopia we then humbly acknowledge what we could have known remains much deeper than what we have achieved so far. This in turn no doubt invites our findings and evidence of Ethiopian sources for a constructive criticism, and again which should leave room for further amendment as other historical data is made available; it is within this understanding that appreciation of a heuristic conclusion is no more than an academic guess.[73]

In writing Ethiopian history, as we have noted above, both Ethio-centric and Ethno-centric writers have to teach themselves that the Ethiopian center–periphery has never been static. In discussing historical notes of a country that we may find from the past, we have many reasons to guide ourselves from not falling in a trap of either "*nostalgic*-driven" or "*denial*-ridden" interpretation of history respectively. In the presence of a dynamic center–periphery, I claim that either "hero*ification*" of one people group over the other, or denial of a possibility of "dominance of a people who had once been subjugated" in history is nothing but an attempt to do little justice to our knowledge of history. A better premise, I affirm, is that a tendency to uplift what is "ours" against the "others" usually ensue when we have been taken away with an overburdened nostalgia and unwarranted denial. It is from the glorification of what is "ours" that we tend to find "saintly" and "godly" figures in the royal courts and political offices, which, I think, is almost impossible; we may need to remind ourselves of an age-old wisdom that saints will not easily fit to the earthly thrones. Admittedly, there seems no reason for us to whitewash the "injustices" of the past purported by aggressive kings of the "center" (usually presented as the "heroes" of the nation), or of the local kings/military powers from the "periphery" (more often portrayed as "saints" stood in defense of the weak). The antidote is to be self-critical with an openness to learn from the other side. Any historical events of the past surely stay within our record and memory—not to be buried but to be highlighted in order to give lessons for today and perhaps more importantly—to project a better future for the nation.

---

72. An excellent and detailed discussion is given by Crummey, "Society," 103–19.

73. And in this case, in the absence of substantial evidence to support our claims, better to do favor to the readers if by admitting the limitations on particular claims. Responsibility is higher when presenting findings; rather than misleading readers who may easily consider the "historical" writings as a presentation of an "objective" and "total history," it is advisable to inform readers the findings are tentative, destined to be amended or discarded upon the availability of new source.

## Conclusion

The historical comments from both Ethno- and Ethio-nationalists are knotted by paradoxes: it is because of the attempts from both sides that our *understanding* of Ethiopian history has been enriched, but at the same time generates some setbacks due to the fact that it was because of the divergent views that *misunderstanding* of many kind emanates. I have come to the conclusion thus that there are some questions left unanswered regarding writing of the history of Ethiopian people, and such an important duty no doubt calls for the importance of a balanced approach in handling historical narratives.

Many writers purposely do injustice to their data due to lack of training in history (as is demonstrated by many of Ethiopian "history" writings, which easily fall into the trap of selection, exclusion, deletion, and generalization). This has produced a core misunderstanding of Ethiopian history that mainly emanates from mishandling of historical data and notes. It is in giving attention to the basic weakness of such a popular approach to Ethiopian history that we see the complex interaction of nations in Ethiopia, and how fragile the proposal of the pseudo north-south divide is. We observe that ethnic identification was so strong that even religious affiliation was undermined[74] and vice-versa. As I have demonstrated, Ethiopian empire/state political alliance/enemy-making cannot be explained in a simplistic north-south divide approach, since it is also evident that such a schism had been evident amongst the "north" at large, even within royal families of the same family, ethnicity and religion.

I assume that we still need to adopt relevant techniques and pertinent methods (both at macro- and micro-level as well as adoption of multi-disciplinary approaches, whether sociological or anthropological) when dealing with the history of Ethiopian diverse peoples who have shared a common country and destiny. In relation to this, problems in history writing, as one can easily observe, arise from lack of knowledge/training in writing an "objective" history, which is probably shaped by biases that overtake one's own ethos, which usually end up in nostalgia that whitewash what is "ours" and ruthlessly blotch what is "theirs." Numerous contentious issues emanate from reflecting on the past events, particularly when some writers, due to lack of humility, impudently comment in a field of study in which they are not adequately trained. More specifically, there is still a need for more professional historians specialized in Ethiopian Medieval history; I assume that understanding of the historical development of the era can possibly direct and redirect the current "historical" discourses for the common

---

74. As a (Christian-oriented) African proverb puts it, "blood is thicker than water."

good. Moreover, since Ethiopia remained a home of diverse peoples who have shared a destiny in one or more ways, analytic and honest handling of the often-conflicting stories and narratives of the land in its long history would no doubt help the growth of "common knowledge" towards a reconstruction and expounded history of Ethiopia.

## Bibliography

Abreham Alemu Fanta. "Ethnicity and Local Identity in the Folklore of the Southwestern Oromo of Ethiopia: A Comparative Study." PhD diss., VU University, 2006.

Asafa Jalata. "Two National Liberation Movements Compared: Oromia and the Southern Sudan." *Social Justice* 27.79 (2000) 152–74.

Atsme-Giorogis Gebre Mesih (Allaqa). የ [ኦሮም] ታሪክ / *History of [the Oromo]* 1. Unpublished Manuscript. Institute of Ethiopian Studies, n.d.

Ayele Teklehaimanot, et al. "Catholicism." In *Encyclopedia Aethiopica*, edited by Siegbert Uhlig, 1:699. Wiesbaden: Harrassowitz Verlag, 2003.

Bahru Zewde. "A Century of Historiography." In *Society, State, and History: Selected Essays*, edited by Bahru Zewde, 13–43. Addis Ababa: Addis Ababa University, 2008.

———. *Pioneers of Change in Ethiopia: The Reformist Intellectuals of the Early Twentieth Century*. Eastern African Studies. Addis Ababa: Addis Ababa University Press, 2002.

Bausi, Alessandro. "Kings and Saints: Founders of Dynasties, Monasteries and Churches in Christian Ethiopia." In *Stifter und Mäzene und ihre Rolle in der Religion, Von Konigen, Monchen, Vordenkern Und Laien in Indien, China Und Anderen Kulturen*, edited by Barbara Schuler, 161–240. Harrassowitz Verlag · Wiesbaden, 2013.

Baxter, P. T. W. "Ethiopia's Unacknowledged Problem." *African Affairs* 77.308 (1978) 283–96.

[Bereket Habte] Selassie. *Conflict and Intervention in the Horn of Africa*. London: Monthly Review, 1981.

Budge. *Queen of Sheba*. N.p.: Routledge, 2016.

Caulk, Richard. "Religion and the State in Nineteenth-century Ethiopia." *Journal of Ethiopian Studies* 10.1 (1972) 23–41.

Clapham, Christopher. *Haile-Selassie's Government*. New York: Praeger, 1969.

Cosmas Indicopleustes. *The Christian Topography of Cosmas, an Egyptian Monk*. Translated and edited by J. W. McCrindle. Cambridge: Cambridge University, 1897.

Crummey, Donald. *Land and Society in the Christian Kingdom of Ethiopia: From the Thirteenth to the Twentieth Century*. Urbana: University of Illinois Press, 2000.

———. "Society, State and Nationality in the Recent Historiography of Ethiopia." *Journal of African History* 31.1 (1990) 103–19.

Dussen, W. J. Van der, and Lionel Rubinoff, eds. *Objectivity, Method and Point of View: Essays in the Philosophy of History*. New York: Brill, 1991.

Ficquet, Éloi. "Understanding Lïj Iyasu through His Forefathers: The Mammedoch Imam-s of Wello." *The Life and Times of Lïj Iyasu of Ethiopia*, edited by Éloi Ficquet and Wolbert G. C. Smidt, 5–29. Zürich: LIT, 2014.

Ficquet, Éloi, and Wolbert G. C. Smidt, eds. *The Life and Times of Lij Iyasu of Ethiopia*. Éloi. Zürich: LIT, 2014.

Getatchew Haile. የአባ ባሕርይ ድርሰቶች አርማችን ከሚመለከቱ ሌሎች ድርሰቶች ጋር [*The Works of Abba Bahrey with Other Documents Concerning the Oromo*]. Translated by Getatchew Haile. Collegeville: Minnesota, 2002.

Getatchew Haile, trans. "The Unity and Territorial Integrity of Ethiopia." *The Journal of Modern African Studies* 24.3 (September 1986) 465–87.

Geubre Heywet Baykedagn. "እጤ ምኒልክና ኢትዮጵያ." In ነጋድራስ ገብረ ሕይወት ባይከዳኝ ሥራዎች [*(Collected) Works of Geubre Heywet Baykedagn*]. Addis Abeba: Addis Ababa University, 2007.

Haile Larebo. "ለምሁኑ በኢትዮጵያ የባሕር ጥቁና ነበር ወይ? [Lemhonu beithopia Yebeher chiqona neber woi?]." *International Journal of Ethiopian Studies* 11.1 (2017) 10–22.

"Historiography." https://qcpages.qc.cuny.edu/writing/history/critical/historiography.html.

Holcomb, Bonnie K., and Sisai Ibssa. *The Invention of Ethiopia*. Trenton, NJ: Red Sea, 1990.

Indicopleustes, Cosmas. *The Christian Topography of Cosmas Indicopleustes*. Edited and translated by Eric Otto Winstedt. N.p.: Forgotten Books, 2010.

Levine, N. Donald. *Greater Ethiopia: The Evolution of a Multiethnic Society*. Chicago: University of Chicago Press, 1974.

Littmann, Enno, et al. *Deutsche Aksum-Expedition, 1905–1910*. Vols. 1–4. Berlin: Verlag der königl Akademie der Wissenschaften, 1913.

Maimire Mennasemay. "Abba Bahrey's Zenahu LeGalla: Towards an Ethiopian Critical Theory." *International Journal of Ethiopian Studies* 6.1/2 (2012) 1–28.

Marjery Perham. *The Government of Ethiopia*. Evanston: Northwestern University, 1969.

Martin, Raymond. "Objectivity and Meaning in Historical Studies: Toward a Post-Analytic View." Review of *Objectivity, Method and Point of View: Essays in the Philosophy of History*, edited by W. J. Van der Dussen and Rubinoff. *History and Theory* 32.1 (February 1993).

Merera Gudina. "Contradictory Interpretations of Ethiopian History: The Need for a New Consensus." In *Ethnic Federalism: The Ethiopian Experience in Comparative Perspective*, edited by David Turton, 119–30. Addis Ababa: Addis Ababa University Press, 2006.

———. "The Elite and the Quest for Peace, Democracy, and Development in Ethiopia: Lessons to Be Learnt." *Northeast African Studies* 10.2 (2003) 141–64.

Merid Wolde Aregay. "Population Movement as a Possible Factor in Christian Muslim Conflict of Medieval Ethiopia." *Symposium Leo Frobenius; Perspectives of Contemporary African Studies* (1974) 266–81.

———. "Southern Ethiopia and the Christian Kingdom, 1508–1708, with Special Reference to the Galla Migration and Their Consequences" PhD diss., University of London, 1971.

Mohammed Hassen. *The Oromo of Ethiopia: A History 1570–1860*. Cambridge: Cambridge University, 1990.

Pankhurst, E. Sylvia. *Ethiopia: A Cultural History*. Essex: Lalibela, 1955.

Pankhurst, Richard. *The Ethiopian Royal Chronicles*. London: Oxford University, 1967.

———. "The Reign of Lij Iyasu—as Avedis Terzian Saw it" *The Life and Times of Lij Iyasu of Ethiopia*, edited by Éloi Ficquet and Wolbert G. C. Smidt, 91–100. Zürich: LIT, 2014.

———. *A Social History of Ethiopia*. Addis Ababa: Institute of Ethiopian Studies, 1990.

Phillipson, David W. *Foundations of an African Civilisation: Aksum and the Northern Horn, 1000 BC–AD 1300*. New York: Boydell & Brewer, 2012.

Sbacchi, Alberto. *Ethiopia Under Mussolini: Fascism and the Colonial Experience*. London: Zed, 1985.

Selassie [Bereket Habte-Selassie]. *Conflict and Intervention in the Horn of Africa*. London: Monthly Review, 1981.

Sergew Hable Selassie. *Ancient and Medieval Ethiopian History to 1270*. Addis Ababa: Haile Selassie I University, 1972.

Shiferaw Bekele. "Gäbrä-Heywät Baykädañ and the Emergence of a Modern Intellectual Discourse." *Sociology Ethnology Bulletin* 1.3 (Feb 1994) 106–20.

———. "Reflections on the Power Elite of the Wärä Seh Mäsfenate (1786–1853)." *Annales d'Éthiopie* 15 (1990) 157–79.

Taddesse Tamrat. "Amhara—the Cultural Background." *The Journal of African History* 8.2 (1967) 352–54

———. *Church and State in Ethiopia, 1270–1527*. Oxford: Clarendon, 1972.

———. "Process of Ethnic Interaction and Integration in Ethiopian History: The Case of the Agaw." *The Journal of African History* 29 (1988) 5–18.

Taye Gebre-Maryam (Allaqa). የኢትዮጵያ ሕዝብ ታሪh [*History of the People of Ethiopia*]. Asmara, 1921.

Tekle Tsadiq Mekuria. አጼ ዮሐንስ እና የኢትዮጵያ አንድነት [*Atse Yohannes ena ye-ithiopia andenet*]. Addis Ababa: Kuraz, 1990.

Wallelign Mekonen. "On the Question of Nationalities in Ethiopia." *Struggle* 17 (1969) 4–7.

White, Hayden, ed. *The Content of the Form: Narrative Discourse and Historical Representation*. Baltimore: Johns Hopkins University, 1987.

Zewde Gabre-Sellassie. *Yohannes IV of Ethiopia: A Political Biography*. Oxford: Clarendon, 1975.

# 3

# Ethnic Diversity and Legal Responsibility in Ethiopia

## Fasil Nahum

MULTIETHNIC TOGETHERNESS, THE BURDEN of this book and a huge subject on its own, is part and parcel of the larger issue of moral responsibility of a human being to another human being. In biblical language the question is, am I my brother's keeper? This moral responsibility is ultimately accountable to the Creator, with intermediate levels of accountability to society and the law. These would be respectively social and legal responsibilities. The former is based on social norms and informal sanctions of the society while the latter follows the formal dictum and machinery of the law. This chapter delves into the narrower issue of ethnic diversity and legal responsibility, taking the Ethiopian constitution as a point of departure. It should be noted at the outset that the Federal State the constitution creates presumes that the system would be lubricated with a lot of give and take as one would expect in a unity-in-diversity model.[1]

People have infinite characteristics based on biology and/or sociology. Biologically we are created as man or woman. Our skin and eye color varies; so do our hair textures. Myriads of specific characteristics are encrypted in our genes. Biologically no two persons are ever exactly alike. Sociologically, depending on how people think and interact with one another and with resources and the environment, under various circumstances, many and varied types of living standards have evolved. Institutions like religion, marriage, and family have developed and following those, clans and similar

---

1. Note the constitution's opening salvo in the fifth paragraph of the preamble referring to mutual support.

groupings have been created. Means of communication, particularly languages, have naturally evolved. As means of living, professions and crafts have sprung up to provide for the needs of society. Security of the person and of the group has brought about a sense of government and institutions, and tools as well as weapons have been invented to accompany them. In these processes, people have forever employed their very many characteristics, biological and sociological, to either bond together or to create separate identity. Ethnicity is one such bio-social characteristic.

## Ethnicity: Melting Pot and Salad Bowl Approaches

Ethnicity is prevalent throughout the world and has been employed for many situations. For family purposes, for instance, endogamous and exogamous marriage relationships prevalent in some societies are based on kinship relationships that encompass ethnicity. Then there is language which is the most conspicuous trait of a people, to such an extent that some prefer to deal with ethno-linguisticity rather than just ethnicity. In my opinion there is nothing wrong in identifying oneself with one's specific characteristics. Others should also recognize and respect one's point of identification as long as it is not illegal or immoral. The sticking question that arises is how and for what purposes is ethno-linguistic identification to be employed?

At this juncture the question should be asked what the constitution and the legal regime in general demand in terms of legal responsibility in employing ethno-linguisticity. When dealing legally with ethnicity there are two broad approaches that can be followed. They may be addressed as the melting pot and the salad bowl approaches. In this kitchen metaphor, the ingredients such as potatoes, onions, tomatoes, carrots, etc., when cut and thrown into a pot on a fire, melt into a soup and lose their individual characteristics. The same ingredients can be dressed up in a salad bowl where each would still retain its characteristics. Constitutions around the world, by and large, employ one or the other approach in dealing with the issue of ethnic identification. The United States has considered itself as the champion of the melting pot approach. As a nation of immigrants, in principle it welcomes all that come legally and stamps them with Americanism. The reality is, of course, not that simple. There are Chinatowns and little Italys in their major cities. It is also common to hear about hyphenated Americans such as Afro-Americans etc. Moreover, lately "Black lives matter" is heard as a resounding motto in American cities. "Equal pay for equal work" (relating to gender) is another cry reverberating in their industries and lately even in sports.

To take another example, this time from home, the Ethiopian constitutions of 1931 and 1955 presumed that the all-important task of nation-building would be furthered by adopting the principle of only one official language for the unitary monarchical state. In this respect schools had an important role to play. Therefore, the language of instruction beginning with grade one had to be Amharic throughout the country. This was the official policy of the government in all schools, public or private. Zealot teachers in some outlying areas went a step further by unilaterally replacing pupils' ethnic names with Amharic ones that were then put into their official report cards. Another unfortunate outcome of this principle was that Oromigna and Tigringna bibles had to be printed abroad and had to be smuggled as contraband into the country. The pros and cons of the melting pot theory can be hotly discussed indefinitely.

On the other hand, the salad bowl approach says, why struggle to knock and whip the eggs together to make an omelet? Let them be as they are. Why try to hide ethnic identities by sweeping them under the carpet as if they do not exist or are not important? It is here that the current Ethiopian constitution reverses the old approach and not only recognizes ethnic identities but goes to the extent of celebrating them; and there are more than eighty ethno-linguistic identities in Ethiopia. Here one historical phenomenon should be injected: all the seventeen armed groups that sprung up to fight the Därg regime and were finally victorious were ethnically composed.

## The Ethiopian Constitution and Ethnicity

Let us examine what the current constitution says about ethnicity. The preamble starts by stating that it is the nations, nationalities and peoples of Ethiopia that adopted the constitution on December 8, 1994. It is not "We the People . . . ," i.e., the people lumped together as in the American constitution, but the people identified via ethnicity. The constitution states that all sovereign power resides in them and the constitution is an expression of their sovereignty. It has to be noted that sovereignty is not divisible. Therefore it is all the nations, nationalities, and peoples of Ethiopia *in toto* that are sovereign.[2] Art. 9 of the constitution affirms its absolute supremacy over any law, customary practice or decision of an organ of state or public institution. It is a sweeping all-encompassing supreme statement.

Moreover, the federation is comprised of states and out of the nine enumerated member states, eight of them are named on the basis of the dominant

---

2. See art. 8 of the constitution: "Constitution of the Federal Democratic Republic of Ethiopia."

ethnic group in the region.³ When we come to the composition of the houses of the federal parliament, the constitution provides for at least twenty seats to be reserved for minority nationalities and peoples out of a maximum of 550 electoral-unit based seats in the house of peoples' representatives. The other house, the house of federation, is fully composed of only representatives of nations, nationalities and peoples of Ethiopia. The constitution goes on to provide for each nation, nationality, and people to be represented by at least one member; and for each one million of its population to be represented by on additional representative.⁴ In article 5 the constitution already provides for all Ethiopian languages to enjoy equal recognition by the state. Moreover, member states of the federation are by law granted the authority to determine their respective working languages. Thus, for instance, Somaligna, Afarigna, Tigrigna, and Oromigna would be the official languages of the respective states. Article 5, due to practical considerations, provides for Amharic (Amarigna) to be the working language of the federal government. Incidentally, the last article of the constitution states that it is the Amharic version of the constitution that has final legal authority.

One has to concede that the notion of ethnicity has a central and conspicuous place in the current constitution of Ethiopia. Incidentally, this central positioning is an answer to the continuous higher institutions students' demand of the 1960s and 1970s to properly address the Ethiopian nationality question. Both in Ethiopia and in Europe and America, Ethiopian student associations kept arranging conferences that *inter alia* would discuss the nationality question. Placing ethnicity on firm ground now begs the question of how it is to be employed for day-to-day living. Here the question of enjoyment of human rights becomes pivotal and paramount.

## Human Rights

The question of human rights which is central to our discussion can be examined by beginning to classify them. Human rights may be classified as generational rights;⁵ freedom from fear and freedom from want rights; political, economic, social, and cultural rights; or human and democratic rights. The

---

3. See art. 47 of the constitution: "Constitution of the Federal Democratic Republic of Ethiopia."

4. The Federal Houses are dealt with in chapter 6 of the constitution. Arts. 54 and 61 provide for membership of the two houses.

5. Human rights are generally classified as first-, second-, and third-generation rights. But there is a discussion going on whether the right of minorities should not constitute a fourth generation.

constitution prefers the last classification of human and democratic rights which easily translate into individual and group rights.

By generational rights we mean first-, second-, and third-generation rights. First-generation rights are rights of the individual that start with the right to life and include the right to liberty and the security of the person. Rights of the individual caught up in the machinery of justice in criminal cases are therefore considered first-generation rights. These include the rights of the persons who are arrested and persons who are accused as well as persons who are held in custody and convicted for crimes committed. A most important right to begin with is the right to the presumption of innocence. In other words, the burden of proof lies in the prosecution to prove that such a crime has been committed by the accused.

Constitutions tend to be specific and detailed when it comes to rights of the person in the criminal case process. The right to be brought to court within forty-eight hours; the right to be promptly informed, in a language one understands, of the reason for one's arrest as well as the right to full access to any evidence presented; and the right to produce one's own defense witnesses are part and parcel of first-generation rights. The right to have legal counsel of one's choice and in special cases to be provided with legal representation at state expense is also included. Another very important right is the right of appeal against an unfavorable decision. This means that a fresh set of judges will review the case and arrive at a decision. All these rights enumerated above assume a fair and unbiased hearing process by neutral and independent judges who shall be directed solely by their conscience and the law. This is what is meant by due process of law.

Of course, humanity has in its long history passed through many stages. As early as just over a century ago institutionalized slavery, an unparalleled inhuman and horrific institution, was still part of the socioeconomic system in many parts of the world. Ethnic groups that were too weak to defend themselves or were defeated in war many a time ended as slaves, bought and sold in the market as chattel. The best-known and recorded stories are from the so-called middle passage slavery. On our continent, western and central African communities found themselves depleted of their young men and women who were forcibly removed to the New World to sweat it out in sugarcane and cotton plantations of European/American slave masters. The *doors of no return* in Senegal, Gambia, Ghana, and many other western and central African countries saw millions of young men and women pass through them, shackled and never hoping to return to their native lands and beloved families. Slavery was an absolute and systematically categorical negation of human rights. That is why modern human rights based international instruments such as the Universal Declaration of

Human Rights and national constitutions like ours declare in the strongest possible language that no one shall be held in slavery.

Then the constitution provides for what it classifies as democratic rights. In principle, democratic rights are those rights necessary for a well-functioning democracy, as the name implies. Democratic rights begin with the right of being able to vote and run for office. But to stop there would definitely be a limited and Spartan way of looking at these rights. Democracy cannot be confined to having elections at prescribed intervals of time and thereby vote and choose one's representatives; democracy is much more and we will presently look at some democratic rights prescribed in the Ethiopian constitution.

The constitution begins providing for democratic rights by stating that everyone has the right of thought, opinion, and expression. The right to hold opinion and the freedom of expression are to be exercised without any interference. These rights then spill over into freedom of the press, widely defined to include any media of one's choice, employing written, verbal, or visual forms. Prohibition of censorship and access to information of public interest as well as freedom of artistic creativity are specifically mentioned as being part of freedom of the press. The constitution places a couple of limitations to the freedom of the press. These are war propaganda and public expression intended to injure human dignity which would amount to criminal activity and are expressly prohibited. What then follow as part of democratic rights are the right to assemble and the right to demonstrate together with others peaceably and unarmed. Closely following is the freedom of association. Associations may be formed for any cause or purpose, be they political, economic, social, or cultural. Naturally political parties are associations established for political reasons.

Then come the right to vote and to be elected. Any citizen without any discrimination based on color, race, nation, nationality, sex, language, religion, political, or other opinion or status has the right to take part in the conduct of public affairs directly or through freely chosen representatives. Every citizen has the right to vote on the attainment of eighteen years of age and to be elected to any office at any level of government. Moreover, elections are to be carried out by universal and equal suffrage and held by secret ballot in order to guarantee the free expression of the will of the electors. That is what is meant by free and fair elections.

Second-generation rights as contrasted to individual rights are group rights or collective rights. Their enhanced application came to the forefront after World War II. Originally the right of workers became a challenge due to the Industrial Revolution of the late eighteenth century particularly in Great Britain and the United States. The labor union federation of America was only established as late as 1886. Earlier on, it even was a crime to form or join labor unions in America. The right of workers was energized by the rise of socialism and Karl Marx's clarion call, "Workers of the world unite!"

In the United Kingdom, the Labor Party, a center-left political party, started as an alliance of trade unionists and leftist thinkers and activists emphasizing social justice. Beginning in 1900 it has affiliated itself internationally with social democratic parties in Europe and elsewhere. Thus, this second-generation human right of laborers has become a significant player in the life of many societies. In Ethiopia it is to be recalled that the Därg had transformed itself into the Workers party, at least in name, and was the only official ruling party until 1991. The current constitution recognizes the right of workers to form associations and to bargain collectively with employers. They not only have the right to express grievances but also to strike. As urbanization and industrialization grow, the strengthening of workers' right can be expected to rise.

Another second-generation right is women's rights. Women's suffrage, i.e., the right of women to vote in elections, only began in Europe in the late nineteenth century when women started working for broad-based economic and political equality. Swiss women did not have the right to vote in federal elections until 1971, incredible as it may sound. In any case, women's rights have been enshrined in United Nations international human-rights instruments from the beginning. The rights of women are today recognized to include the right to equality, to non-discrimination, to education and to live as full members of society in all aspects. The Ethiopian constitution considers the right of women so fundamental that it deals with in great detail. But much work still remains to translate the constitution into everyday reality as far as women's rights are concerned.

Still another second-generation right is the right of children, with particular attention to the rights of special protection and care afforded to minors. The United Nations Convention on the Rights of the Child was signed in 1989 and came into force in 1990. Currently 196 countries are parties to the treaty—the largest number of member states ever in the history of treaties of the United Nations. Ethiopia as a member state has taken it seriously and the constitution which was adopted less than half a dozen years later has had the opportunity to include all the pertinent points covered by the UN Convention on the Rights of the Child. Obviously, prescription is one thing and application another. As the Ethiopian population surpasses the hundred million mark and about a third of the population is young, the socioeconomic challenges are immense. In article 36, the constitution has comprehensively covered the rights of children and the telltale phrase employed is "the primary consideration shall be the best interests of the child." Women's and children's rights are second-generation rights which are still in the process of unfolding.

Third-generation rights, also known as solidarity rights, sprung up in the fight against colonialism and apartheid. Although the issues are as old as humanity itself, third-generation rights are chronologically the latest and newest of rights. The struggle against colonialism was won in Africa in the 1960s when much of Africa became independent.

Although third-generation rights started in the political arena they have moved on to encompass life as a whole. Thus, once political independence of subjugated peoples has been largely achieved, other nonpolitical demands have sprung up. The right to development, for instance, as articulated by the African Charter on Human and Peoples' Rights in 1981 recognizes it as an inalienable human right, by virtue of which all peoples are entitled to participate in, contribute to, and enjoy economic, social, cultural, and political rights.

Another third-generation right is the right to a clean and healthy environment. It is the right that mankind requires and deserves. In addition to having the right to food, clean water, sustainable shelter, and education, a safe and sustainable environment is paramount as all other rights depend upon it.

## Human Rights: Positivistic and Naturalistic Jurisprudence

Where do rights come from? In other words, what is the source of human rights? Here two broad jurisprudential approaches can be considered. These are the *positivistic* and *naturalistic* jurisprudences. Hans Kelsen, professor of law and author of the 1920 Austrian constitution, would argue strongly that one has rights because the state through its laws has given you these rights. What the extents of the rights are and how they are to be enjoyed is also defined and determined by the law. Therefore the state is the provider of rights. This is known as positive law jurisprudence.[6] Authoritarian states would be comfortable with this approach.

On the other hand, there is the natural law jurisprudence which is enshrined in the current Ethiopian constitution. This approach assumes that ethics and morality are the basis of law and the rule of law should be distinguished from rule by law. The constitution reads "Human rights and freedoms, emanating from the nature of mankind are inviolable and

---

6. Kelsen, *Theory of Law*.

inalienable." Therefore, what the constitution does is only to affirm and to provide for the enjoyment of these rights.

Having answered the question of the origin of human rights, that is, that they are not state-given and that the constitution only affirms their existence and protects them, the next issue is identification of these rights. To begin with, the constitution states that citizens and people's rights shall be respected.[7] Moreover, additionally, what this means is that the current Ethiopian constitution places on par individual and group rights and by no means superimposes one over the other. Both individual and group rights are equally treated and equally protected.

The respect and enforcement of human rights is moreover the responsibility and duty of all federal and state legislative, executive, and judicial organs at all levels of government. The constitution goes on to require that human rights be interpreted in conformity to the Universal Declaration of Human Rights, International Covenants on Human Rights, and international instruments adopted by Ethiopia. In other words, Ethiopia is not an island drifting on its own and has to follow best practices around the world with respect to human rights.[8]

The reference to international human rights in the constitution is not an afterthought. Already when the constitution was on the drafting board international human rights instruments were canvassed and carefully examined. The current Ethiopian constitution, as a Johnny-come-lately, has benefited from its international predecessors and particularly the UN human rights instruments. Having created a constitution very liberal in its broad dosage of human rights it was also important to safeguard it from legislative standard-lowering and hence the hefty amendment process. Obviously the constitution's main duty is to deal with the basic issues of the nation by providing enforceable guidance; thus it had to orient itself as a problem solver.

One principal undercurrent that flows throughout the constitution is the right to equality. I quote: "All persons are equal . . . without discrimination on grounds of race, nation, nationality, or other social origin, color, sex, language, religion, political or other opinion, property, birth or other status." Again I quote: "All persons are entitled to equal protection of the law and the law shall guarantee to all persons equal and effective protection."[9] The whole

---

7. See art. 10(1) and (2) of the constitution: "Constitution of the Federal Democratic Republic of Ethiopia."

8. See art. 13 of the constitution: "Constitution of the Federal Democratic Republic of Ethiopia."

9. See art. 25 of the constitution: "Constitution of the Federal Democratic Republic of Ethiopia."

gamut of human rights, beginning with the right to life—the mother of all rights, and spreading to personal, political, economic, social, and cultural rights, be they of first-, second-, or third-generation classification, fall in line and have to be equally available to all persons.

## Examples of Constitutional Principles under Duress

The scope of this chapter does not permit going through a more detailed enumeration and examination of the human rights enshrined in the constitution. But let us take some examples of what the constitution provides by way of some basic rights. Next to its peoples, land may be considered Ethiopia's greatest asset. Article 40(3) states, "the right of ownership of rural and urban land . . . is exclusively vested in the State and in the Peoples of Ethiopia. Land is a common property of the Nations, Nationalities and Peoples of Ethiopia and shall not be subject to sale or to other means of exchange." Two specific constitutional rules can be extracted from this article. First, that all land is public and not private property.

Second, that all land in Ethiopia belongs to the state and to *all* the nations, nationalities and peoples of Ethiopia as common property. It is not the constitution's intention to parcel out land on the basis of ethnicity. This can be shown by the fact that the enacting of law for the utilization and conservation of land is specifically given to the federal government under article 51(5) and not to the states. Then, article 55, which deals with the powers and functions of the federal house of peoples' representatives, under subarticle 2(a) stipulates that it is this federal house that has the power to enact specific laws on the utilization of land. The administration of land in accordance with federal laws is then provided to member states under article 52(2d) of the federal constitution. In other words, all land in Ethiopia is first public and not private property; and secondly, it belongs to the state and to the nations, nationalities, and peoples of Ethiopia as a whole. That is why laws on land utilization are promulgated by the federal government through the house of peoples' representatives. The role of member states of the federation is only to administer the land on the basis of the federal laws.

To move on to another specific right, article 32 of the constitution stipulates that any Ethiopian has the right to liberty of movement and freedom to choose their residence and engage freely in economic activity and pursue a livelihood of their choice within the national territory of Ethiopia. In other words, an Ethiopian national can decide to reside anywhere in the country and pursue the livelihood of their choice.

Still another example emanates from the famous phrase *interstate commerce* which is embedded in article 55(2b) of the constitution. As part and parcel of the broad powers it is provided within a parliamentary democratic system, the federal house of peoples' representatives has the power to enact laws on interstate commerce. This telltale phrase has its origin in the American constitution; when the issue of federal vis-à-vis state power arose, the US Federal Supreme Court interpreted *interstate commerce* in such a way as to give broad powers to the federal government vis-à-vis state governments. The main reason has been so that the free flow of commerce between states should not be impeded.

Coming back home, the Ethiopian constitution, already in its preamble, mentions the desiderata of *one economic community*. Since interstate commerce is to be handled by the federal government, communication, transportation, and fiscal policy dealing with interstate commerce have to be the responsibility of the federal government as provided for in article 55(2c). This means that highways and railways linking states, interstate lakes, and rivers as well as airports are squarely the responsibility of the federal government.

But taking into account recent and disturbing developments in Ethiopia, one may ask, why the massive human displacement, killing, maiming, and property destruction, as well as the closing of roads based on ethnicity? Why is government not enforcing the rule of law as it should, which is its primary duty, and as a matter of fact the *reason d'etre* of its existence and sustainability? Is it too weak and the destabilizing forces too strong? Is it that it cannot marshal the power needed by bringing the society together because it is undermined by legitimacy issues? It should not be forgotten that government can enhance its ordinary powers by declaring a state of emergency and putting it in place for as long as necessary to solve a strained constitutional situation and manage serious crises as provided in article 93 of the constitution.

## Conclusion: Justice versus Transitional Justice

One possible major reason could be the government's juggling feat involving the manipulation of transitional justice and hoping for the attainment of lasting peace. Transitional justice at its core is a way of addressing the past employing largely extra-legal measures to ensure a better future. Transitional justice assumes that stable and enduring peace can be achieved by addressing the demands of justice and reconciliation in the society. But justice and reconciliation do not necessarily pull together in the same direction all the time. Justice requires and demands that any time a crime is committed the perpetrator should be hunted down and delivered to court for an enforceable legal final decision. Reconciliation as restoration of friendly relations many a time prefers to work extra-legally via customary practices and norms involving social bodies such as elders and traditional peacemakers. Religious leaders and informal practices hark back to the good old days. Truth and reconciliation commissions by whatever name they may appear basically work extra-legally. In the long run, transitional justice does not and cannot replace justice. Transitional justice at best has a window of opportunity in which to operate and is limited by time. Wisdom lies in what manner and when and for how long to employ transitional justice.

What has happened in the recent past in Ethiopia is that all the disgruntled forces that were operating for decades against the government agreed to lay down their arms, come back home, and pursue their vision via the ballot box. This major achievement and the peace with neighboring Eritrea are closely intertwined. It is at this juncture that transitional justice became the preferred *modus operandi*. The forces that have been unleashed by such extraordinary phenomena, particularly at ethnic levels, have, however, created deep-seated problems for the rule of law that cannot be allowed to linger.

The time has come for the constitution and the legal regime as a whole to be properly understood and implemented by state organs at all federal and state levels. The failure of state organs from now onwards not to do their duty and enforce the constitution and the legal regime may create the spiraling up of unfortunate incidents. For such mob behavior to subside and normal life to return, the enforcement of the rule of law is absolutely essential, mandatory, and fundamental.

## Bibliography

"The Constitution of the Federal Democratic Republic of Ethiopia." *Negarit Gazeta* Year 1 No. 1 (1995). https://ethiopianembassy.be/wp-content/uploads/Constitution-of-the-FDRE.pdf.

Fasil Nahum. *Constitution for a Nation of Nations: The Ethiopian Prospect*. Asmara: Red Sea, 1997.

Kelsen, Hans. *The General Theory of Law and State*. Cambridge: Harvard University Press, 1945.

Stone, Richard D. *The Interstate Commerce*. Santa Barbara, CA: Praeger, 1991.

Weber, Max. *On Law in Economy and Society*. Edited by Max Rheinstein. Austin, TX: Touchstone, 1967.

Zurcher, Arnold J. *Constitutions and Constitutional Trends since World War II*. New York: New York University Press, 1951.

# 4

## "Deeply Mediatized" and "Deeply Ethnicized" Politics in Ethiopia (2014–19)

Signposts toward Moral Articulation for a Digital Space

———— Sara Abdella Kedir ————

Reflecting on the current state of Ethiopia, Achamyeleh Tamiru, a diaspora activist of the "Amhara Resistance" movement, expresses his concern over the gradual closure of interethnic dialogical space as follows: "We may occupy the same space but we do not live in the same dimension."[1] I find this sentence quite interesting for three reasons: (1) his use of the first person "we" while he resides in the United States, with implied suggestion that cohabitative space spans international boundaries; (2) this "we" referring to people with different ethnic loyalties including himself; (3) the discontent in his tone for the discrepancy between occupying "the same space" and living "in the same dimension." Though I am not sure whether Achamyeleh was consciously thinking of the digital space in his reflection, I find his sentence thought-provoking: how can Ethiopians, whose ethnic loyalties are diverse and who occupy the same (digital) space, live together (or "in the same dimension" to borrow from Achamyeleh)?

This question of togetherness, shot through with the ambiguity of spatiality due to the overlap of the digital space with social and physical space, carries within it a moral interrogation since morality is concerned

---

1. Achamyeleh, "My Perception," para. 2.

with living well together. Living together is now largely dependent on digital media, and hence living *well* together requires moral reflection on the digital space. Returning to Achamyeleh's discontent, what does this mean, if anything, for the politics of ethnic identity in Ethiopia? This chapter is concerned with this question, which includes both an interrogation of whether digital media matters to the politics of ethnic identity in Ethiopia and how it does so. I answer the first question with a "Yes" and attempt to outline how it operates. The main argument is that the uses of digital media for the politics of ethnic identity have resulted in and hence now occur in more mediatized and ethnicized milieu, making the digital space worthy of serious moral rumination.

As such, I am seeking an explanation for the correlation between, on the one hand, the challenge of living together capitulated in Achamyeleh's observation and, on the other, the uses and governances of digital media, and more particularly social media. To this end, I take a practice-based approach. A practice-based approach is one of the strongest approaches that pay attention to the limitation of structures on actors without altogether curbing their agency. This emphasis on the dialectics between structure and agency makes this approach fit for my purposes of pointing out signposts for moral articulation. As such, I will highlight how a triad of practices—i.e., practices of digital media use, the state's practices of internet governance, and the politics of ethnic identity—have coproduced each other in Ethiopia from 2014 to 2019.

In the case of Ethiopia, discussing "deep mediatization" as a recent and ongoing phenomenon would require engaging the apparent discrepancy this phenomenon has with the "digital divide" and "suppressive internet governance practice." After such discussion, I will take a demonstrative approach and look at mediatized practices of belonging and those of what I call "group diachronicity" to demonstrate how the nature of the relationship between digital media and social reality poses a moral dilemma to the politics of ethnic identity in Ethiopia. The demonstrative nature of section 3 means that instead of being a full-blown moral articulation, or an exhaustive explanation, this chapter will only be a signpost to such articulation and further sociological explanation. Since I am taking a practices-approach to the problem, I first have to take time to explain what I mean by such an approach.

## A Practices-approach to the Politics of Ethnic Identity in a Digital Era

This section is a sort of throat-clearing: I will outline what I mean by a practices-approach to the politics of ethnic identity in a digital era. A look at Ethiopia's digital history of the past half-decade in relation to the politics of ethnic identity exposes some useful observations as starting points for analysis. First and most clearly, Ethiopia's digital history is marked by continued pressure from the authoritarian-hand of the state.[2] The second and more recent phenomenon involves the role of different uses of the digital for the construction of ethnic identities. This second observation lacks empirical grounding as it relates to an emerging phenomenon. As a way of supplementing the lack of this empirical grounding, I will attempt to outline how "deeper ethnicization" of politics in Ethiopia is involved with "deeper mediatization."

These two observations upon Ethiopia's digital history give us three non-exhaustive, interrelated domains of action: the *digital* in its relationship to the *nation-state* and the *politics of ethnic identity*. As a domain of action, the digital is far more complex as it is an important but non-exclusive space of action for both the state and the politics of ethnic identity, on the one hand, and that it has a transnational nature as actions of both users and the state as a governing body are governed by transnational corporations. Instead of including transnational corporations as separate units of analysis, for the sake of brevity and clarity of my analysis, I will assume their "algorithmic" presence throughout this chapter. Given this, if one would like a practices approach to the politics of ethnic identity as it relates to the digital and internet, therefore, three respective interrelated practices related to these domains come to mind: practices of the politics of ethnic identity, practices of use of digital media, and practices of regulation of digital media and internet.

However, before I go on discussing these practices and their interrelations, it would be appropriate to outline what I mean by the term "practice" itself. Though this word is of major contention in contemporary sociology, I have neither the desire nor the need to enter this strenuous debate. All the major proponents of practices theory agree, according to Theodore Schatzki, that "practices are the central moment in social life because they are the site where understanding is carried and intelligibility articulated."[3] Thus,

---

2. See, for instance, "10 Most Censored Countries, 2015"; Téwodros, "Digital Cleansing?," 102–24; Habtamu, "Powers and Limits"; Yohannes, "Internet Shutdown," 208–24.

3. Schatzki, *Social Practices*, 210.

following Marlies Glasius and Marcus Michaelsen's helpful insight, borrowed from Schatzki's Wittgensteinian conceptions, I use the word "practice" to identify an object of inquiry that is characterized by "patterned actions that are embedded in particular organized contexts [ . . . as] a set of doings and sayings organized by a pool of understandings [and/or] a set of rules."[4]

This definition of practice in relation to the phrases "a pool of understanding" and "a set of rules" as mutually non-exclusive alternatives is intentional. On the one hand, some practices are not guided by "a set of rules," but have a rather loose and dynamic sense of order in which "understanding is structured and intelligibility articulated" (à la Schatzki). Other practices, particularly practices of regulation, however, are organized by a set of explicit rules since they are (and their intelligibility depends on) juridical articulations of normativity. While "digital media practices" and "practices of the politics of ethnic identity" resemble the former, "internet governance practices" resemble the latter.

Having that in mind, when my inquiry is related to digital media practices, I am asking rather loose questions, such as "what are people (individuals, groups, institutions) doing in relation to media across a whole range of situations and contexts? How does people's media-related practice relate, in turn, to their wider agency?"[5] These questions are, therefore, the questions of use. One should note that the use of digital media in the age of Web 2.0 is not limited to consumption of content produced elsewhere, but is a more complex interrelation of production and consumption. As a user of YouTube, I can easily record a video of an event and upload it or watch, like, comment on, or share what someone has produced, simultaneously acting as producer and consumer. This has significant implications for practices related to the politics of ethnic identity.

When my inquiry is related to internet governance practices, on the other hand, I am asking the following questions: "What is the state machinery, as an agent of regulation of the practices of use, doing to citizens' access to and privacy on the internet? What national and international legal frameworks does it employ? What narratives underpin and legitimize its regulatory patterns? How do its regulating activities relate to its agency, particularly in light of the transnational and 'democratizing' gist of digitization?"

The practice of regulation as such has a relationship to the practices of use. To be more specific, digital media practices and internet governance practices coproduce each other. In an introduction to the edited book titled

---

4. Glasius and Michaelsen, "Illiberal and Authoritarian Practices," 3799 [Additions mine].

5. Couldry, *Media, Society, World*.

*The Net and the Nation-State*, Uta Kohl and Carrie Fox construe online communities and the modern nation-state (or national communities) as "two oppositional and at the same time co-constituting forces in the context of internet governance" in the same way that action and reaction, force and counterforce, power and resistance coproduce each other in Newton's Third Law.[6] This is because the transnational nature of digital media undermines the state's sovereignty, extending the range of (political) communication in such a way that is not mediated primarily through state machinery.

The third set of practices are those related to the politics of ethnic identity. I will simply define some of the practices in this set, instead of entering the huge conceptual jungle of politics of ethnic identity itself. Trying the latter would derail the discussion by dragging me into solving the riddles of the nature and types of collective identity, the meaning of ethnicity, etc. Moreover, as I have mentioned in the introduction, the intent of this chapter is not to be exhaustive regarding which types of activities underpin which practices or what happened within this half-decade. Therefore, I will only mention two non-exhaustive sets of practices related to the politics of ethnic identity: practices of belonging and of group diachronicity.

Before going to this discussion, however, this chapter needs to address the potential obstacles to a significant overlap of these three practices since moral articulation means that they are significantly related. In other words, one might have a suspicion about whether or not I might be making far-fetched assumptions about the capacity of digital media to so significantly overlap with the politics of ethnic identity that it appears to pose normative dilemmas. Especially so given aspects that may hinder media's influence on Ethiopian society: due to the low internet penetration and the government's history of surveillance and censoring of digital practices. If one is following Ethiopian politics closely, one might not have such doubt. However, even in that case, I would like to address this suspicion because it touches upon some normative dilemmas associated with digital practices.

## Ethiopia Deeply Mediatized?: From Polarities of Hindrance to a Triad of Practices as a Complex Moral Space

Framed in technical terms, the above two suspicions are suspicions about the extent to which Ethiopia is "mediatized," especially given the fact that it is at the bottom of "the digital divide" and that its government practiced

---

6. Kohl and Fox, "Introduction," 1–2.

suppressive internet governance for the longer duration of our period of inquiry (2014–19). In what follows, I will take a long detour through the apparent contradictions of a "deeply mediatized society" being *at the bottom of the digital divide,* and that of *"deep mediatization* of society" ruled by "a state that practiced a suppressive internet governance." This section claims that the coproduction of deep mediatization and the digital divide, as opposed to their radical polarity, along with Ethiopia's history of conscious mediatization for the politics of resistance has an aftermath for the politics of ethnic identity: the Ethiopian political milieu is being deeply mediatized, rendering the region of overlap of the practices triad a place for moral rumination.

## "Deeply Mediatized" and "at the Bottom of the Digital Divide"?

Andreas Hepp et al. define mediatization as an analytic concept used to analyze "the interrelation between the change of media and communication on the one hand and the change of (fields of) culture and society on the other hand."[7] Thus, "deep mediatization" refers to the deepening of this inter-relationship in the digital age. This depth is related to two things. First, it relates to how the emergence of the internet and digital apparatuses contributed both to the contemporary ubiquity of media in everyday life and the very deep dependence of the social world we inhabit on these mediations.[8] Such ubiquity and dependence are coupled by a logic of coproduction, giving media its power. The more digital tools such as smartphones, tablets, and computers connected to the internet are ubiquitous and embedded in a society's everyday activities and its organization of social interactions, the more dependent that society and its actors are on these tools and their logics of operation.

Second, the depth in deep mediatization also refers to what digital media researchers call "datafication," the process of the abstraction of the data generated by the user's communicative actions from the user's communicative intent and of its manipulation to create new relations.[9] As such, "communicative agency" is no longer limited to simple human agency but is also *extended* to automated algorithms. These algorithms produce the 'metadata' of our social networks and past online decisions. Such metadata are used to predict our future behavior *and*, to a significant degree, determine the kinds

---

7. Hepp et al., "Mediatization," 8.
8. Hepp et al., "Rethinking Transforming Communications," 6.
9. Hepp et al., "Rethinking Transforming Communications," 6.

of friends that we make, kinds of products that we love, and what sorts of videos we would like to watch through tailored suggestions.

I will demonstrate how aspects of deep mediatization (i.e., both the ubiquity of the media in everyday life and datafication) have particular implications for the politics of ethnic identity. Here, I am simply addressing the suspicion against the claim that Ethiopia is "deeply mediatized." As it is one of the least digitized countries in the world with only 18.6 percent internet penetration, according to the Internet World Stats report on 30 June 2019,[10] Ethiopia is also at the bottom of "digital divide": the divide in access, use, engagement with ICT and their actual and perceived outcomes along economic, cultural and geopolitical lines.[11] One may attempt to address the suspicion caused by such a geopolitical digital divide by simply pointing to an empirically intelligent prediction of future internet penetration in light of the high rate of penetration, and hence head simply towards preventive ethics.[12]

However, I take a different route: an answer based on the relationship between "deep mediatization" and "digital divide," since it forms an important basis for a sign-post-like discussion of the concept of "ethnic digital outskirts," and avoids the pretension that morality for deeply mediated politics is only forward-looking. This relationship is, I think, deeply ingrained in the critical tone of the digital divide discourse itself, i.e., in the fact that it resembles critical social theory in a sense of addressing the coproduction of digital divide and other lines of inequalities. The presumption is that the digital is now deeply ingrained in the ways we amass different sorts of capital and are placed in the social field. This is just another way (i.e., a Bourdieusian way[13]) of framing deep mediatization.

Thus deep mediatization produces geopolitical inequalities, which in turn produce the divide since the divide is based not only on one's awareness and access to the internet but also on one's capacity to afford new technologies. This renders the digital divide itself a dark underbelly of "deep

---

10. "Africa Internet Users, 2019." Between 2000 and 2019 internet penetration in Ethiopia has grown by 204.972%, and therefore further and speedier penetration can be expected in the coming few years.

11. Selwyn, *Defining the "Digital Divide."*

12. "Africa Internet Users, 2019."

13. Pierre Bourdieu reconceives the Marxian concept of "Capital" as "a wider system of exchanges whereby assets of different kinds are transformed and exchanged within complex networks or circuits within and across different fields." (Moore, "Capital," 102.) Thus digital divide, understood in the Bourdieusian way, is difference in access and quality of use of the digital to produce other goods that locate agents within different social classes in the social field.

mediatization," what Nick Couldry calls the "vicious circle of connectivity"[14] that may further exclude the already-excluded. In other words, digital divide is a deep mediatization of inequality and exclusion.

Moreover, the ubiquity of the digital and its embeddedness in everyday life (i.e., deep mediatization) in parts of the world that are at the bottom of the divide also largely depends on the continuous attempt to close the divide. For instance, a poor country such as Ethiopia attempts to increase internet penetration as a way of fostering participation in the digitized global market economy. This is a conscious attempt to close the digital divide, but at the same time a provision for society to be "deeply mediatized." Thus the "rest" of the world's attempt to trail behind the "west" as closely as possible shows us that the reality of digital divide and the attempt to overcome it also produces "deep mediatization."

This co-production therefore points to the scalability of both digital divide and mediatization. Based on different levels of digitization in different geopolitical regions, there are different depths of mediatization and divides. There is a difference between the depth of mediatization between Ethiopia and Singapore, and hence national digital divide. Simultaneously, there is also a different sort of mediatization among different regional states of Ethiopia, and hence a regional divide. On yet another level, there are digital divides of rural parts of a region and its urban parts.

This awareness of the scalability of digital divide and deep mediatization offers helpful insights into the study of digital practices in Ethiopia in relation to the politics of ethnic identity. Even more so given that the administrative structure in Ethiopia is an ethnic-based federalist one, and that there is a quasi-regionalized trend of urbanization and economic growth.[15] If Ethiopia is deeply mediatized, which does not exclude digital divide, does this have implications for the politics of ethnic identity?

Let me begin this moral rumination by quoting Couldry's third type of media injustice: "until such time as we regard being visible through media as intrinsic to human life, then there will be no automatic injustice from not having access to the possibility of speaking through media."[16] Deep mediatization creates the illusion of the mediated totality of social reality, in the sense that being human in our century implies being capable of "mass self-communication." This illusion is created through the mediatization of practices that *frame* social reality.[17] This framing does not determine just who exercises explana-

---

14. Couldry, *Media, Society, World*, n.p.
15. World Bank Group, "Ethiopia Urbanization Review," 14.
16. Couldry, *Media, Society, World*.
17. Couldry, *Media, Society, World*.

tory power in relation to social reality, but also who gets to shape or "mold" social reality. This is the conviction behind concepts such as "media power" (Kent Asp),[18] the "molding force of media" (Hepp),[19] and even "the mediated construction of social reality" (Hepp and Couldry).[20]

As such, if the moral dilemmas of deeper mediatization are to be addressed through a practices-approach, the digital divide calls for a kind of methodological reflexivity since there are not only groups that do something on digital media, but those who cannot and do not. Thus, based on the logic of the coproduction of deeper mediatization and digital divide, we may pause for moral consideration: if media plays a significant role in the construction of social reality via digital practices, the digital divide outskirts some. In the case of Ethiopia, which is a museum of peoples, such outskirts can be ethnic too, rendering them "Ethnic Digital Outskirts."

This calls for institutional balance that does not buy into the illusion of a digitally mediated totality of social reality. Such institutional balance should include, in addition to attempts to close the divide, conscious provision of platforms for representational practices that can minimize the invisibility caused by the coproduction of the divide and mediatization. Such practices may include journalistic coverage, intentional archiving of events and social realities, social research, etc., of less mediatized societies.

Having reflexively pointed out a limit to the practices-approach to deeply mediatized practices of the politics of ethnic identity, and thus asking my reader to note a caveat, I move to tackle the second challenge. Why should one take seriously a discussion of "deep mediatization" for the construction of the politics of ethnic identity in Ethiopia, a country with records of censorship and repression? Taking a long quasi-historical detour through the politics of resistance in our period, I next show how conscious digital media practices for ethnic-based politics of resistance has left the political air of Ethiopia more deeply mediated and "ethnicized," both at the same time.

## Ethnic-based Politics of Resistance (2014–18): A Story of "Deeper Mediatization" and "Deeper Ethnicization"

As mentioned above, Kohl and Carrie have observed that, globally, the use and regulation of the internet are mutually coproduced, in a form of force and counter-force, action and reaction, power and resistance. The same is true in

---

18. Asp, "Mediatization," 349–73.
19. Hepp, "Mediatization and the 'Molding Force,'" 1–28.
20. Couldry and Hepp, *Mediated Construction of Reality*.

Ethiopia: the politics of resistance and suppressive internet governance practices have coproduced each other. The more people used the internet to garner the politics of resistance, the tighter the states' regulatory measures became; and the tighter the regulation, the more creative practices of use were employed by the leadership of activists and journalists, as clearly outlined in the empirical research carried out by Iginio Gagliardone and Matti Pohjonen.[21] Is this a vicious circle or does it spiral towards emancipation? Communication scholars who study Ethiopia, including Gagliardone and Pohjonen themselves as well as Téwodros Workneh and Habtamu Dugo, all whose research focused on the period from 2014 to 2017, are ambiguous about emancipation as a result of such coproduction between social-media-based activism and authoritarian internet governance.[22] Thus, they wrote in an emancipatory tone, perhaps with the intent of supporting the resistance.

Workneh and Dugo particularly focus on exposing the discrepancies in the narratives that underpin the state's legally sanctioned suppressive practices of internet governance, the jurisprudential vagueness and contradictions that allow abuses and suppressions related to use of digital media, and implementations that violate rights of citizens and the diaspora.[23] The state's practices, according to these communication scholars, cast a shadow on the digital's potential to be a means for emancipation.

A curious case then: how did the politics of ethnic identity, which had a shape of resistance then (i.e., 2014–18), manage to use social media effectively? In a time marked by so much fragmentation and waning of collective action, how did people manage to galvanize patterned collective action that lasted for almost four years if not more? Some have claimed that the interactive nature of Web 2.0 platforms garner popular agency by undermining the producer/consumer divide, a logic that pervaded traditional mainstream media and earlier forms of the web. There is some truth in such optimism about new media, though it needs some serious qualification. As Paulo Gerbaudo rightly argues, the myth of absolute spontaneity and mere "horizontality" cannot stand: just as much as a well-performed choreography requires a "script" written by someone in which different actors can coordinately participate, an effective politics of resistance requires leaders and mobilizers who make the best use of Web 2.0.[24]

---

21. See, for instance, Gagliardone and Pohjonen, "Engaging in Polarized Society," 25–44. In this article, Gagliardone and Pohjonen discuss how "FreeZone9ers" went global and also viral on social media due to the state's attempt to take tighter action.

22. Téwodros, "Digital Cleansing?"; Habtamu, "Powers and Limits."

23. See also Yohannes, "Internet Shutdown."

24. Gerbaudo, "Populism 2.0," 44.

A look at a few instances of diaspora-initiated digital activism confirms the same point concerning ethnic-based politics of resistance in Ethiopia. Let me first look at an article written by the Ethiopian-born American Journalist/Activist Jawar Mohammed, who is one of the diaspora at the forefront of the Oromo resistance. Writing in 2011, Jawar claims that Web 2.0 offers a golden opportunity for an emancipative political practice:

> A picture or video clip taken on a cheap cell phone in rural Ethiopia can instantly wind up on social media . . . At the moment dictators are at a great disadvantage. This is a golden moment that needs to be seized by all oppressed people yearning for freedom.[25]

In a presentation in 2016 at a conference titled "Social Media Activism in Ethiopia" held in Washington DC on September 18, Mohammed pointed out why social media is an effective medium of resistance politics despite the government's tight measures:

> በጣም አፋኝ በሆነ ሥርዓት ውስጥ እነዚህ እንቅስቃሴዎች በአጭር ጊዜ ውስጥ ከፍተኛ ድል ሊያስገኙ የቻሉት ሚዲያው የህዝብ መሆን በመቻሉ ነው. . . ሶሻል ሚዲያ የኢንፎርሜሽን ፍሰውን ሆሪዞንታል፣ አግዞምሽ እንዲሆን አድርጎታል፤ ከላይ ወደታች ሳይሆን አግድሞሽ እንዲሆን አድርጎታል.
>
> These [resistance] movements achieved high rates of success in such a short time despite an extremely suppressive regime because the media now belongs to the people. Social media has made the flow of information horizontal; not vertical, but horizontal.[26]

Here, he is again referring to the interactive nature of the use of media which challenges the producer/consumer divide. However, a deeper look at Jawar's argument reveals how activism during our period of history broke the vicious circle and turned it into a spiral towards emancipation.

In the 2011 article, Jawar argues that the use of social media requires careful planning, especially given the fact that fewer than 1 percent of Ethiopians had access to the internet and that the state will probably "unplug" the internet once it realizes that resistance is buttressed through it.[27] While resistance movements can make good use of deep mediatization qua ubiquity of media with Web 2.0 advantages, the other danger lies in the ubiquity–dependence coproduction. If more use creates dependence, unplugging of the

---

25. Jawar, "Nonviolent Struggle."
26. EthioTube, "EthioTube የኦርም ተጋድሎ," 07:38–45. Translation and addition mine.
27. Jawar, "Nonviolent Struggle."

internet creates total devastation on politics of resistance, argues Mohammed.[28] How can resistance movements overcome this? Mohammed points to alternative internet supplies and locally based face-to-face interaction to spread news and garner collective action for a nonviolent struggle.

Mohammed was not alone in his affirmations of the need for a kind of digital tutelage. Habtamu Dugo's paper, presented at an Oromo Community Conference held in 2012 at Howard University, emphasizes the dire need of the Oromo to adopt and utilize Diaspora-based new media practices. In this paper he writes his hopes about the role of new media practices that have been enthusiastically adopted by Oromo youth after the second half of 2000s:

> Both nationally and globally, Oromumma, as a unifying architecture and as an instrument of Oromo collective actions towards their holistic liberation, requires new media technologies that can help deliver effective nation-building communications.[29]

In the same breath, however, he asserts that the new media practices of the Oromo youth, though enthusiastic, "are diverse, fragmented, individualized, and even polarized, hampering the development of Oromummaa as the pan-Oromian national identity."[30] Therefore, Habtamu proposes "some strategies toward the integration of emergent Oromo new media practices."[31]

For now, I am interested not only in his proposals but also in the fact *that* he proposes and in *why* he proposes. *That* he, and others such as him, propose the organization of media practices affirms the same point Gerbaudo was making: the choreographic nature of resistance politics and activism on Web 2.0. *What* he proposes includes one media network that unites all Oromos and a robust communal funding for this, the culture of civility and *Safuu* among the Oromo, recognizing the power of platforms such as Facebook, Twitter, and YouTube and engaging in content sharing.[32]

For now, let us focus on *why* he proposes: "to *adapt* to an ever-changing *communication landscape* that requires matching changes in approaches,"[33] *and* to counter "Oromo youth disengagement and demotivation as opposed to Habesha youth who *outnumber* and *out-engage* Oromo youth on political

---

28. EthioTube, "EthioTube የኦሮም ተጋድሎ"
29. Habtamu, "Powers and Limits," 3.
30. Habtamu, "Transcontinental Emerging New Media," 1.
31. Habtamu, "Transcontinental Emerging New Media," 1.
32. Habtamu, "Transcontinental Emerging New Media," 10.
33. Habtamu, "Transcontinental Emerging New Media," 2.

issues on social media platforms such as Twitter and Facebook."[34] These two rationales are interesting because they point to the "scalability" and co-production of digital divide outlined the previous section. Habtamu is arguing that Oromo youth need to cope *not only* with the changing realities of the mediatized world, *but also* with what he perceives to be a quantitative (i.e., "outnumbered") and qualitative (i.e., "out-engaged") gap related to new media practices between "the Habesha" and "the Oromo." Both of the rationales point to Dugo's desire to close two types of digital divides, the first one created by an ever-changing nature of communicative technology, and another one created along sociopolitical lines of inequality. (Note: I am not interested so much in whether Habtamu's assessment of this inequality is correct as what the assessments performatively achieve.)

One can make an intelligent guess, say, that Habtamu's desire is eventually endorsed by those who participated in the Oromo resistance, though such a claim would require further empirical validation. However, I can point to a few preliminary observations as to the performative force of Habtamu's proposal. First, in light of his proposal of a media network that unites all Oromos, and for a robust communal funding for this media network, one can note that Oromo Media Network (OMN) has emerged as a media giant in Oromo Politics of Resistance. Its mission of producing "original and citizen-driven reporting on Oromo and Oromia"[35] incorporates also connecting "the growing Oromo diaspora to its homeland using innovative digital tools and people-centered storytelling techniques."[36] Since its establishment in 2014, it has grown in its role in offering a sense of such mediated center, and is largely funded by the Oromo mass.

In addition to the proposal of the mediated center, one can note also that there is currently a relatively much more organized Oromo digital practice on social media as compared to what Habtamu describes in his 2012 article. Habtamu was dissatisfied with YouTube-based media practices and he highlights that Youtube was used only for sporadic "Music, comedy, YouTube-based radios and television shows, videos"[37]—instead of organizing Oromo collective action.

---

34. Habtamu, "Transcontinental Emerging New Media," 9.

35. See OMN's YouTube channel at https://www.youtube.com/user/OromiaMedia/about.

36. See "About Us" at https://oromiamedia.com/about/; "OMN–YouTube".

37. Habtamu, "Transcontinental Emerging New Media," 8.

Currently, however, YouTube channels started between 2014 and 2018 such as Raya Studio,[38] Yayo Studio,[39] and Urji Oromia[40] are geared towards explicitly promoting the culture and art of Oromo. Moreover, there are channels such as Obsa Techno[41] and Oro Mp4[42] which are directed at a kind of "Oromo Technology." Note, for instance, an excerpt from the channel Obsa Techno: "*Ilmaan Oromoo Sammuu isaanii Qaroomsuu fi Duubatti Hafummaa ilmaan oromoo irraa balleessuuf Qofa kan Hojjatuudha*"[43] (my translation: "[Obsa Techno] is exclusively committed to informing the minds of the children of Oromo and removing any kind of backwardness from among them"). [44]

The rise of mediatized politics of resistance which has an ethnic nature is not limited to Oromo politics of resistance, however. The so-called "provincial annexation" of the Amhara in Wolqait, a small area of land at the borders of Tigray region and Amhara region, gave rise to an articulated Amhara politics of resistance organized through #AmharaResistance over social media around mid-decade.[45] Achamyeleh Tamiru, a leader of the resistance movement claims that this movement, *inter alia*, contests a construal of the Amhara people as the hegemon in Ethiopian politics by countering the narrative of the "Tigrayan regime." This narrative, Achamyeleh argues, sanctions the enactment of the regime's desire of erecting a Tigrayan dynasty on the death of Amhara, including the placement of systemic genocidal techniques.[46] Therefore this resistance is a vanguard of Amhara's existence as a people and this calls for an organization of Amhara resistance, hence the call "ተደራጅ!" which means "get organized!"

Thus, one can reasonably assume intentionality, and therefore conscious agency, not only in the process of mediatizing politics of resistance but also in that of rendering it more ethnically centered. Mohammed, in a tweet posted on September 7, 2019, says:

38. "Raya Studio–YouTube." This channel has since been deleted by YouTube.

39. See Yayo Studio Tube's YouTube channel at https://www.youtube.com/channel/UCGZQdfugGkPoJAVEcOgn7Lw.

40. See Urji Oromia Tube's YouTube channel at https://www.youtube.com/channel/UCGafDQwJD2T21z3HtSWybbg/about.

41. See Obsa Techno's YouTube channel at https://www.youtube.com/channel/UCIYjWy8kGig8BguPtylaWew.

42. See Neima Abdurahman's YouTube channel at https://www.youtube.com/channel/UCyXv48Dg9RVIYPpyfSiyqoA.

43. See Obsa Techno's YouTube channel.

44. See Obsa Techno's YouTube channel.

45. Achamyeleh, "Forceful Annexation."

46. Achamyeleh, "የአማራ ተጋድሎና መንስዔው."

Amharizing the Amhara has been the most useful accomplishment of this change. The 'Ethiopian' mask used by the Amhara elite to camouflage their ethnic interest has been a barrier to a real dialogue. Now the mask has been removed, real negotiation and discussion is possible.[47]

So, what do these two changes, deeper mediatization and deeper ethnicization, mean for Ethiopia and its political practices? The state practices have changed. After the coming to Premiership of Laureate Dr. Abiy Ahmed as a result of the politics of resistance garnered by both the Oromo and later the Amhara, "a New Digital Chapter" dawned on Ethiopia. The "New Digital Chapter" is "new" precisely because there are changes in the way the state's practices of internet governance. For instance, Ethiopia ranked fourth in the "10 Most Censored Countries" after Eritrea, North Korea and Saudi Arabia in 2018, according to a report by Committee to Protect Journalists (CPJ),[48] yet leaves the list in 2019.[49] Similarly, Freedom On the Net's 2018 analysis on "Rising Authoritarianism" also reports the dawn of freedom of speech on the net for Ethiopia.[50]

All of these examples mean that the three practices in the three domains have changed: (1) the digital practices of politics of resistance have resulted and hence now occur in a more mediatized setting; (3) internet governance has loosened its grip; (3) the political air has not only been mediatized, but also become more ethnocentric. This makes the digital space an important and urgent location of moral rumination concerning the politics of ethnic identity. As highlighted throughout this section, though, the response to the suspicions this section attempts to respond to do not necessarily need such a long conceptual and historical detour. I have highlighted earlier that this long detour was intentional and relates to normative dilemmas related to the politics of ethnic identity. This brings me to the next section.

## Deeply Mediatized Practices of the Politics of Ethnic Identity: Moral Dilemmas

The above three changes (deeper mediatization, more loose internet governance, and further ethnically centered politics) result in a number of normative

---

47. See Jawar Mohammed's Twitter account: https://twitter.com/Jawar_Mohammed/status/1170307265825583105.
48. "10 Most Censored Countries, 2015."
49. "10 Most Censored Countries, 2019."
50. Shahbaz, "Digital Authoritarianism," 5.

crossroads: (1) to the state, *a crossroad of governance*: finding relatively newer paths or relapsing to suppressive measures? (2) the practices of use *at a moral crossroad*: (ir)responsible exercise of human communicative *power*? (3) the politics of ethnic identity, which had a nature of resistance against the states suppressive nature, now stands at *some moral crossroads*, which I will discuss below in combination with the second crossroad. I thus consider here the combination of the latter two in one term: deeply mediatized practices of the politics of ethnic identity. The first, *crossroad of governance*, is equally important. However, it is outside of the scope of this chapter.

As I noted in the first section, I will neither attempt to define the politics of ethnic identity nor list an exhaustive set of practices. Instead, since the purpose of this essay is to render the use of the digital for the politics of ethnic identity an object of moral rumination, I will discuss only two sets of digital practices of the politics of ethnic identity: the practices of belonging and those of group diachronicity.

## Belonging in the Algorithmic Ethnic?

The first and foremost set of practices related to the politics of ethnic identity are the practices of belonging, which aim to create and/or maintain feelings of being at home, curating a kind of ontological security in relation to an ethnic group: "I *am* where I *belong*." These relations of belonging and the sense of ontological security are not only the outcomes of practices of belonging but also form conditions for them.[51] One of the preoccupations of such practices is to delineate who belongs and who does not, practices of inclusion and exclusion in relation to individuals.

Here I will discuss YouTube music as an outcome of the practices of ethnic-based inclusion and exclusion. Let me focus, for brevity, on particular YouTube channels: Rayaa Studio, a channel dedicated to the exclusive production and dissemination of Oromo Music, and Heni Tube, a channel that releases some music related to Amhara politics of resentment. This digital practice can be called "Ethnic YouTubing," also carried out by other YouTube channels delineated above.

From among Rayaa Studio's productions, some of the music clips include "geerarsaa," a genre often used as war bravado among Oromo people. In these videos "Kessumma" ("guest") is recurrently used as a metaphor for the other. Oromo politics of resentment is marked by colonial reading of Ethiopia's history of state formation, arguably started by Emperor Minilik II of Shoa. As such, the settlers from the north who came as a result of Minilik's native

---

51. Nolan et al., "Australian Media," 7.

colonization, according to this reading, are the *Kessumma* who are nonetheless the colonizers. Since Minilik is understood to be *bineensa* (hyena)[52] in this reading, the ethnic *kessumma* are also construed as *bineensa*. Let us, for instance, take a look at two songs published in the middle of the heated politics of resistance leading to "the Irrecha Massacre 2016: Ittiqaa Tafarii's "Itti Muddi, Itti Muddi" ("Hurry Up! Hurry Up!"), published on YouTube in May 2016, and Galaana Garoomsa's "Sodaa Qaawwee hin Qabnu" ("We Are Not Scared of Guns"), published in July 2016.

Ittiqaa's clip, which has reached over half a million views and 2,400 likes, appeals to the Oromo to hurry because there is weed in the wheat:

> Inkirdaada qamadii kessama argama maloo jarana
> Wajjin haamani inkirdaadi kessaa gubani.[53]

> Lo and behold! There's weed in the wheat
> And you harvest them together and burn the weed.
> [Translation mine]

The wheat are those who, appearing to be relatives ("fira fakkaachisani"), are in reality man-eating guests devouring on their hosts ("maali keessummaan nama nyata"). Much of the bravado is synchronized with a visual scene of someone firing a gun, almost every time Ittiqaa says "Itti muddi" or hurry up, in a fashion similar to swift and unhesitant action required from someone defending themselves from a beast.

Gelaanaa's song has close to a million views (888,639 views) and is liked by thousands (3,200).[54] This song also starts by using the word *Kessumma* in a rather negative way, "du'eetan bada malee, kessummaan dinqa hin qabu" ("I will rather die than care about the guest"). On the one hand this song has a nonviolent gist which talks about "buqqisuu" (uprooting) of the enemy by "du'uu" (dying). On the other hand, however, it defeats its own nonviolent turn by including phrases such as "the other is a hyena, and a river that takes you away as you play with" ("Alagaan bineenchisa, bishaan sinyaatu si kofalchiisa"). He does this to supplant his appeal, "lammii sii wayya" ("you better side with your own people"), by pointing to friendship with the ethnically other as radically enigmatic and untrustworthy. Note the mutual opposition of "lammi" and other:

> Tulluun sitti jiguumoo lammin sii jiguu wayyaa
> Afaan namaan dubbatta akka tamboofi gayaa

---

52. Mulualem, "Theses and Antitheses of Anoole Statue," 45.
53. Ittiqaa, "Itti Muddi."
54. Gelaanaa, "Soodaa Qaawwee."

> Duutus awwalcha hin qabdu, baddu barbaacha hin qabdu
> Koo lammikee sii wayya, koo lammiikee si wayya.[55]
>
> Is it better if a mountain falls on you, or your people fall for you?
> You speak in the language of others as if you're addicted to it,
> You have none to bury you if you die, or none to look for you if you go missing,
> Come stick to your own people, Come stick to your people.
> [Translation mine]

These two songs deepen the sense of ontological insecurity, insisting that one's home is always unsafe so long as there are guests in it. Therefore, Ittiqaa calls, hurry-up and destroy your "guest," your enemy from among you ("ballessi diinakee") and disturb them ("booressi diinakee"). Gelaanaa's construal of the ethnic other as enigmatic and untrustworthy is used to garner loyalty to the "lammi." As such, inclusion is constructed by its limit: the excluded ethnic other as monstrous.

These practices of the Oromo are not alone though; rather, the polarization of the Oromo and the Amhara is done from both sides. During the years 2016 to 2018, these two ethnic groups were united in their resistance captured by the conglomerate word "OrAmhara." However, as Daniel Mekonen's 2019 article points out, these groups have relapsed to their old habits of mutual ridiculing after the Tigrayan regime has been done with and Laureate Dr. Abiy Ahmed came to power.[56]

Though empirical backing is admittedly lacking, the ethnic other is often called "*Jiboch*" in Amharic or "*Bineensa*" in Afan Oromo, both meaning hyena, and "*Aganintoch*," meaning demons. These insults are sometimes accompanied by visual contents that are highly offensive, sometimes even to the extent of sexualized derogation: social media posts of altered pictures of a person from one ethnic group appearing to be raping another prestigious person from the other group, and the mention of cutting of the other person's genitalia as a way of directing offense at the Oromo for their narrative of Minilik II's mutilation. One can note that Facebook has lately been swarmed with appeals such as "አዲስ አበቤ ተደራጅ" ("The children of Addis Ababa get organized") and "ፋኖ ተደራጅ" (which calls to the Amhara counterpart of Qeerroo to be organized), with a connotation of buying a gun.

Some of the music clips published on Heni Tube can be examples of violent proclivities in some of these calls for organization, particularly

---

55. Gelaanaa, "Soodaa Qaawwee."

56. Daniel, "የኦሮማራ ጥምረትና አዙሪት ያስከተለው ሀገራዊ ስጋት" ["yeOroMara Timretina azurite yasketelew hagerawi sigat," in Amharic].

fantasies of gunning down the offender. Let us consider Mebre Mengste's "ዋ በለው" (*wa belew*), published on October 21, 2019, having 306,417 views and 4,100 likes.[57] This clip is directed at both the Amhara as a bravado, since it includes the genre of ቀረርቶ (an Amhara bravado for war) and those who agitate the Amhara, since the word "ዋ" (*wa*) is an Amharic word used to warn/threaten. Summoning the Amhara from border to border, Mengste warns as follows: "ሾዋ ነፍሰቢሱ፣ ሲከፋው ባሩድ ነው ድግሱ" ("Shoa the soul-less, feasts on gunpowder when grieved"); "መውዜሩን ወልውሎ ይዛል በትከሻው" ("he has wiped his gun clean and is holding it on his back"); "መሬን አትነካኩት . . . ከላሽ ውበቱ ነው" ("do not agitate the embittered, since his gun is his beauty"). The motion-graphic is marked by recurrent gunfire. As such, gunning down is both normalized and aesthesized.

These simulations of self-other relations, both in Oromo and Amhara practices, hint at the emergence of exclusionary politics. Miroslav Volf, in *Exclusion and Embrace*, calls such politics the politics of "the good and the just imprisoned in their own conscience," borrowing from Nietzsche's *Thus Spoke Zarathustra*.[58] These "prisoners" are caught in the illusion of having a perfect knowledge: of the other as the evil enemy, and of themselves as "impersonations of the absence of evil."[59] The utterly good, therefore, obliterate the other, construed as utterly evil, from amongst themselves.

While the violent notion of these simulations needs attention, there is yet another dimension that comes to the fore when one thinks of datafication. Datafication further buttresses such polarization of self-other identities. The kinds of videos one shares on Facebook contribute to the kinds of friends one makes since one's befriending is mediated by algorithm-based friend suggestions. As such, the kind of ethnic that one belongs to may be called, though hesitantly, an "algorithmic ethnic." One will be surrounded by those like-minded who further solidify the "imprisonment" in one's conscience, and ostracizing whoever challenges this conscience. This, of course, is not exclusive of the choreographic nature of political practices over Web 2.0 platforms I have mentioned above.

Therefore, one asks, is Mohammed's hopes about the dialogical opening as a result of "Amharization of the Amhara" founded? Or could the merging of deeper datafication and "ethnicization" be a closure of dialogical space due to people becoming more and more imprisoned in the "algorithmic ethnic" that construes the self as "the good and the just" and the other as the monstrous to be destroyed?

57. Heni Tube, "Mebre Mengste." See also Heni Tube, "Mebre Mengste."
58. Volf, *Exclusion and Embrace*, 61.
59. Volf, *Exclusion and Embrace*, 61.

Achamyeleh's observation mentioned at the beginning of this chapter (i.e., "We may occupy the same *space* but we do not live in the same dimension"[60]) points to something dangerous for the digital *space* as a place of cohabitation of different ethnic groups. The closure of this space, moreover, is not limited to synchronic practices such as watching, liking and sharing a video, but also relates to war of memories.

## Warring Digital Diachronicities and Deeply Mediatized *Anamnesis*

The second type of practices of the politics of ethnic identity are what I call practices of group diachronicity, aimed at securing continuity across time. From among these, I will address what I call practices of memory, which include, in my discussion, two sets of practices: commemorative and archival practices. Commemorative practices are the present's attempt to steward the memory of the past while archival practices are the present's attempt to steward the memory of the future. As such, they are both attempts of the present to extend itself in time, therefore the name "diachronicity."

One of the reasons people from different ethnic groups talk past each other while "occupying the same space," has to do with the war of memories that have reached a *cul de sac*: Ethiopian politics of ethnic identity is often polarized into a "colonialist reading" of Ethiopian history by the Oromo-nationalists and "imperial-nationalist" reading by the Amhara and other Pan-Ethiopianists (See Afework's chapter in this volume). This has resulted in practices and counter-practices of commemoration. This polarity is well-captured by the opposition between commemorations centered around the monument of Emperor Minilik II in Addis Ababa, and the monument of Anole at Hetiso.

The monument in Addis Ababa commemorates Minilik II as the victorious Emperor who founded the capital, secured the Victory of Adwa, and founded Ethiopia as a nation. On the other hand, the erection of the monument Anole in Hetosa, Oromia region, on April 6, 2014 commemorates the Oromo martyrs who were victims of Minilik's army during his 1889 march southward to subjugate the Cushite peoples, including the Oromo, to found a modern Ethiopian state. The monument, a statue which depicts a mutilated right hand holding a mutilated female breast, stands for the alleged mutilations of the right hands of men and breasts of women in Hetosa in 1888.

60. Achamyeleh, "My Perception."

These warring memories are getting more polarized by the day, manifesting themselves through online and offline enactments. On the one hand, on September 14, 2018, the Qerro, the Oromo mass of young people organized through social media, attempted to bring down the monument in Addis Ababa, resisting a celebration of Minilik II.[61] On the other hand, some Amhara youth started a practice of changing their profile pictures to portraits of Minilik II, and/or their Facebook names to something that includes either "Menelik" or "*Neftegna*" ("gun holder", a name given to the gun-owning feuds in Minilik's *neftegna–gabbar* feudal system; now given to the Amhara to indicate that they are the heirs of Minilik's politics of coercive subjugation).

This war of commemorations is also further extended into the war of archives. The archiving of brutality and killing has long been an aspect of the practices of Oromo politics of resistance: in addition to reports on OMN and hashtags such as #anoolee and #neverforget on social media, qerroo.org also archives the number of the dead every month, sometimes with pictures. Amahara resistance has also taken up this practice.

Let me point out some of these concerning the event of the last week of October 2019. During that week, there was a wide-ranging ethnic conflict, mainly between the Amhara and the Oromo, resulting in the deaths of at least eighty-six people in a duration of less than two weeks. People have died from both ethnic groups according to official reports. Amhara social media activists have been involved in the archiving of the death of the Amahara and the alleged brutality committed against them. For instance, the Facebook page known as "ልሳነ ዐማራ Amhara Press" also archived the list of dead people with their ethnicity and religious affiliation.[62] Achamyeleh also uses Facebook as a site of archive. Note his post on October 30, 2019, as a commentary on the video that he posted there, shared 1500 times:

በዶዶላ በጃዋር መሐመድ መንግሥት ቄሮዎች ጡታቸው የተቆረጠው የሁለቱ እናትማማቾች ግፍ ተመዝግቦ ይቀመጥ!

ጥቅምት 15 ቀን 2012 ዓ.ም. የጀዋር መሐመድ መንግሥት ወታደሮች [ቄሮዎችን ማለቴ ነው] በዶላ የሁለት እናትማማቾችን ጡት መቁረጣቸውን እነሆ የዐይን ምስክሩ ይናገራል! ይህ ለኔ በግል ከተላከው የጋም እናት ጡት መቆረጡን ከሚያሳየው ዘጋናኝ ቪዲዮ ተጨማሪ ነው።

---

61. Yonas, "Addis on the Edge."

62. See this post on ልሳነ ዐማራ Amhara Press's Facebook page at https://www.facebook.com/AmharaPress/photos/a.158858051178508/876938769370429/?type=3&permPage=1.

በጃዋር መሐመድ መንግሥት ወታደሮች ጡታቸው የቆረጡዋና ቡሉቱ
እነትማማቾች ላይ የተፈጸመው ጭካኔ ከጡት ቆራጮቹ ወገን ከፀመው ከዐቢይ
አሕመድ አገዛዝ ፍትሕ ባያገኝም ወደፊት ትውልድና ታሪክ ይፋድርበት ዘንድ
በሰባተኛው ንጉሥ በዐፄ ዐቢይ አሕመድ ዘመነ መንግሥት በተሰዋጩ መንግሥት
በጃዋር መሐመድ ወታደሮች ጡት መቆረጡን የሚያረጋግጠው ይህ የዐይን ምስክሩ
ማስረጃ ለታሪክ ተመዝግቦ ይቀመጣል፡፡

በተስፋዬ ገብረአብ ልብወለድ አኛሌ ላይ የተቆረጠ ጡት ሐውልት ያቆሙትና
መቆሙን የደገፉ የኦሮም ብሔርተኞች አንዲህ የዐይን ምስክር ማስረጃ ላለው
በጃዋር መሐመድ ቄሮዎች ጡታቸውን ለተቆረጡ አነትማማቾች ሐውልት
ያቆሙላቸው ይሆን?[63]

Let the atrocious mutilation of the breasts of the two sisters in Dodola committed by Jawar Mohammed's Qerroos be recorded!

Note that an eye witness testifies Jawar Mohammed's soldiers (I mean Qerroos) had mutilated the two sisters' breast on October 24, 2019. This is in addition to the horrendous video sent to me as a clear display of the mutilated breasts.

Even if this atrocious mutilation carried out by the soldiers of Jawar Mohammed's government has not met justice that should have been served under the rule of Abiy Ahmed, who stands on the side of the mutilators, this record of the eye witness will be retained so that it will be an evidence that the soldiers of the succeeding government of Jawar Mohammed have mutilated breasts under the rule of Emperor Abiy Ahmed, the Seventh King.

Will the Oromo nationalists who erected the monument of a mutilated breast in Anole and those who supported such commemoration, just based on nothing but Tesfaye Gebreab's fiction,[64] also erect a monument for these sisters whose breasts were mutilated by Qerroo? [Translation mine]

Deep mediatization, however, poses moral dilemmas concerning such archives. As Ricardo L. Punzalan and Michelle Caswell rightly point out, archival practices can be acts that largely contribute to social justice by documenting human rights violations.[65] But, as Couldry points out, in a deeply mediatized setting "all sorts of information persist into the present as open archive."[66] The ubiquity of media means the ubiquity of the archive. This is

---

63. See Achamyeleh's Facebook page at https://www.facebook.com/achamyeleh.tamiru.3.

64. Tesfaye Gebreab, የቡርቃ ዝምታ.

65. Punzalan and Caswell, "Archival Approaches," 1–18.

66. Couldry, *Media, Society, World*.

shot through with dilemma: on the one hand, as I just mentioned, archiving violations can be considered a contribution to social justice; on the other hand, however, these archives are open to be retrieved by anyone. Does that result in a more just coexistence or a more vengeful society?

As a kind of *anamnesis* (i.e., a conscious recollection of the past) digital forms of retrieval also pose another dilemma. For instance, consider Facebook's algorithmic retrieval of the past: its *annual reminding*. This retrieval makes *anamnetic* practices algorithmically mediated, altering human *anamnetic* agency. Achamyeleh's archive of the alleged mutilation of breasts has been shared 1,500 times. This would mean that 1,500 pages, whether individual or collective, will be annually reminded of this online event, and from among those, those who *chose* the memory to resurface will give their social networks a "News Feed," creating further opportunity for large-scale algorithmically mediated *anamnesis*.

This creates a platform for dangerous speech done not just by humans but also by humans whose *anamnetic* capacity and agency is extended through algorithms. This means, if I may emphasize by way of hyperbole, we do not remember just as humans anymore but as algorithmically "aided" humans. Thus our *anamnetic* agency is placed in what Holger Pötzsch calls "post-comprehension era of information processing."[67] This poses a moral challenge for deeply mediatized ethnic archival practices in Ethiopia.

## Concluding Remarks: Moral Signposts

I began this chapter with Achamyeleh's thought-provoking sentence: "We may occupy the same space but we do not live in the same dimension."[68] And following that provocation, I posed a thought-provoking question: how can Ethiopians, whose ethnic loyalties are diverse and who occupy the same (digital) space, live together? This chapter has not been an answer to this question, but rather a path toward such an answer. Instead of heading right to moral articulation for togetherness, I have taken a quasi-theoretical, quasi-historical detours to discuss the space between a triad of practices—the practices of use of digital media, the practices of internet governance and those of the politics of ethnic identity. I have argued that consciously mediated highly ethnicized politics of resistance has left the political air of Ethiopia both further ethnicized and more mediatized. I have also argued that any moral articulation concerning ethnic diversity should take into consideration this reality, and therefore take morals for a digital space seriously.

67. Pötzsch, "Archives and Identity," 3316.
68. Achamyeleh, "My Perception."

This moral reflection for the digital space, I have argued, also needs to be reflexive of the practices-approach. Especially given Ethiopia's ethnic-based federalism and quasi-regional economic development and urbanization, "ethnic digital outskirts" should be taken seriously. As such, this is a signpost towards moral articulation for the digital space and its outer limit. I have pointed to journalism, archival practices, and social studies as possible moves towards social justice to consider these outskirts, and challenge the illusion of the mediation of total social reality for a more just society despite the coproduction of deep mediatization and digital divide. Social research, I would like to mention, can particularly bridge the gap of empirical validation in the insights this chapter attempts to offer, which are meant to be only signposts.

That being the first signpost, the next signpost was related to belonging in what I hesitantly called "the algorithmic ethnic" which takes on and also contributes to embodied and materialized practices of the politics of ethnic identity. I have particularly focused on practices of exclusion and, marginally, inclusion, arguing that they are more and more polarized. In other words, it is becoming the case that to be included in one's ethnic group is more and more associated with excluding others, either in the form of dispelling the guest and/or killing them. Moreover, a look at some Amhara practices also shows the normalization and aestheticization of violence against the other as a response to agitation. Both point toward the solidification of the friend/enemy distinction, the violent turn to the enemy, and hostile attitude to the guest or the alien. I have pointed out how algorithmic creation of social networks contributes to the polarization of friend/enemy distinction and hence offer communal validation of the violent and inhospitable turn to the other. These insights can give us the second, third, and fourth signposts toward moral articulation for a digital space: articulations of the love of the enemy, of nonviolent resistance, and the ethics of hospitality.

Finally, I have considered warring digital diachronicities by looking at digital practices of commemorative and archival practices. I have argued that our *anamnetic* agency is now largely mediatized both through the ubiquity of open archive, and its algorithmic retrieval. In the context of warring memories of the Amhara and the Oromo, such retention not only solidifies the friend/enemy distinction, but also, to a certain extent, foretells the danger of the returns of memories of violent events. These memories of violent events, whether factual or fabricated, can throw society into a vicious circle of animosity.

Moral articulations, therefore, are required for responsible *anamnesis*, the fifth signpost. Christian tradition, with its nonviolent commemoration of the violent event of the death of its God, carries a unique moral resource in this regard. Theologians and communities in Ethiopia, I suggest, benefit greatly from a moral rumination on the Eucharist in light of this, enabling people to receive violent memories with non-violent attitudes, transforming hearts towards forgiveness and reconciliation.

## Bibliography

"10 Most Censored Countries." *Committee to Protect Journalists*, 2015. cpj.org/2015/04/10-most-censored-countries.php.

"10 Most Censored Countries." https://cpj.org/reports/2019/09/10-most-censored-eritrea-north-korea-turkmenistan-journalist/.

Achamyeleh Tamiru. "Forceful Annexation, Violation of Human Rights and Silent Genocide: A Quest for Identity and Geographic Restoration of Wolkait-Tegede, Gondar, Amhara, Ethiopia." http://ethioforum.org/wp-content/uploads/2016/08/Wolqait-Tegede-AT-Edited-Version-5-with-corrections-and-remarks.pdf.

———. "My Perception of and Reflection on the State of Ethiopia." https://www.ethioreference.com/archives/17583.

"Africa Internet Users, 2019 Population and Facebook Statistics." https://www.internetworldstats.com/stats1.htm.

Asp, Kent. "Mediatization: Rethinking the Question of Media Power." In *Mediatization of Communication*, edited by Knut Lundby et al., 349–73. Handbooks of Communication Science 21. Boston: De Gruyter Mouton, 2014.

Couldry, Nick. *Media, Society, World: Digital Media Practice*. Epub. Cambridge: Polity, 2012.

Couldry, Nick, and Andreas Hepp. *Mediated Construction of Reality*. Malden: Polity, 2017.

Daniel Mekonen. "የኦሮማራ ጥምረትና አዙሪት ያስከተለው ሀገራዊ ስጋት." *Ethio-Think-Thank*, April 2019. https://ethiothinkthank.com/2019/04/07/the-dismay-and-threats-of-oromara-coalition/.

"Ethiopia Urbanization Review: Urban Institutions for a Middle-Income Ethiopia." Washington, DC: World Bank, 2015. https://openknowledge.worldbank.org/handle/10986/22979.

EthioTube. "EthioTube የአማራ ተጋድሎና መንስዔው: Social Media Activism in Ethiopia. - Achamyeleh Tamiru on የአማራ ተጋድሎ | Sep. 18, 2016." *YouTube*, September 21, 2016. https://www.youtube.com/watch?v=7It1qgm2cig&t=309s.

Gagliardone, Iginio, and Matti Pohjonen. "Engaging in Polarized Society: Social Media and Political Discourse in Ethiopia." In *Digital Activism in the Social Media Era: Critical Reflections on Emerging Trends in Sub-Saharan Africa*, edited by Bruce Mutsvairo, 25–44. Cham: Palgrave Macmillan, 2016.

Gelaanaa Gaaromsaa. "Soodaa Qaawwee Hin Qabnuu." *YouTube*, July 2016. https://www.youtube.com/watch?v=HuigkRXTAzs&has_verified=1.

Gerbaudo, Paulo. "Populism 2.0: Social Media Activism, the Generic Nternet User and Interactive Direct Democracy." In *Social Media, Politics and the State: Protests, Revolutions, Riots, Crime and Policing in the Age of Facebook, Twitter and YouTube*, edited by Daniel Trottier and Christian Fush, 67–87. New York: Routledge, 2015.

Glasius, Marlies, and Marcus Michaelsen. "Illiberal and Authoritarian Practices in the Digital Sphere | Prologue." *International Journal of Communication* 12 (2018) 3795–813.

Habtamu Dugo. "The Powers and Limits of New Media Appropriation in Authoritarian Contexts: A Comparative Case Study of Oromo Protests in Ethiopia." *Africology: The Journal of Pan African Studies* 10.10 (November 2017).

———. "Transcontinental Emerging New Media Practices and Oromo Youth in Galvanizing Oromummaa." Paper presented at the Oromo Community-DC Seminar on Oromummaa, Howard University, September 1, 2012.

Heni Tube. "Mehari Degefaw - Gitem Alegn | ግጠም አለኝ - New Ethiopian Music 2019 (Official Video)." *YouTube*, April 21, 2019. https://www.youtube.com/watch?v=uORB6yJ-CQg.

———. "Mebre Mengste - ሙብሬ መንግስቴ (መዉዜር አማርኛ) / ዋ በለው / New Ethiopian Music 2019 (Official Video)." *YouTube*, October 21, 2019. https://www.youtube.com/watch?v=eGnwGGFVioQ.

Hepp, Andreas. "Mediatization and the 'Molding Force' of the Media." *Communications* 37.1 (1 January 2012) 1–28.

Hepp, Andreas, et al. "Mediatization: Theorizing the Interplay between Media, Culture and Society." *Media, Culture & Society* 37.2 (March 2015) 314–24.

Hepp, Andreas, et al. "Rethinking Transforming Communications: An Introduction." In *Communicative Figurations: Transforming Communications in Times of Deep Mediatization*, edited by Andreas Hepp et al., 3–15. Cham: Palgrave Macmillan, 2018.

Ittiqaa Tafari. "Itti Muddi, Itti Muddi." *YouTube*, May 26, 2016. https:/www.youtube.com/watch?v=v4rxPTr1KD0.

Jawar Mohammed. "Nonviolent Struggle: Ethiopian Exceptionalism?" *OPride*, February 28, 2011. https://www.opride.com/2011/02/28/nonviolent-struggle-ethiopian-exceptionalism/.

Kohl, Uta, and Carrie Fox. "Introduction: Internet Governance and the Resilience of the Nation State." In *The Net and the Nation State: Multidisciplinary Perspectives on Internet Governance*, edited by Uta Kohl, 1–24. New York: Cambridge University Press, 2017.

Moore, Robert. "Capital." In *Pierre Bourdieu: Key Concepts*, edited by Michael Grenfell, 101–19. Key Concepts. Stocksfield: Acumen, 2008.

Mulualem Daba Tola. "The Theses and Antitheses of Anoole Statue in the Ethiopian Polity." *Research on Humanities and Social Sciences* 7.9 (2017) 43–49.

Nolan, David, et al. "Australian Media and the Politics of Belonging." In *Australian Media and the Politics of Belonging*, edited by David Nolan et al., 3–18. London: Anthem, 2018.

Pötzsch, Holger. "Archives and Identity in the Context of Social Media and Algorithmic Analytics: Towards an Understanding of IArchive and Predictive Retention." *New Media & Society* 20.9 (September 2018) 3304–22.

Punzalan, Ricardo L., and Michelle Caswell. "Critical Directions for Archival Approaches to Social Justice." *The Library Quarterly* 86.1 (2016) 1–18.

Schatzki, Theodore. *Social Practices: A Wittgensteinian Approach to Human Activity and the Social*. Cambridge: Cambridge University Press, 1996.

Selwyn, Neil. *Defining the "Digital Divide": Developing a Theoretical Understanding of Inequalities in the Information Age*. Cardiff: Cardiff, 2002.

Shahbaz, Adrian. "The Rise of Digital Authoritarianism." https://freedomhouse.org/report/freedom-net/2018/rise-digital-authoritarianism.

Tedla Desta. "Comments on the Digitalization and Digital Divide in the Horn of Africa (HoA), Kenya and Ethiopia: The Media Perspective." *Global Media Journal* 16.30 (February 2018) 1–7.

Tesfaye Gebreab. የቡርቃ ዝምታ [*Ya'Burka Zimita*]. Addis Ababa, 2000.

Téwodros Workneh. "Digital Cleansing? A Look into State-Sponsored Policing of Ethiopian Networked Communities." *African Journalism Studies* 36.4 (October 2015) 102–24.

Volf, Miroslav. *Exclusion and Embrace: A Theological Exploration of Identity, Otherness, and Reconciliation*. Nashville: Abingdon, 1996.

World Bank Group. "Ethiopia Urbanization Review: Urban Institutions for a Middle-Income Ethiopia." Washington, DC: World Bank, 2015. https://openknowledge.worldbank.org/handle/10986/22979.

Yohannes Eneyew Ayalew. "The Internet Shutdown Muzzle(s) Freedom of Expression in Ethiopia: Competing Narratives." *Information & Communications Technology Law* 28.2 (May 2019) 208–24.

Yonas Abiye. "Addis on the Edge." *The Reporter Ethiopia English*, September 15, 2018. https://www.thereporterethiopia.com/article/addis-edge.

"ልሳነ ዐማራ– Amhara Press." Facebook Page. Facebook, November 4. https://www.facebook.com/AmharaPress/photos/a.158858051178508/876938769370429/?type=3&permPage=1.

# Part III

# Unity and Diversity: Moral Visions of Togetherness

# 5

# Identity in the Light of Unity-in-Diversity

— Daniel Assefa Kassaye (Abba) —

> Behold, how good and how pleasant it is for brothers to dwell together in unity!
>
> (Ps 133:1, NASB)

DEBATES OVER SHARED IDENTITIES often reflect strong tensions. Antagonisms surface easily, leading to deadlocks. Solutions seem distant and extreme positions slip easily into meaningless discussion. However, the question of the one and of the many is a pleasant mystery of creation. Certainly, some opt for the "one," others for the "many." Having said that, is unity a threat to diversity or its guarantee? Does diversity warrant unity or impede unity? Is it possible to conceive diversity without unity, or unity without diversity? When does diversity become beautiful? When does unity lead to happiness? Can we reduce identity to membership to any given community? Does not Christian identity transcend all identities based on membership to a community? Inspired by the Christian message, this chapter aims at showing the intrinsic and beneficial connection between unity and diversity for a healthy understanding of identity.

## Defining Narrative Identity

Identity here refers to the labels one puts on an individual or a community. Identity is the answer to the questions "Who is a person?" or "What is a community?" Both unity and diversity are connected with identity. Defense of unity implies affirmation of the identity of a given community, be it an association, an ethnic community, or a country.[1] Similarly, defense of diversity infers the affirmation of a community in relation to other communities. Unity focuses on the identity of various individuals or communities with a rather vertical direction. Its risk is assimilation or uniformity. Diversity claims horizontal recognition. Its risk is division and separation.

The answer to the questions "Who is this person?" or "What is this community?" has a narrative form. Identity includes what one thinks and what one does, lest it becomes a very limited and poor description. Paul Ricoeur, in his conclusion of his trilogy on *Time and Narrative*[2] affirms the following:

> To state the identity of an individual or a community is to answer the question, "who did this?" "who is the agent, the author?" We first answer this question by naming someone, that is, by designating them with a proper name. But what is the basis for the permanence of this proper name? What justifies our taking the subject of an action, so designated by his, her, or its proper name, as the same throughout a life that stretches from birth to death? The answer has to be narrative. To answer the question "who?" as Hannah Arendt has so forcefully put it, is to tell the story of a life. The story told tells about the action of the "who". And the identity of this "who" therefore itself must be a narrative identity. Without the recourse to narration, the problem of personal identity would in fact be condemned to an antinomy with no solution.

Kevin Vanhoozer,[3] in his explanation of Ricoeur's thesis, says:

> Finally, in giving us a historical consciousness, narrative bestows an identity as well. Indeed, Ricoeur suggests that personal identity is inherently narrative in nature. To understand who we are is to be able to follow our stories. Narrative also provides the all-important link between the continuity and discontinuity of the self. As historical, the self-changes; yet it remains itself.

Ricoeur opposes identity denoting "sameness," which he calls *idem*, to identity denoting "selfhood," which he names *ipse*. For Ricoeur there is a dialectics of selfhood and sameness expressed in the Latin terms *idem* and *ipse*, and showing the paradoxical nature of narrative identity whereby there

---

1. One speaks also of the European community.
2. Ricoeur, *Time and Narrative*, 244–49.
3. Vanhoozer, *Biblical Narrative*, 103–4. Besides, one may learn more about one's identity by identifying oneself with characters of other stories and histories.

is sameness and change.[4] Besides, Ricoeur uses the expression "permanence in time" to explain the concept of characters and the concept of being faithful to one's word or promise. "Habit," says Ricoeur, "gives history to character" and that history implies change, in the sense that it includes "sedimentation" that inclines "to cover over the innovation which preceded it."[5] Narratives of individuals or of communities are rewritten with corrections and alteration.[6] One may consider here the impact of narrative on identity.

Narratives play a crucial role by either helping to overcome pride or by triggering arrogance. They can propose new perspectives and enable one to see outside the box. They can show the value of humility. Unhealthy narratives of unity or of diversity create unhealthy understanding of identity. Identity needs constant purification lest it become discriminative, or victim of egoism or exclusivism.

Both unity and diversity can entertain violent narratives. Both can become ideologies that romanticize and absolutize one aspect of reality and hide another dimension of the whole truth. Both can inculcate hatred and dualism by rejecting other perspectives. An aggressive narrative is deficient. A narrative that nourishes fear, hatred, competition, or greed will harm unity, diversity, and identity. Identity needs a peaceful and positive definition.

## Good Can Come from Outside

When one speaks of the identity of an individual or a community one can easily slip into caricatures and prejudices. One needs to stop and reflect in order to avoid fallacious definitions and descriptions. It is easy to make mistakes over the identity of an individual and a community. What is worse is that the mistake can lead into wrong conduct causing others to suffer by one's action.

Let us take, for example, the commandment to love one's neighbor (Lev 19:18). This commandment is associated with the commandment of divine love. The question would be "Who is my neighbor?" Only the person who belongs to my community, be it ethnic or religious or political? When the lawyer put this question to Jesus (Luke 10:29) it was not with good intention. He was not motivated by a desire to learn. Perhaps, with some cynicism, he seemed to imply that the commandment to love one's neighbor is not applicable to all human beings. The fact that Jesus mentions a Samaritan

---

4. Ricoeur, *Oneself as Another*, 113–39.

5. Ricoeur, *Oneself as Another*, 122.

6. Ricoeur, *Time and Narrative*, 247. For a reflection of these concepts in an Ethiopian context, see Theodros, *The Politics of Metanoia*, 71–74.

as a model is significant. Does a Samaritan qualify to be a good example for the understanding of the commandment to "love one's neighbor"? The answer could have been negative for the lawyer. A Samaritan, for him, is a heretic and schismatic; he cannot be a neighbor.[7]

There is however another important point. Jesus' answer is focused on the action of the neighbor. The question becomes, then, "What does a neighbor think and do" rather than "to which community does a neighbor belong." Accordingly, a neighbor is someone who shows compassion. Being a neighbor becomes a quality.

This contrasts with human tendency and human temptation of delimiting the community whose neighbors deserve to be loved. It is not then easy to admire and appreciate outsiders whatever the quality of the community to which one belongs. Yet, admiring individual and communal values of outsiders creates good relations, peace, and harmony. If diverse communities imagine stories where compassion becomes a trait of a "Samaritan" there is more room for modesty and wisdom. There will be more chances to explain individual and communal limitations, human incompleteness, and gratefulness.

In the book of Jonah, the seamen who do not know the law of Moses fear the Lord. They pray before throwing Jonah into the sea. They do not want to offend God; they do not want to be guilty of innocent blood (Jonah 1:14–15). The people of Nineveh, who were not part of the covenant of Sinai or the promise, repent; even the animals of Nineveh fast and repent (Jonah 3:5–10). From the book of Jonah, one can thus learn that good can come from outside.

Ruth, the Moabite, does not seem to have the credentials for being an ancestor of King David and eventually of Jesus (Ruth 1:4, 24; 2:2, 21; 3:5, 10; Matt 1:5). In asserting the identity of diversity, one can fall in the trap of pride. The book of Amos challenges such boasting (Amos 9). Paul too challenges such boasting (Phil 3). Paul does not deny his Jewish identity. In fact, in Roman 9, he deplores that his kin have not believed in Jesus. He however subdues all identities of belongingness to the Christian identity, to being in Christ.

## The Language of Identity

Conflicts are often triggered and sustained because words used to define identity may carry aggressive connotations. Besides, words that include positive connotations are shunned, rejected, and condemned, just because

---

7. McKenzie, *Dictionary of the Bible*, 765–66.

they are used by outsiders. Above and beyond, lack of attention and listening can create problems. Are definitions fundamentally different or are people saying the same things with different words? Do people understand each other even when they use the same words? Do not words show a multiplicity of meanings? Much energy can be wasted, and no harmony found, when polysemy is ignored or denied. Ricoeur's interest in language can be significant here.

> In certain contexts, the other words eliminate the undesirable connotations of a given word; such is the case with respect to technical and scientific language, where everything is explicit. But 'in other contexts, [the] connotations are liberated; these are most notably the contexts in which language becomes figurative, and especially metaphorical.' Such discourse can be said to involve a primary level and a secondary level of meaning at the same time. Its meaning is multiple; play on words, implication, metaphor, and irony are some particular cases of this polysemy. It is important here to say multiple meaning rather than ambiguity, because, properly speaking, we are confronted with ambiguity only when one meaning alone of two possible meanings is required, and the context does not provide us grounds for deciding between them. But literature precisely does confront us with discourse where several things are meant at the same time, without the reader being required to choose between them.[8]

In this above mentioned paragraph, Ricoeur underlines the difference between "scientific" or "technical" language, on the one hand, and the use of language in other circumstances on the other. The scientific language is supposed to confer just one meaning. Equivocal words and expressions must be avoided. In literature and ordinary life, where one also speaks often of identity there is indeed room for multiplicity of meanings, which is neither sign of deficiency nor an indication of a problem.

Contexts are important for determining the meaning of a word or a sentence. The same is true when one speaks of identity, unity and diversity. After affirming that polysemy, far from being a "case of vagueness" or a pathological phenomenon, is the "outline of an order," Ricoeur says that

> A language without polysemy would violate the principle of economy, for it would extend its vocabulary infinitely. Furthermore, it would violate the rule of communication, because it would multiply its designations as often as, in principle, the

---

8. Ricoeur, *Rule of Metaphors*, 105–6.

diversity of human experience and the plurality of subjects of experience demanded. We need a lexical system that is economical, flexible, and sensitive to context, in order to express the spectrum of human experience. It is the task of contexts to sift the variations of appropriate meanings and, with the help of polysemic words to devise discourse that is seen as relatively univocal—that is, giving rise to just one interpretation, that which the speaker intended to bestow on his words.[9]

## The Intrinsic Relation between Diversity and Unity

Diversity without unity can never be appealing. It does not even deserve to be called diversity. It would rather be called alienation. In order to admire various flowers, I need also to admit that I am dealing with flowers. If I deny the identity of flowers, if I say that only one species deserves to be called flowers and the others are not flowers, I also ignore variety.

Unity is not worthy of the name if it does not have room for diversity. Unity deprived from diversity has no meaning. In order to be united we must at least have two entities. Diversity becomes beautiful when it transcends uniformity. Diversity without unity is cold. Unity without diversity suffocates. It is nice when diversity and unity are harmonized and embrace one another. There is enough liberty for diversity when unity and hope reign. There is enough prosperity when there is space for unity. Wealth will thus not fail. There is no scarcity for there is sharing and caring for.

Unity is threatened when there is domination of a member in a community or a community in various communities. However, it is not only unity that is threatened. Diversity too is threatened because one cannot harm unity without harming diversity. Whether I underline diversity or unity, I am asserting identity. The only difference is the type of identity I want to assert. The identity asserted by the unity defender defers from the identity claimed by the defender of diversity. Yet both are asserting identity. One of the reasons for underling diversity is safeguard of identity. Is diversity guaranteed for identity?

Ignoring common points and similarities is no less harmful than denying differences. Diversity becomes problematic when it leads individuals and communities to forget or undermine universal dimensions like the one being created in the image of God, creativity, the capacity of language, and other similar traits. Fear comes when unity or diversity are threatened. Is unity a

---

9. Ricoeur, *Rule of Metaphors*, 134.

threat for diversity? Is diversity a threat for unity? Does it have to be so? In a family, harmony presupposes both unity and diversity.

## The Word of God, Unity and Diversity

The Scriptures underline the values of both unity and diversity. The word of God as a two-edged sword penetrates the inner self (Eph 6:17). If after so many years people still quarrel over issues of identity and do not find a solution, it means that they need new perspectives, new visions, new reflections. It means secret emotions should be addressed and redeemed through the penetrating word of God that is sharper than a two-edged sword (Heb 4:12).

Two thousand years ago Christ gave himself for the love of human beings. Yet he did not discriminate people on the basis of one's provenance. In this he left a great message: to love one's enemy. He glorified diversity while praising unity. When the lawyer asked him who his neighbor was (Luke 10:29) Jesus answers by telling a fascinating parable. By presenting a Samaritan as a model of compassion he shook the terrain on which the lawyer was standing. He showed that one is not supposed to delimit the scope of brotherly love. One ought not restrict the profile of a person or a community that deserves Christian love, lest it loses entirely any Christian nature.

Again, about two thousand years ago the apostle Paul taught a great lesson on identity and belongingness. He harmonized diversity with unity. He did not neglect unity when he held diversity. He did not suppress diversity when he proclaimed unity. It is noteworthy to consider how he connected unity with diversity. His is precious in the eyes of philosophers and for the wise on earth. My identity should not be reduced to the communities to which I may belong. My identity is more than membership. To be a Jew, a Greek, or a Roman, to be a man or a woman is to illustrate diversity (Gal 3:28). Paul says also that "neither circumcision nor uncircumcision is anything; but a new creation is everything!" (Gal 6:15, NRSV)

When we expect the Jew to live exactly like the Greek, or the Greek to be exactly like a Jew, we harm diversity. For their culture is their beauty. Yet they become even more beautiful when there is a Christological truth that unites them. It bestows them with a beauty more glittering than before. What transcends does not destroy what was before. It rather makes it grow. It perfects it. To limit one's identity to a community is to limit oneself. It is to obstruct beauty.

In 2 Cor 5:17, Paul affirms that to be in Christ is to become a new creation, hence, to acquire a new identity. The first letter of Peter (1 Pet 1:22–23, NRSV) has also strong words in this connection.

> Now that you have purified your souls by your obedience to the truth so that you have genuine mutual love, love one another deeply from the heart. You have been born anew, not of perishable but of imperishable seed, through the living and enduring word of God.

Let alone human beings, even other creatures are interrelated. In a Christian context, Christ becomes a source of unity. Through baptism, people of diverse cultures all become heirs (Gal 3:26). Children of the same father are brothers and sisters. How could brotherhood and sisterhood be expressed in a community? When is blood thicker than water?[10] When is community stronger than baptism? Would this unity bring about a distinction between Christians and non-Christians?

To be created in the image of God is a universal source of unity and equal dignity. Paul calls for the beauty of unity. Yet is it not unity based on ethnic diversity? The issue can also concern diversity in Charisms. The Christians of Corinth were aspiring to spiritual gifts but were also divided on various terms. The division was condemned and criticized by Paul (1 Cor 1:12–13; 3:4—6:22). Unity in diversity is asserted in 1 Corinthians 12:4–20.

There is a healthy self-esteem and a sickening egoism. When we say "we," there is also a difference between a healthy and a sick one. Beauty will be enjoyed, unity experienced, peace tasted, prosperity welcomed only and only when there is unity which transcends community. Time and space, mother earth and history cry for the vindication of innocent victims. When they run short of words all these plead for the help of poetry. Love overcomes fear. Hope is medicine both for diversity and for unity.

## Identity Is Not the Only Cause of Conflicts

It is wrong to think that all problems are solved by asserting either identity of unity or identity of diversity. Reducing all issues to questions of identity is misleading. After all, the conflict between Cain and Abel had nothing to do with questions of identity. According to the narrative they come from the same parents. They do not belong to different ethnic communities. Yet this did not save them from the tragedy of fratricide. Envy, greed, and

---

10. See Katongole, "Blood of Tribalism," 319–25.

egoism do not have borders. They can manifest at all levels and in all contexts and thus can poison relationships.

Identity, unity, and diversity become challenged when there is "privatization" of power.[11] One should ask the following questions: "Diversity for whom?" "At what level?" Both diversity and unity are best fostered with humility. Both are worst served with pride and jealousy. The tension between unity[12] and diversity[13] is sometimes disagreement over the radius of communities' circles. Unity seems to propose a larger or longer radius. Nevertheless, in both cases, the debate is about the circle. The self can, however, transcend all circles.

A flower alone, a tree alone, does not make a paradise. Various flowers, different trees together, make a paradise. They will get water in concert. They share the light and warmth of the Sun in unison. They are beautified by the moon and the stars. Yet a flower may not know that she is beautiful. She needs a human being to appreciate her splendor, to enjoy her fragrance. Human beings, on the other hand, can know themselves. How curative can be to stop for a while and admire the glory of a flower. A lesson about unity and diversity!

Flowers do not declare war against flowers. Humans, on the contrary, do not realize how much they hurt their fellow creatures. They ignore that every human being is their relative. Mountains, plants, and animals would confess the kinship of all human beings if they were given a chance to talk.

Peace brings about safety. Yet, it is not enough just to desire peace. One needs to admit this truth, to be an instrument of peace and to respect everything that leads to peace. Peace does not harm except for those who have another agenda. Peace can only be good for those of good will, for innocents. In order to build peace, in order to ensure justice and reconciliation, truth needs to be linked with compassion.

---

11. Bongmba, *Dialectics*, 12.

12. Much violence and atrocities have been perpetrated in the name of fight for unity.

13. According to Bongmba, political elites in Africa have used ethnicity to incite violence and promote their own goals. Atieno Odhiambo argues that the politics of ethnicity in Kenya under Jomo Kenyatta and Daniel Arap Moi responded to the socioeconomic, political, and symbolic world of each ethnic community. Both Kenyatta and Oginga Odinga cultivated ethnicity in their anticolonial politics, which was driven especially among the Kikuyu by their anger over stolen lands. But the post-Mau Mau era was marked by a nationalist agenda that seemed to put ethnic politics at the background. However, when independence came, Kenyatta and the African National Union (KANU) consolidated power in their hands and sidelined members of other ethnic communities. Kenyatta organized traditional oath-taking to ensure that power remained with the Gikuyu; see Bongmba, *Dialectics*, 31.

Peace is guaranteed when one appreciates a narrative whereby the other has valuable and beautiful elements. Besides, peace needs to be experienced since childhood. To live in fullness is to make children taste peace and love. If unity and diversity are God's gifts, they need to be offered to children as the best of treasures. Economy, money, and power do not lead to plenitude without love. The greatest investment is the one of love. How wonderful it would have been if love was taken into consideration when budgets are prepared. How much the interest would have been! Love that transcends and includes responsibility is a big asset of economy.

The narratives transmitted to children are far from being harmless. A child who is told to hate a certain individual or community will have difficulties appreciating that individual or community afterwards. Are not perhaps Christians scandalizing their children by telling them stories that incite ethnic hatred?

It is a great pleasure to look at the face of a baby. The smile of child is charming to everybody. It invites more smiles. It wins over unity and diversity. Love beautifies diversity. Hatred makes diversity ugly. Generosity is more heroic than egoism; forgiveness is more heroic that revenge. What about smiles, laughing, playing, being creative in art? These are virtues that transcend all borders of identity. They enable to ignore tensions and embrace a win-win situation. How nice it would be if people focus more on planting trees! Not one tree but a lot of trees! Not one type of tree, but various kinds of trees! Trees of unity and diversity! For one tree or one type of tree is never enough. Diversity cannot be appealing without unity. Unity cannot last without diversity.

## Conclusion

Narratives are critical. Identity, unity, and diversity are expressed through narratives. The best way to improve human understanding of identities is to examine, investigate and compare narratives. Attention should be given to the narratives of opponents too. Narratives on unity are not necessarily against stories on diversity. The two are not inevitably incompatible.

The best condition for an examination of narratives of identity is to stop for a while and reflect. In happiness and sadness, in peace and affliction, it is always good to enter in one's interior self. Those moments are fundamental for discernment. A critical view is necessary to distinguish between various narratives. Although one may be afraid to be alone, there is some positive one may get from solitude.[14] It gives conditions of purification

14. One may remember here Zara Yacob, the Ethiopian philosopher of the

from biased ideas, ideologies, and superficial thoughts. Jesus used to go often to the wilderness to pray (Luke 5:16). The theologian too needs such solitude for wisdom and enlightenment.[15]

Some solitude enables the theologian to observe the surrounding and to learn from the beauty of the created world. Indeed, to explore the mystery of the one and the many, it is nice to observe the lakes, to listen to the songs of birds, to be attracted by the green plants, the animals, and the beauty of the sky. For nature has both diversity and unity. What a harmony of colors! What a symphony! How sad and unfortunate when human beings do not learn from creation! Why so much division when miracles follow collaboration and agreement? Is diversity a cause of enmity or is there another reason behind unnecessary opposition? Do not solutions come from serenity, listening and meditation, from looking for the truth that transcends human egoism?

Here, a wisdom parable is worth reflecting upon:[16]

> It was said that there were three friends who were not afraid of hard work. The first chose to reconcile those who were fighting each other, as it is said, "Blessed are the peace-makers" (Matt. 5). The second chose to visit the sick. The third went to live in prayer and stillness in the desert. Now in spite of all his labours, the first could not make peace in all people's quarrels; and in his sorrow he went to him who was serving the sick, and he him also disheartened, for he could not fulfil that commandment either. So they went together to see him who was living in the stillness of prayer. They told him their difficulties and begged him to tell them what to do. After a short silence, he poured some water in a bowl and said to them, "Look at the water," and it was disturbed. After a little while he said to them again, "Look how still the water is now", and as they looked into the water, they saw their own faces reflected in it as in a mirror. Then he said to them, "It is the same for those who live among men; disturbances prevent them from seeing their faults. But when a person is still, especially in the desert, then he or she sees his or her failings."

Among other things, tranquility and stillness enable persons and communities to analyze narratives, the meaning of words, and affirmations. Narratives that promote both unity and diversity can provide healthy

---

seventeenth century, who chose solitude in an effort to think critically beyond prejudices.

15. An authentic theologian is a person of prayer (Evagrius Ponticus, *Orat.* 61).

16. Ward, *Wisdom*, 1.

definitions and stories of identity, beyond ambiguities and propagandas. Stillness helps to detect discourses of manipulators. Even to understand unity and diversity, to create narratives of harmony, individuals as well as communities need serenity and the blessing of listening. Silence gives the conditions to transcend identities limited by belongingness and to explore identities based on conducts and on Christian new creation. Silence helps to realize that Christ, the peace of all, has broken down the dividing wall between communities (Eph 2:14 NRSV). All cultures of all communities need to be evangelized. All cultures need to be purified by the Gospel. When individuals and communities fulfill the will of God, they become part of new family, relatives of Jesus (Mark 3:35). It is in Jesus, through and with Jesus, that one may dare to say, "Our Father."[17]

John, in his vision, did not see a heaven that set apart just one community or one individual. On the contrary, he saw in heaven that people should start building on earth:

> After this I looked, and there was a great multitude that no one could count, from every nation, from all tribes and peoples and languages, standing before the throne and before the Lamb, robed in white, with palm branches in their hands. (Rev 7:9, NRSV)

## Bibliography

Bongmba, Elias. *The Dialectics of Transformation in Africa*. New York: Palgrave Macmillan, 2006.
Jeremias, Joachim. *The Lord's Prayer*. Philadelphia: Fortress, 1964.
McKenzie, John. *Dictionary of the Bible*. Bangalore: Asian Trading Corporation, 2002.
Katongole, Emmanuel. "'A Blood Thicker than the Blood of Tribalism': Eucharist and Identity in African Politics." *Modern Theology* 30.2 (2014) 319–25.
Ricoeur, Paul. *Oneself as Another*. Chicago: University of Chicago Press, 1992.
———. *The Rule of Metaphors: The Creation of Meaning in Language*. London: Routledge, 2003.
———. *Time and Narrative*. Vol. 3. Chicago: University of Chicago Press, 1988.
Theodros A. Teklu. *The Politics of Metanoia: Towards a Post-Nationalistic Political Theology in Ethiopia*. Frankfurt am Main: Lang, 2014.
Vanhoozer, Kevin. *Biblical Narrative in the Philosophy of Paul Ricoeur: A Study in Hermeneutics and Theology*. Cambridge: Cambridge University Press, 1990.
Ward, Benedicta, trans. *The Wisdom of the Desert Fathers: Systematic Sayings from the Anonymous Series of the Apophthegmata Patrum*. Oxford: SLG, 1986.

---

17. Ancient Christians gave special reverence to the prayer of the Lord: our Father; they used to recite it with holy fear and reverence; see Jeremias, *Lord's Prayer*.

# 6

## "Ethnic" and "Christian" Identity

Ethiopian Reflections from the Epistle to the Galatians

Nebeyou Alemu

Conflicts that arise out of ethnic issues are widespread across Africa. As most scholars endorse, in Africa most wars are caused by ethnic tension.[1] A search for cultural identity, self-expression, and power amid a constantly changing world are the causes of ethnic conflict. So ethnic issue is not just a theoretical issue in Africa, but rather one we face it daily.

In post-nationalistic Ethiopia, society is divided by issues of identity, political ideology, and religion.[2] Ethno-political conflicts have been on the increase in contemporary Ethiopia. The heterogeneous ethnic composition of the country is used by political entrepreneurs to create a feeling of suspicion, distrust, and hatred among members of various ethnic groups. People have been displaced and killed because of their ethnic identity. In such a context how should we read the Bible responsibly and faithfully while accounting for such realities of daily life? The Bible is still capable of influencing people if interpreted creatively to address pertinent issues.

---

1. Togarasei, "Rethinking Christian Identity," 101; Kunhiyop, *African Christian Ethics*, 108; Merera, *Ethiopia*, 26–27.

2. I borrowed the phrase "Post-nationalist Ethiopia" from Theodros, *Politics of Metanoia*. The term "Post-nationalist Ethiopia" refers to a period after 1991. Ethiopia used to be a unitary state before 1991 and the current regime redrew the country based on ethno-linguistic lines, to balance between the centripetal forces and centrifugal forces.

Paul addressed the Judean–gentile ethnic divide in Galatians using ethnic and kinship language and he creates a bond between Jews and gentiles by tracing their origin back to Abraham. These results can form a significant foundation for a study that asks how Paul's strategies and skills in Galatians can be adopted in a contemporary Ethiopian situation. It is my conviction that understanding ethnic identity in relation to Christian identity has a lot to contribute to the study of early Christian definition and has contemporary ecclesiological significance.

John Barclay, reflecting exegetically on Paul's words that "there is neither Jew nor Greek" (Gal 3:28), concludes that Paul envisions or attempts to create "church communities which were multiethnic and multicultural."[3] He further comments that this alternative form of community "could bridge ethnic and cultural divisions by creating new patterns of common life."[4]

Within the African context, a call to integrate ethnic and biblical studies has recently been sounded by Peter Nyende.[5] African biblical scholarship, he argues, should rise to the occasion and begin addressing ethnicity via biblical studies. In Ethiopia, Christians "see" the Bible as a resource for influencing their choices. Our theology must therefore respond creatively to negative ethnicity. Reading the bible for contemporary significance while interpreting it within its historical realities informs this study. Thus a brief overview of the latter is needed.

## Galatians and Paul

When early Christianity expanded across ethnic lines to include gentiles it encountered some difficulties. One such difficulty was the ethnic conflict that occurred within the emerging Christian movement. Such process helped the early church to forge its identity amidst conflicts.[6] The type of Christianity that was propagated by Paul was not attached to a particular ethno-cultural or geopolitical identity; rather it was trans-ethnic and did not require gentiles to renounce their gentile identity. However, as Christianity expanded into gentile territory issues related to identity started to surface.

The majority of scholars agree that Paul wrote Galatians somewhere between forty-eight and mid-fifties AD,[7] most likely to congregations in central Asia Minor. Paul and Barnabas established the church while working

---

3. Barclay, "Neither Jew Nor Greek," 210.
4. Barclay, "Neither Jew Nor Greek," 210.
5. Nyende, "Addressing Ethnicity," 122–39, and "Ethnic Studies," 132–46.
6. See Bennema, "Early Christian Identity Formation," 26–48.
7. Keener, *Galatians*, 4.

as missionaries of the church of Antioch. Even if there is still a debate on the identity of the recipients, it is clear that the recipients were living in a city dominated by Greek culture and had more recently come under Roman rule. The majority of Paul's audience were gentiles.[8] The Jewish communities in Galatia, albeit being colonized and assimilated to the dominant Hellenism and at the same time influenced by the mingling of cultures because of urbanization and migration, kept their unique identity and position, and in some ways their identity was liminal.[9]

It is generally believed by scholars that Paul wrote Galatians in response to those who urged gentiles to be circumcised.[10] But there is a disagreement about the identity of the advocators of circumcision and from where they came.[11] At least they can be grouped into four categories: 1) gnostics, 2) Jewish Christians from Jerusalem, 3) gentile or Jewish Christians from Galatia, and 4) two different groups, one legalistic and the other "pneumatic of a libertine tendency."[12] It is not the intention of this chapter to discuss this issue in great length.

The letter of Galatians depicts inter-Christian debate concerning the social relation between Jewish and gentiles and the inclusion of gentiles into the people of God without passing through circumcision and following the law.[13] To understand this social issue, scholars employ a sociological approach to Paul's letters and conclude that justification by faith is to be understood in light of social issues.[14] James Dunn argues, "Unless this social, we may even say national and racial, dimension of the issues confronting Paul is clearly grasped, it will be well-nigh impossible to achieve an exegesis of Paul's treatment of the law which pays proper respect to historical context."[15]

---

8. Keener, *Galatians*, 7.

9. See Barclay, *Jews*; Goodman, *Mission*; Trebilco, *Jewish Communities*.

10. Matera, *Sacra Pagina: Galatians*, 1.

11. Different names are attributed to these advocators: "agitators," "A Law-observant mission," "Paul's opponents," and "Judaizers."

12. For scholars' different opinions about Paul's opponents, see Sumney, "Studying Paul's Opponents," 7–58; Matera, *Sacra Pagina: Galatians*, 2–6; Nanos, *Irony of Galatians*, 115–92.

13. See, e.g., Hansen, *Abraham in Galatians*; Martyn, *Galatians*, 13–34; Dunn, *Epistle to the Galatians*.

14. See Malherbe, *Social Aspects of Early Christianity*; Meeks, *First Urban Christians*; Meggitt, *Paul, Poverty and Survival*; Stambaugh and Balch, *New Testament*; Theissen, *Social Setting of Pauline Christianity*; Holmberg, *Sociology and the New Testament*.

15. Dunn, *Jesus, Paul and the Law*, 219.

Philip Esler's work employs a social-scientific reading of Paul's letters to the Galatians using Mediterranean social-identity theory.[16] Esler particularly gives attention to the relationship between Paul's theology in Galatians and the social dimension of the Galatian context. His primary focus is on intergroup processes and the distinction made between in-group and out-group members. Esler argues that Paul wrote the letter to create and to maintain the identity of the Christ-following group in Galatians, composed of both Judeans and non-Judeans. This identity can be created and maintained through boundary-making with these two groups. This makes Paul an architect of group identity.[17] Paul's goal was not to make each subgroup to abandon its own cultural identity; rather he wanted to widen the scope of Christian group identity to incorporate both. In that case, the common group identity superseded each subgroup while individual subgroup boundaries would become more permeable.[18]

## Paul and the New Perspective

How did Paul understand the law? This is one of the central questions in Pauline Studies and particularly central to Galatians as well. Historically, Paul's opponents have been perceived as Judaizers who argued for justification based on works of the law. Luther developed this view in the context of his polemic against the Roman Catholic Church's merit-oriented concept of salvation. As a continuation of Lutheran tradition, the founder of the Tübingen School, F. C. Baur, and his followers, read the New Testament using Hegelian philosophy as an analytical tool. This reading of the New Testament tended to interpret Paul's writings in terms of conflict between Hellenistic Christianity (Paul and Apollos) and Jewish Christianity (Cephas and the "Christ party") along ethnic lines.[19] According to Baur, Paul

---

16. Esler, *Galatians*. See also Esler, "Family Imagery," 121–49; Esler, "Group Boundaries," 215–40; Esler, "Making and Breaking," 285–314.

17. Esler also studied Romans by giving a focus for intragroup processes and the development of a common in-group identity; *Conflict and Identity in Romans*. A similar case has been made by Esler for the Gospels of Matthew and John. See Esler, "From *Ioudaioi* to Children of God," 106–37; Esler, "Judean Ethnic Identity," 193–210.

18. Some notable studies after Esler which use social identity theory: Faulkner, "Jewish Identity"; Tucker, "You Belong to Christ"; Kuecher, "Spirit And the 'Other'"; Marohl, *Faithfulness*; Shkul, "Reading Ephesians".

19. William S. Campbell said the following regarding Baur: "he [Baur] contributed enormously to the tendency in the Paulinism of the last century and a half to denigrate the image of Judaism in the New Testament" (Campbell, *Paul*, 16). Shawn Kelley further argues, "For Baur, Christianity, despite its origins in the East, is the Western religion. Consequently, his task is to define the essence of Christianity by purging it of

introduced Christian universalism (the antithesis) over against Jewish nationalistic particularism (the thesis) which is based on the Torah.[20] This tension continued up until the emergence of the orthodox, hierarchical church (the synthesis) to the end of the second century. Many scholars criticized Baur's view for failing to recognize diversity within both Judean and non-Judean Christianity.

However, the introduction of the "new perspective on Paul"[21] in New Testament studies provides a platform to reconsider the above reading of Baur. E. P. Sanders (1977) and J. Dunn (1988, 1990) contributed significantly in this direction.[22] The New Perspective in Pauline studies "has considered a shift in focus from conversion in light of a reassessment of Paul in light of first-century intra-Jewish, and not modern Protestant-Catholic or Christian-Jewish, conflicts."[23] The New Perspective on Paul argues that Paul should be understood better within his Jewish context. This, in turn, affects one's approach and interpretation of Paul and a re-evaluation of Paul in light of the re-reading of first-century Judaism is required. E. P. Sanders, by studying Jewish texts written between 200 BCE and 200 CE, argued that Judaism was a religion of grace, while the human response is understood in terms of response to that grace.[24] Sanders claimed that the Judaism of the first-century was not a religion where the Jews obeyed the Law for their salvation because they considered themselves as already saved people by God's choice and their salvation from Egyptian slavery.[25] Sanders introduced the phrase "covenantal nomism" to describe the Judaism of the first-century as a religion in which the Jews obeyed the Law (*nomos*) in reverence to their covenant God as they were in covenant with their God, their Savior.[26] It means that "obedience to the Torah is a matter of maintenance of the covenant membership, rather than one of entrance into the covenant. So

anything that smacks of Judaism or the Orient, of nationalism, legalism, and particularism" (Kelley, *Racializing Jesus*, 76).

20. Leander, "Reading Paul," 184–205, 190.

21. Stendahl, a Swedish Lutheran scholar based at Harvard University, contributes significantly to the emerging "new perspective on Paul." In his essay, "The Apostle Paul and the Introspective Conscience of the West," he argues that categorizing Judaism as a religion of works-righteousness is unfounded. He said that such a view emanates from Luther's critique of sixteenth-century Catholicism than Paul's critique of first century Judaism (Stendahl, "Apostle Paul," 201).

22. James G. Dunn is the first to use the term "the New Perspective" in his article entitled "New Perspective," 95–122.

23. Lopez, *Apostle to the Conquered*, 121.

24. Sanders, *Paul and Palestinian Judaism*, 33–59.

25. See Sanders, *Paul and Palestinian Judaism*, 18.

26. Sanders, *Judaism*, 262.

there is a sharp distinction between "getting in" and "staying in."[27] Since Jewish people didn't believe that they earn salvation via obeying the law, Paul was not criticizing Judaism in general; rather he was against the belief that restricts salvation to the Jews.[28]

Sanders' idea was further developed and promoted by James Dunn with a fresh analysis of Romans and Galatians using Sanders' interpretation of first-century Judaism, offering a new interpretation of Paul through the rereading of Pauline literature. While affirming Paul's Judean ethnic identity, Dunn differs from Sanders in maintaining that Paul did not reject his ethnic identity or criticize the law. Paul was simply critical of the misuse of the law that created social barriers. Dunn said, "to a remarkable and indeed alarming degree, throughout this century the standard depiction of the Judaism which Paul rejected has been the reflex of Lutheran hermeneutic."[29] Dunn argues that Paul was not against the idea of covenant or the law rather he was against a particular Jewish *attitude* to the law, i.e., Jewish *nationalistic exclusivism*. The Jews boasted because of their membership in the covenant and such a view distorted the law into a means of excluding gentiles.[30] According to Dunn, Paul's polemic against the law is not directed to the law itself but against the works of the law, especially circumcision, food laws, and Sabbath (e.g. Gal 2:16; 3:2, 5, 10; Rom 3:27; 4:2; 9:32; 11:6). Certain elements of the law were used as boundary markers designed to exclude gentiles.[31] When these certain elements of the law retain some significance in the church they divide the single body of Christ. Dunn insists that Paul's teaching of justification should be understood in light of his mission to the gentiles. In his own words:

> [J]ustification by faith is the banner raised by Paul against any and all such presumption of privileged status before God by virtue of race, culture or nationality, against any and all attempts to preserve such spurious distinctions by practice that exclude and divide.[32]

---

27. Sanders, *Paul, the Law*, 6.
28. Sanders, *Paul, the Law*, 55.
29. Dunn, "New Perspective," 97.
30. Dunn, *Partings*, 137–38.
31. Dunn, "New Perspective," 114, 117, 120; Dunn, "Work of the Law," 520.
32. Dunn, "New Perspective," 205.

According to Dunn, justification by faith has ecclesiological or sociological dimensions. It is faith in Christ, not the works of the law, which serves as the badge of membership in the new covenant people of God.[33]

The so-called "New Perspective on Paul" ignites an interest in the "ethnic" dimension of Paul's thought. The advocates of the "New Perspective" argue that much of Paul's theological reflection and argumentation are intended to address practical concerns as he attempts "to set up multi-ethnic 'alternative communities' of Christ-followers across the Greco-Roman world."[34] The New Perspective takes Paul's argument as a concern for (ethnic) group boundaries among the Jesus followers and while emphasizing the social aspect of the problem, even if the problem is with deep theological implications.[35] It means that Paul's letters were not written to communicate abstract answers but instead written to address concrete social issues which affect the churches. For the adherent of the New Perspective, the "Jew–gentile question" is not a peripheral issue for Paul; it stands at the heart of his theology."[36] Not all Pauline scholars, of course, accept this new perspective. Critics of the new perspective argue that this idea, instead of being inspired by a right reading of Paul, is inspired mainly by contemporary Jewish–Christian relations in light of the Holocaust.[37] This chapter approaches Paul in line with the recent Pauline scholarship that acknowledges the Jewish character of Pauline communities as well as the ethnic character of Paul's vision.

## Reading Paul Ethnically

Samuel Vollenweider argues that Paul was aware of "what we today call "ethnicity."[38] As Charles Cosgrove pointed out, "Paul never offers us a definition of ethnic identity, but we can get an idea of how he understood ethnicity by placing what he says about being a Jew in the wider context of Hellenistic-Jewish views of ethnic identity."[39] Paul depicts all humanity in ethnic terms. Paul was a diaspora Jew and it must be the case that he experienced multiethnicity in his life, Jewish and Greco-Roman. Paul was called as an apostle for the gentiles (Gal 1:16; 2:7) and his missionary call for gentiles led him to travel

33. Dunn, "New Perspective," 194–98.
34. Stanley, "Ethnic Context," 177.
35. Matera, "Galatians in Perspective," 236–37.
36. Stanley, "Ethnic Context," 177.
37. See for the thoughtful critique of the new perspective by Stephen Westerholm in *Israel's Law*; Seifrid, "'New Perspective on Paul,'" 4–18.
38. Vollenweider, "Are Christians a New 'People'?," 293, 293–308.
39. Cosgrove, "Did Paul Value Ethnicity?," 271.

to the eastern part of the Mediterranean and engage with mixed communities of diverse ethnic and cultural background.

Ethnicity plays a great role in identity formation and maintenance. It is one of the fundamental factors in human life and a phenomenon that is intrinsic to human life. However, a concept like ethnicity is very elusive, complex and often very controversial. What is the definition of ethnicity? How do ethnic groups form? What differentiates the boundaries between different ethnic groups? These are some of the important questions that need to be dealt with in relation to ethnic identity. Two approaches dominate the discourse on ethnicity. The first one is often called primordialism and the second one is referred to as "instrumentalist"/"social constructivism."[40] The first theory considers ethnicity as a stable category whereas the latter emphasizes its fluid character.

Primordialists argue that an ethnic group is a group of humans whose members identify with each other through a common heritage (real or assumed). This shared heritage may be based upon supposed common ancestry, shared territory, history, religion, language, nationality or physical appearance and serves as a means of deep and overwhelming attachment for the ethnic group.[41] This theory views ethnicity as universal, natural, and inherent in human nature,[42] and considers it fixed and constant and thus must be maintained.[43] Primordialists emphasize the emotional aspect of the relationship among ethnic members, for ethnic members "express an intense solidarity and a passion that is overpowering and coercive."[44] Such bonds are further considered "to have a 'sacred' quality."[45]

The Instrumentalist approach to ethnicity considers ethnic markers as social, political, and cultural resources that are utilized by different interests and status groups.[46] This theory of ethnicity emerged as a response

---

40. These two theories are associated particularly with Clifford Geertz and Fredrik Barth, respectively. For a survey of theoretical literature on ethnicity see Thompson, *Theories of Ethnicity*.

41. Jones, *Archaeology of Ethnicity*, 65.

42. Smith, "Culture, Community and Territory," 72; Smith, *Ethnic Origins of Nations*, 3, 210.

43. See Hutchinson and Smith, *Ethnicity*, 67. See also Banks, *Ethnicity: Anthropological Constructions*, 151. Many scholars criticized primordial approaches to ethnicity for presenting a "static" and "naturalistic" view of ethnicity. Certain identity markers can evolve; people can also possess multiple identities. See Hutchinson and Smith, *Ethnicity*, 8.

44. Duling, "Whatever Gain I Had," 800.

45. Duling, "Whatever Gain I Had," 800.

46. Hutchinson and Smith, *Ethnicity*, 8–9.

to primordialism in 1969 by the Norwegian Fredrik Barth.[47] Instrumentalists view ethnicity as "a resource to be mobilized, or an instrument to be employed."[48] The instrumentalist argues that ethnic identity is not something historically given, rather it is created by the society (or manufactured by the elite) for ideological and political purposes. It is an adoptive and malleable phenomenon. Anthony Smith argues,

> Human beings are continually moving in and out of these collective identities. They choose, and construct, their identities according to the situation in which they find themselves. Hence, for instrumentalists, identity tends to be "situational" rather than pervasive.[49]

As a result, ethnicity is a "strategic choice."[50] Unlike in the past, the majority of contemporary scholars believe that identity in general, and ethnic identity in particular, is flexible and fluid rather than stable and static.[51] It is *"socially constructed and subjectively perceived."*[52]

As Christopher Stanley pointed out, Paul lived in an ethnically diverse context "where ethnic identities were fluid and contested and interethnic tensions were woven deeply into the social fabric."[53] As a result, recent scholarship on Paul has a strong interest in ethnicity and ethnic identity in relation to Pauline and other writings of the New Testament. The introduction of the New Perspective on Paul directed scholars to investigate the "ethnic" dimension of Paul's thought and writings. Paul's usage of the nomenclature of "Jews" and "gentiles" began to be interpreted within the real interaction between "Jews" and "gentiles" in the communities that Paul was addressing. Besides this, "Paul's language about 'Jews' and 'Gentiles' came to be viewed in more instrumental terms as a strategy for overcoming actual divisions that were hindering the unity of the socially diverse communities of Christ-followers."[54]

Numerous forms of identity theory and models are used as an interpretive framework for understanding identity issues in the New Testament. In our case, in Paul's letter to the Galatians, we see Paul using the primordial

---

47. See Barth, *Ethnic Groups and Boundaries.*
48. Smith, "Politics of Culture," 707.
49. Smith, *Nations,* 30.
50. Bell, "Ethnicity," 171.
51. Lim, "Race," 120.
52. Hall, *Ethnic Identity,* 19, italics original.
53. Stanley, "Ethnic Context," 177.
54. Stanley, "Paul the Ethnic Hybrid?," 110.

concept of ethnicity (e.g., Abraham as a common ancestor for Jews) while also using the instrumentalist approach when placing the gentile Christians as the sons of Abraham. Paul used ethnic vocabulary and logic of kinship to persuade his readers that they have a common ancestor (Abraham) and a common homeland ("in Christ") from which their identity derives. Paul incorporated gentile Galatians in the genealogy of Abraham, hence they are the inheritors of the blessing and the promise given to Abraham. As Karin Neutel puts it, "In Paul's characterization, Abraham is not solely a Jewish ancestor, he is a universal ancestor."[55]

## "Christian" Identity in Galatians

In the past, almost all scholars used the term "Christian" without any ambiguity in relation to the New Testament writings.[56] However, using the term "Christian" for the Christ groups in the first-century setting is considered by some scholars as anachronistic.[57] As a result, instead of this term, scholars used terms like "the Jesus movement";[58] "Christ followers";[59] "Christ-believers";[60] "believers";[61] "saints";[62] "Christ-confessing communities";[63] and "a follower of the Way."[64] However, some scholars suggested that many of the characteristics of "Christians" and "Christianity" in the first century were present in the later years of Christian history. Hence, they argue that it is not anachronistic to use the term Christianity within the first hundred years of its history.[65] In this article, the term is not used with the more developed sense of the term of the fourth century CE.[66]

---

55. Neutel, "Neither Jew Nor Greek," 291.

56. The term "Christian" occurs only thrice in the New Testament (Acts 11:26; 26:28; 1 Pet 4:16).

57. See Bennema, "Early Christian Identity Formation," 27.

58. Horsley, *Sociology and the Jesus Movement*.

59. Esler, "Keeping It in the Family," 157.

60. See generally Tellbe, *Christ-Believers*.

61. Jewett, *Romans*, 27, 525.

62. Friesen, "Poverty in Pauline Studies," 323, 334, 348.

63. Stegemann and Stegemann, *Jesus Movement*, 262–87.

64. Klassen, "Normative Self-Definitions of Christianity," 92.

65. Trebilco, *Self-designations and Group Identity*, 3–4.

66. For an extended treatment of how early "Christians" used various "self-designations" or "labels" to address on another or call each other see Trebilco, *Self-designations and Group Identity*.

"Christianity" started as an intra-Jewish messianic renewal movement in about 30 CE.[67] The movement developed into a religion distinct from Judaism in the second century. Yet, from its inception, Christianity conflicted with its mother, Judaism, and therefore adherents were persecuted by Jewish authorities. This informs us that, despite the movement being, undoubtedly, a Jewish phenomenon, the identity-forming boundaries between Jews and Christ-believers were present from the start.

As Christianity expanded across varied territories it started to accommodate various groups consisting of people who recognize the death and resurrection of Christ, irrespective of ethnicity, social position, or nationality. The death and resurrection of Jesus and the experience of receiving his Holy Spirit was the central belief of early Christians and were a crucial identity marker.[68] These are the doctrinal aspects of identity markers and are shared by Christians across borders and varied cultural locations. This makes Christian identity distinct from Jewish identity since Christian identity is a group identity. Here, the main question is to understand in what way these doctrinal aspects of identity affect the cultural/social identity of the followers of Christ.

Besides the doctrinal aspects, Jennifer Slater identifies inclusiveness, "legal ethics," "mystical ethics," and love as characteristics of Christian identity in Paul's letter to the Galatians.[69] In her study, she points out that Paul aims to come up with a type of Christianity, which includes Jews and gentiles, males and females, free and slave, based on their common baptism in Christ. She reads the book of Galatians against the Roman Empire.[70] The Roman Empire found it difficult to embrace many different ethnic groups. On the contrary, Paul in Galatians introduced inclusivity in Christ and his Holy Spirit. As Slater argues, Paul's proposal has key social implications that can be utilized as a tool to help us overcome divisions of race, culture, nationality, or ethnicity.

Many scholars in the past viewed early Christian identity as "universal," in effect, non-ethnic in nature. On the other hand some contemporary readers of Paul began to view it in ethno-racial terms similar to that of other ethnicities or races. Denise Kimber Buell argues that the modern concept of depicting Christianity as a "universal" religion in contrast to Judaism and considering it as transcending ethnicity and race, though it seems anti-racist,

---

67. Early Christianity was a diverse movement and for a good treatment of the subject, see Dunn, *Unity and Diversity*.

68. Brett, *Ethnicity and the Bible*, 11.

69. Slate, *Christian Identity Characteristics*.

70. For an introductory discussion of "empire" studies in the New Testament see Winn, *Empire*.

is a misguided understanding of early Christian self-definition.[71] She pointed out that such an understanding is racist and has anti-Jewish tendencies by exhibiting some dislike to Judaism by portraying it with "particularity."[72] To address the above-perceived problem, she presents a comprehensive argument against such a notion and argues that ethnicity and race were central to how early Christians defined themselves.[73]

Buell further develops her argument in an article with Caroline Johnson Hodge and argues that the Pauline vision of unity in Christ does not erase ethnic differences, but is rather to be understood as a form of "ethnic reasoning."[74] This claim presupposes that religion did not exist as a separate category during antiquity. The claim of being in Christ does not imply to be ethnically neutral; on the contrary, it is a way of being *Ioudaios*, i.e., as a particular form of Jewish or Judean identity. Through baptism, non-Judean peoples are thus included in God's promises to Israel, get Abraham as the forefather, and join an ethnic community of culture and descent. Thus, the in-Christ identity is located under a Judean umbrella that has ethnic significance. To quote their own words, "there is no ethnically neutral "Christianity" implied in Galatians 3:28."[75]

The in-Christ identity does not abrogate other ethnic belongings. Paul has an *Ioudaios* identity while being in Christ, and the same applied to Titus, who remained a Greek (Gal 2:3). Similarly, Paul continued to refer to his audience as Galatians even if they had been baptized (Gal 3:1). As Paul argues in Galatians, being a follower of Christ has ethnic implications of receiving Abraham as the forefather and joining a community of culture and descent, but this does not prevent one from at the same time belonging to other ethnic groups. Being in Christ (Gal 3:28) for Paul can thus be viewed as a form of open ethnic identity that can be combined with other ethnicities and could, therefore, be paraphrased, with Sze-kar Wan, as "You are both Jew and Greek . . . for you are all one in Christ."[76] As Alain Badiou, puts it, "although it is true . . . that there is 'neither Greek nor Jew,' the fact is that there are Greeks and Jews."[77] Therefore, the acquired ethno-religious Abrahamic identity adds to, rather than replaces, previous ethnic belongings. Even if the

---

71. Buell and Hodge, "Politics of Interpretation," 236.

72. Buell, "Rethinking the Relevance of Race," 449–76.

73. Buell, "Rethinking the Relevance of Race", 449–76; Buell, "Race and Universalism," 432–41.

74. Buell and Hodge, "Politics of Interpretation," 247. The term ethnic reasoning has been coined by Buell "Rethinking," 451.

75. Buell and Hodge, "Politics of Interpretation," 250.

76. Wan. "Diaspora Identity," 127.

77. Badiou, *Saint Paul*, 98.

in-Christ formula does not erase ethnic difference, it does transform the way we see others. The unity in Christ involves a "new creation" (Gal 6:15) and challenges the notion of cultural supremacy.[78]

As a conclusion,

> the hybrid nature of the Pauline vision of Judeans and Greeks as one in Christ was therefore not foreign to the Jewish context in which it emerged. Jewish Diasporic Torah-based faith as well as Paul's Christ-centered faith use ethnic reasoning as well as religious practices in their forming of group identities, thereby in complex ways both establishing and transcending ethnic borders.[79]

A Jew or Greek becoming a Christian did not cease being Jewish or Greek, and yet the Christian *ethne* is not simply added to the Jewish or Greek *ethne* but also permeates and transforms them. As Holmberg states,

> To some extent, they [Jews and Gentiles] all remained what they had always been. On the other hand, none of them remained what they had been. . . . [W]e see both Jews and Gentiles in the Christian movement slowly sliding out of their earlier identities, becoming something that none of them had ever been before.[80]

## Galatians 3:28: The Baptismal Formula

> There is no longer Jew or Greek, there is no longer slave or free, there is no longer male and female; for all of you are one in Christ Jesus. (Gal 3:28)

Hans Dieter Betz rightly pointed out that Galatians 3:26–29 is "the goal towards which Paul has been driving all along."[81] Stanley argues that scholars wrongly assume that the term "Greek" in Galatians 3:28 is a synonym for "Gentile." According to him, both "Jew" and "Greek" should be regarded as labels indicating ethnicity and Paul's reference in this regard

---

78. Wan, "Diaspora Identity," 126–27. Buell and Hodge criticized such a reading of Paul. Based on Romans 11:17–24, they argued that Paul used the olive tree as a metaphor to show some privilege to Judeans over against the Greeks. See Buell and Hodge, "Politics of Interpretation," 249.

79. Leander, "Reading Paul in Post-Lutheran Sweden," 198.

80. Holmberg, "Early Christian Identity," 176–77.

81. Betz, *Galatians*, 181.

makes sense if one takes into account the history of interethnic conflict in that part of the Roman Empire.[82]

What does it mean that there is "neither Jew nor Greek in Christ?" "Gal 3:28, is taken by some as a representation of a de-ethnicized identity."[83] Dunn makes a convincing case that Galatians 2–3 is not about earning salvation but instead makes an argument against ethnic assimilation. He also builds a similar case for Romans 2–3 and argues that Paul's primary aim was not to establish universal human sinfulness in general but to undermine Jewish superiority in particular.

Galatians 3:26–29 is commonly considered as the baptismal unity formula with social implications,[84] in which Paul's vision for ethnic unity of the church is reflected. For Paul, both Jews and Greeks are now the one people of God with shared ancestry. The gentile Galatians who are baptized into Christ and belong to Christ are said to be "seed of Abraham, heirs according to the promise." (3:29).

In this section, Galatians 3:26–29, Paul climactically announces the new corporate identity which are central to chapter 3: "in Christ Jesus, you are all children of God through faith" (3:26); "baptized into Christ" (3:27); "all of you are one in Christ Jesus," "you belong to Christ," "you are Abraham's offspring" (3:29); "heirs according to the promise" (3:29). These interconnected identity statements sum up the arguments of 3:6–25,[85] in which Paul redefines the very foundations of the Jew versus Greek division.

Using this baptismal formula of 3:28, Paul declares social unity in Christ: "for all of you are one in Christ Jesus," and the abolition of the very exclusion dividing the Galatian church, "There is no longer Jew and Greek." Leander Keck explains baptism into Christ as "the 'objective' transference into a domain of power. To be baptized into Christ is to be included in the domain of Christ, his field of force."[86]

In Galatians 3:6–25 Paul supports this claim by redefining the very foundations of the Jew versus Greek division, namely Abrahamic descent and law observance.[87] As Bruce Hansen puts it, "This apocalyptic

---

82. Stanley, "'Neither Jew nor Greek,'" 101–24.

83. This interpretation is referred to as "fusion theory" by Caroline Johnson Hodge. She rejected this theory for it makes ethnicity irrelevant by advocating a melting of differences into one Unified identity in Christ. See Hodge, *If Sons*, 126–27.

84. Horrell, *Solidarity and Difference*, 104–106.

85. Hansen, "*All of you are one*".

86. Keck, *Paul*, 57–58.

87. There is a broad consensus that these are the main topics dividing Paul and his opponents. See Dunn, *Galatians*, 159; Martyn, *Galatians*, 302–06; R. Longenecker, *Galatians*, xcvi–xcviii, 114; Betz, *Galatians* 142, no. 29. Witherington, *Grace in Galatia*,

disruption into historical Israel's ethnic reckoning encapsulates the continuity–discontinuity tension throughout Galatians. Paul has produced a genealogical construction of the church derived from that of Israel but radically reconfigured by the cross of Christ."[88]

This new social solidarity gained by being in Christ did not erase the previous disconnection of being a Jew or a Greek, rather it encompasses both in a new sphere of belonging and reevaluates them with real social implications.[89] As Bennema points out: "Being 'in Christ' is ethnically neutral, not in the sense of denying one's particular ethnicity but of ethnicity being irrelevant for joining this group. At the same time, however, being 'in Christ' permeates and transforms any existing ethnic identity, whether Jewish or Greek."[90]

Therefore, from the baptismal formula of Paul, we can infer that "in Christ" identity does not obliterate the Jewish and Greek identities, but rather accommodates them and transforms them by directing them to Christ, causing Christian identity to transcend other identities. Against Buell and Hodge Christian, identity does not prioritize Judaean/Jewish ethnos and it does not suggest that being 'in Christ' means to adopt the Judaean ethnos.[91] On the contrary, the Christian community is not identified with one particular form of ethnicity, nationality, or cultural domination.[92] For this reason, Christian identity is a unifying identity that incorporates diverse identities "and converges them towards Christ in terms of beliefs, practices, behaviour, and ethos."[93]

## Reading Galatians in the Ethiopian Context

John Mansford Prior, speaking of his Indonesian context, pointed out that interpreting Galatians 3:27–28 in spiritualized ways has caused the church to become irrelevant and insignificant in a multiethnic and multi-religious context such as that of Indonesia.[94] We exhibit the same problem in the Ethiopian Evangelical/Pentecostal context. Galatians 3:28 is mainly

---

218–19, 227.

88. Hansen, "All of You Are One," 102.

89. Horrell, *Solidarity and Difference*, 126.

90. Bennema, "Early Christian Identity Formation," 26–48

91. Bennema, "Early Christian Identity Formation," 26–48; see Buell and Hodge, "Politics of Interpretation," 247.

92. Hansen, "All of You Are One," 104.

93. Bennema, "Early Christian Identity Formation," 26–48.

94. Prior, "Integration, Isolation or Deviation," 71–90.

interpreted in a spiritual sense and as a result it has no impact on the Christian community and beyond. Thus, a social reading of Galatians 3:27–28 is needed. The spiritual reading of the Bible fails to analyze the concrete realities in which the Bible is being interpreted. Hence, a shallow application follows. However, the social reading analyzes both the reader's and the biblical context and informs how we should order our lives. Ethnic issues are real in Ethiopian churches and this demands a creative reading of biblical texts to address the issue.

The first century Greco-Roman world and modern Ethiopian society share significant features. In both environments, religion plays a prominent role in social life and as an important identity marker. People in the ancient Mediterranean were strongly group-oriented individuals.[95] The same can be argued for the Ethiopian context. This means that groups play a prominent role in the social identity of an individual. In this kind of society there exists a clear demarcation between the in-group and out-groups based on social boundaries. However, it should be noted that social boundaries are fluid and change over time in response to social changes. So in dealing with New Testament, particularly Pauline Epistles, we should ask how the Judeans constructed their unique/distinct sense of self. How did the Judeans of Paul's time perceive their own identity and how did "others"/"outsiders" perceive them?

How does one social identity (e.g., being an Ethiopian, Oromo, Amhara, Afar) relate to other forms of social identity (i.e., being a Christian)? African theologians considered identity as a theological issue that has serious implications for Christians living in contemporary Africa.[96] In current Ethiopia, like in the book of Galatians, both the primordial and constructivist methods are used to construct one's group or individual identity.

Ethiopia is a heterogeneous society with multiethnic groups and religious affiliations. In his discussion about African nations, Hans Haselbarth writes, "Historical development has brought together tribes who, forced together and growing together into a wider fellowship, are finally identified as a nation."[97] This statement is true of Ethiopia. Ethnic groups in Ethiopia have been influenced by centuries of migration and interaction between people, which has created a complex pattern of ethnic, linguistic, and religious groups. Therefore, in a pluralistic society like that of Ethiopia, the issue of ethnic relations can become a matter of tension

---

95. See Kok and Eck, *Unlocking the World of Jesus*.

96. See Tiénou, "Right to Difference," 31; Bediako, *Theology and Identity*, 6, 31–33; Ferdinando, "Christian Identity," 121.

97. Haselbarth, *Christian Ethics*, 185.

and misunderstanding. Language and ethnicity are hot and sensitive issues in Ethiopia.[98] While most Christians would like to think they are not prejudiced against peoples of other ethnic groups, the attitude of ethnocentrism may be present nonetheless.

There is much debate on what it means to be "Ethiopian," and who has the legitimacy to define it. Currently, it seems the case that ethnic identity is overshadowing national identity. Some politicians and activists want the current federal system, which is organized along ethno-linguistic lines, to continue, while others argue for a different structure, which is not based on ethno-linguistics (maybe a pan-Ethiopian one). This ongoing identity politics is very much affecting churches in Ethiopia and the society at large.

Negative ethnicity poses a threat to Ethiopian society, and this calls for a multi-disciplinary approach involving all spheres of society to look for unique and creative ways of responding by all sectors of society, including the church. In Ethiopian society, religion plays a prominent role and can, therefore, act as an agent of change. The Ethiopian churches include a variety of ethnic groups, who in the past felt hostility toward each other. As a result, churches in Ethiopia are struggling to triumph over the historical and cultural prejudices that they have inherited and are striving to use the gospel to build Christian unity in the midst of cultural diversity.[99]

Ethnocentrism is a serious problem in Africa and particularly in Ethiopia. The negative nature of ethnicity is termed as "ethnocentrism," "negative ethnicity," or "tribalism." In the Ethiopian context, the Amharic terms racism (ዘረኝነት), tribalism (ጎሰኝነት), and ethnocentrisms (ብሔርተኝነት) are used. Ethnocentrism is an attitude and a practice of embracing the strong feeling of loyalty to one's ethnic group or tribe by excluding or demonizing those "others" who are considered outside of one's group.[100]

The churches in Ethiopia have failed to provide an articulated response to the problem of negative ethnicity. There is a tendency to view those who highlight their ethnic identity as *racist* (ዘረኛ). However, such a view is not right. As we have observed from our reading of Paul, being in-Christ (a Christian) does not abrogate our other identities. It is therefore important to recognize that we have multiple identities. As a result, we should be allowed to promote our ethnic identity without being antagonistic to others or in a

---

98. Cohen, "Regional & Local Languages," 171. Cohen comments: "Language should be used to facilitate development and self-expression, but in Ethiopia it has gained greater significance as the marker of identity. Language issues have become increasingly politicized . . . Language is, therefore, an unreliable marker of ethnicity" (Cohen, "Regional & Local Languages," 171).

99. See Hays, *From Every People and Nation*.

100. Nothwehr, *That They May Be One*, 5.

manner that goes in line with our newly added identity that we get, by being in-Christ, through the Spirit's work of placing ("baptizing") us in Christ. However, as pointed out above, our ethnic identity should be transformed by our Christian identity, i.e., our Christian values and ethos.

## Conclusion

In this chapter, I have tried to understand Paul in a way that interacts with a contemporary location where issues of ethnic difference and belonging matter in an existential way. Reading Paul ethnically enables us to appreciate variant cultural traditions and gives us a resource to tackle ethnocentric tendencies. As argued above, even though early Christians used ethnic reasoning or ethno-racial terms, Christian identity transcends other identities and relativizes ethnic identities.

## Bibliography

Badiou, Alain. *Saint Paul: The Foundation of Universalism*. Translated by Ray Brassier. Stanford: Stanford University Press, 2003.
Banks, Marcus. *Ethnicity: Anthropological Constructions*. London: Routledge, 1996.
Barclay, John M. G. *Jews in the Mediterranean Diaspora*. Edinburgh: T. & T. Clark, 1996.
———. "Neither Jew Nor Greek: Multiculturalism and the New Perspective on Paul." In *Ethnicity and the Bible*, edited by M. G. Brett, 197–214. Leiden: Brill, 1996.
Barth, Fredrik, ed. *Ethnic Group and Boundaries: The Social Organization of Culture Difference*. Boston: Little, Brown, 1969.
Bediako, Kwame. *Theology and Identity: The Impact of Culture Upon Christian Thought in the Second Century and in Modern Africa*. Regnum Studies in Mission. Oxford: Regnum, 1992.
Bell, Daniel. "Ethnicity and Social Change." In *Ethnicity: Theory and Experience*, edited by Nathan Glazier and Daniel P. Moynihan, 141–74. Cambridge: Harvard University Press, 1975.
Bennema, Cornelis. "Early Christian Identity Formation Amidst Conflict." *Journal of Early Christian History* 5.1 (January 2015) 26–48.
Betz, Hans Dieter. *Galatians: A Commentary on Paul's Letter to the Churches in Galatia*. Hermeneia. Philadelphia: Fortress, 1979.
Brett, Mark G. *Ethnicity and the Bible*, edited by M. G. Brett, 215–40. Leiden: Brill, 1996.
Buell, Denise Kimber. "Race and Universalism in Early Christianity." *Journal of Early Christian Studies* 10 (2002) 432–41.
———. "Rethinking the Relevance of Race for Early Christian Self-Definition." *Harvard Theological Review* 94 (2001) 449–76.
Buell, Denise Kimber, and Caroline E. Johnson Hodge. "The Politics of Interpretation: The Rhetoric of Race and Ethnicity in Paul." *JBL* 123.2 (2004) 235–51.
Campbell, William S. *Paul and the Creation of Christian Identity*. Library of New Testament Studies 322. New York: T. & T. Clark, 2006.

Cohen, Gideon. "The Development of Regional & Local Languages in Ethiopia's Federal System." In *Ethnic Federalism: The Ethiopian Experience in Comparative Perspective*, edited by David Turton, 165–80. Addis Ababa: Addis Ababa University Press, 2006.

Cosgrove, Charles H. "Did Paul Value Ethnicity?" *Catholic Biblical Quarterly* 68.2 (April 2006) 268–90.

Duling, Dennis. "'Whatever Gain I Had . . .': Ethnicity and Paul's Self-identification in Philippians 3:5–6." *HTS* 64.2 (2008) 799–818.

Dunn, James D. G. *The Epistle to the Galatians.* Black's New Testament Commentary. Peabody, MA: Hendrickson, 1993.

———. *Jesus, Paul and the Law.* Grand Rapids: Eerdmans, 2011.

———. "The New Perspective on Paul." *Bulletin of the John Rylands Library* 65 (1983) 95–122.

———. *The Partings of the Ways: Between Christianity and Judaism and Their Significance for the Character of Christianity.* London: SCM, 1991.

———. *Unity and Diversity in the New Testament: An Inquiry into the Character of Earliest Christianity.* London: SCM, 1990.

———. "Works of the Law and the Curse of the Law (Galatians 3.10–14)." *New Testament Studies* 31.4 (October 1985) 523–42.

Esler, Philip. *Conflict and Identity in Romans: The Social Setting of Paul's Letter.* Minneapolis: Fortress, 2003.

———. "Family Imagery and Christian Identity in Gal 5:13 to 6:10." In *Constructing Early Christian Families as Social Reality and Metaphor*, edited by Halvor Moxnes, 121–49. London: Routledge, 1997.

———. "From Ioudaioi to Children of God: The Development of a Non-Ethnic Group Identity in the Gospel of John." In *Other Words: Essays on Social Science Methods and the New Testament in Honor of Jerome H. Neyrey*, edited by Anselm C. Hagedorn et al., 106–37. Social World of Biblical Antiquity, Second Series, 1. Sheffield: Sheffield Phoenix, 2007.

———. *Galatians.* London: Routledge, 1998.

———. "Group Boundaries and Intergroup Conflict in Galatians." In *Ethnicity and the Bible*, edited by M. G. Brett, 215–40. Leiden: Brill, 1996.

———. "Judean Ethnic Identity and the Matthean Jesus." In *Jesus—Gestalt und Gestaltungen. Rezeptionen des Galiläers in Wissenschaft, Kirche und Gesellschaft*, edited by Petra von Gemünden et al., 193–210. FS Gerd Theissen. NTOA 100. Göttingen: Vandenhoeck & Ruprecht, 2013.

———. "'Keeping It in the Family': Culture, Kinship and Identity in 1 Thessalonians and Galatians." In *Families and Family Relations as Represented in Early Judaisms and Early Christianities: Texts and Fictions*, edited by J. W. van Henten and A. Brenner, 145–85. Leiden: Deo, 2000.

———. "Making and Breaking an Agreement Mediterranean Style: A New Reading of Galatians 2:1–14." *BibInt* 3 (1995) 285–314.

Faulkner, Anne. "Jewish Identity and the Jerusalem Conference: Social Identity and Self-categorization in the Early Church Communities." *eSharp* 6.1 (2005) 1–19. http://www.gla.ac.uk/media/media_41174_en.pdf.

Ferdinando, Keith. "Christian Identity in the African Context: Reflections on Kwame Bediako's Theology and Identity." *Journal of Evangelical Theological Society* 50.1 (2007) 121–43.

Friesen, Steven J. "Poverty in Pauline Studies: Beyond the So-called New Consensus." *JSNT* 26.3 (2004) 323–61.
Goodman, M. D. *Mission and Conversion*. Oxford: Clarendon, 1994.
Hall, Jonathan M. *Ethnic Identity in Greek Antiquity*. Cambridge: Cambridge University Press, 1997.
Hansen, Bruce. "'All of You Are One': The Social Vision of Gal 3:28, 1 Cor 12:13 and Col 3:11." PhD diss., University of St. Andrews, 2007.
Hansen, G. W. *Abraham in Galatians: Epistolary and Rhetorical Contexts*. Journal for the Study of the New Testament Supplement Series 29. Sheffield: JSOT, 1988.
Haselbarth, Hans. *Christian Ethics in African Context*. Nairobi: Uzima, 1976.
Hodge, Caroline Johnson. *If Sons, Then Heirs: A Study of Kinship and Ethnicity in the Letters of Paul*. Oxford: Oxford University Press, 2007.
Holmberg, Bengt. "Early Christian Identity—Some Conclusions." In *Exploring Early Christian Identity*, edited by Bengt Holmberg, 176–77. Wissenschaftliche Untersuchungen zum Neuen Testament 226. Tübingen: Mohr Siebeck, 2008.
———. *Sociology and the New Testament*. Minneapolis: Fortress, 1990.
Horrell, David G. *Solidarity and Difference: A Contemporary Reading of Paul's Ethics*. London: T. & T. Clark, 2005.
Horsley, Richard A. *Sociology and the Jesus Movement*. New York: Crossroad, 1989.
Hutchinson, John, and Anthony D. Smith. *Ethnicity*. Oxford Readers. Oxford: Oxford University Press, 1996.
Jewett, Robert. *Romans: A Commentary*. Hermeneia. Minneapolis: Fortress, 2007.
Jones, Sian. *The Archaeology of Ethnicity: Constructing Identities in the Past and Present*. New York: Routledge, 1997.
Keck, Leander E. *Paul and His Letters*. Proclamation Commentaries. Philadelphia: Fortress, 1979.
Keener, Craig S. *Galatians*. New Cambridge Bible Commentary. Cambridge: Cambridge University Press, 2018.
Kelley, Shawn. *Racializing Jesus: Race, Ideology, and the Formation of Modern Biblical Scholarship*. London: Routledge, 2002.
Klassen, William. "Normative Self-Definitions of Christianity in the New Testament." In *Common Life in the Early Church: Essays Honoring Graydon F. Snyder*, edited by Julian V. Hills, 91–105. Harrisburg: Trinity Press International, 1998.
Kok, J., and Ernest Van Eck, eds. *Unlocking the World of Jesus*. Pretoria: Biblaridion, 2012.
Kuecher, Aaron. "The Spirit And the 'Other': Social Identity, Ethnicity and Intergroup Reconciliation in Luke–Acts." PhD diss., University of St. Andrews, 2008.
Kunhiyop, Samuel Wajo. *African Christian Ethics*. Grand Rapids: Zondervan, 2008.
Leander, Hans. "Reading Paul in Post-Lutheran Sweden." *Studia Theologica—Nordic Journal of Theology* 68.2 (2014) 184–205. http://dx.doi.org/10.1080/0039338X.2014.961200.
Lim, Sung Uk. "Race and Ethnicity Discourse in Biblical Studies and Beyond." *Journal for the Study of Religions and Ideologies* 15.45 (2016) 120–42.
Lopez, Davina C. *Apostle to the Conquered: Reimagining Paul's Mission*. Minneapolis: Fortress, 2008.
Malherbe, A. J. *Social Aspects of Early Christianity*. 2nd ed. Philadelphia: Fortress, 1983.
Marohl, Matthew J. *Faithfulness and the Purpose of Hebrews: A Social Identity Approach*. Eugene: Pickwick, 2008.

Martyn, J. L. *Galatians: A New Translation with Introduction and Commentary*. Anchor Bible 33A. New York: Doubleday, 1997.
Matera, Frank J. "Galatians in Perspective: Cutting a New Path through Old Territory." *Interpretation* 54.3 (2000) 236–37.
———. *Sacra Pagina: Galatians 9*. Edited by Daniel J. Harrington. Collegeville, MN: Liturgical, 1992.
Meeks, W. A. *The First Urban Christians*. New Haven: Yale University Press, 1983.
Meggitt, J. J. *Paul, Poverty and Survival*. Edinburgh: T. & T. Clark, 1998.
Merera Gudina. *Ethiopia: Competing Ethnic Nationalism and the Quest for Democracy, 1960–2000*. Addis Ababa: Chamber, 2003.
Nanos, Mark D. *The Irony of Galatians: Paul's Letter in First-Century Context*. Minneapolis: Fortress, 2002.
Neutel, Karin B. "'Neither Jew Nor Greek': Abraham As A Universal Ancestor." In *Abraham, the Nations, and the Hagarites: Jewish, Christian, and Islamic Perspective on Kinship with Abraham*, edited by Martin Goodman et al., 291–306. Leiden: Brill, 2010.
Nothwehr, Dawn M. *That They May Be One: Catholic Social Teaching on Racism, Tribalism, and Xenophobia*. New York: Orbis, 2008.
Nyende, Peter. "Addressing Ethnicity via Biblical Studies: A Task of African Biblical Scholarship." *Neotestamentica* 44.1 (2010) 122–39.
———. "Ethnic Studies: An Urgent Need in Theological Education in Africa." *International Review of Mission* 98.1 (2009) 132–46.
Prior, John M. "Integration, Isolation or Deviation: Reading Galatians 3:27–28 in Indonesia Today." *Mission Studies* 27.1 (2010) 71–90.
Sanders, Ed Parish. *Paul and Palestinian Judaism: A Comparison of Patterns of Religion*. Philadelphia: Fortress, 1977.
———. *Paul, the Law, and the Jewish People*. Philadelphia: Fortress, 1983.
———. *Judaism: Practice and Belief, 63BCE–66CE*. London: SCM, 1992.
Seifrid, Mark A. "The 'New Perspective on Paul' and Its Problems." *Themelios* 25.2 (2000) 4–18.
Shkul, Minna. "Reading Ephesians: Exploring Social Entrepreneurship in the Text." PhD diss., University of Sheffield, 2008.
Slate, Jennifer. *Christian Identity Characteristics in Paul's Letter to the Members of the Jesus Movement in Galatians: Creating Diastratic Unity in a Diastratic Divergent South African Society*. Bloomington: Authorhouse, 2012.
Smith, Anthony D. "Culture, Community and Territory: The Politics of Ethnicity and Nationalism." *International Affairs (Royal Institute of International Affairs)* 72.3 (1996) 445–58.
———. *The Ethnic Origins of Nations*. Oxford: Basil Blackwell, 1986.
———. *Nations and Nationalism in a Global Era*. Cambridge: Polity, 1995.
———. "The Politics of Culture: Ethnicity and Nationalism." In *Companion Encyclopedia of Anthropology*, edited by Tim Ingold, 706–33. London: Routledge, 1994.
Stambaugh, J. E., and D. L. Balch. *The New Testament in Its Social Environment*. Library of Eearly Christianity 2. Philadelphia: Westminster, 1986.
Stanley, Christopher D. "The Ethnic Context of Paul's Letters." In *Christian Origins and Hellenistic Judaism: Social and Literary Contexts for the New Testament*, edited

by Stanley E. Porter and Andrew W. Pitts, 177–201. Early Christianity in its Hellenistic Context 2. Leiden: Brill, 2013.

———. "'Neither Jew nor Greek': Ethnic Conflict in Graeco-Roman Society." *Journal for the Study of the New Testament* 64 (1996) 101–24.

———. "Paul the Ethnic Hybrid? Postcolonial Perspectives on Paul's Ethnic Categorization." In *The Colonized Apostle: Paul Through Postcolonial Eyes*, edited by Christopher D. Stanley, 110–26. Minneapolis: Fortress, 2001.

Stegemann, Ekkehard W., and Wolfgang Stegemann. *The Jesus Movement: A Social History of Its First Century*. Edinburgh: T. & T. Clark, 1999.

Stendahl, Krister. "The Apostle Paul and the Introspective Conscience of the West." *Harvard Theological Review* 56.3 (1963) 199–215.

Sumney, Jerry L. "Studying Paul's Opponents: Advances and Challenges." In *Paul and His Opponents*, edited by Stanley Porter, 7–58. Pauline Studies. Leiden: Brill, 2005.

Tellbe, Mikael. *Christ-Believers in Ephesus: A Textual Analysis of Early Christian Identity Formation in a Local Perspective*. Wissenschaftliche Untersuchungen zum Neuen Testament 242. Tübingen: Mohr Siebeck, 2009.

Theissen, Gerd. *The Social Setting of Pauline Christianity*. Philadelphia: Fortress, 1982.

Theodros A. Teklu. *The Politics of Metanoia: Towards a Post-Nationalistic Political Theology in Ethiopia*. Frankfurt am Main: Lang, 2014.

Thompson, Richard H. *Theories of Ethnicity: A Critical Appraisal*. Contributions in Sociology 82. New York: Greenwood, 1989.

Tiénou, Tite. "The Right to Difference: The Common Roots of African Theology and African Philosophy." *African Journal of Evangelical Theology* 9.1 (1990) 24–34.

Togarasei, Lovemore. "Rethinking Christian Identity: African Reflections from Pauline Writings." *Perichoresis* 14.1 (2016) 101–14.

Trebilco, Paul. *Jewish Communities in Asia Minor*. Cambridge: Cambridge University Press, 2006.

———. *Self-designations and Group Identity in the New Testament*. Cambridge: Cambridge University Press, 2014.

Tucker, J. Brian. "You Belong to Christ Paul and the Formation of Social Identity in 1 Cor 1–4." PhD diss., University of Wales Lampeter, 2009.

Vollenweider, Samuel. "Are Christians a New 'People'? Detecting Ethnicity and Cultural Friction in Paul's Letters and Early Christianity." *Early Christianity* 8.3 (2017) 293–308.

Wan, Sze-kar Wan. "Does Diaspora Identity Imply Some Sort of Universality? An Asian–American Reading of Galatians." In *Interpreting Beyond Borders*, edited by Fernando F. Segovia, 107–32. Sheffield: Sheffield Academic, 2000.

Westerholm, Stephen. *Israel's Law and the Church's Faith: Paul and his Recent Interpreters*. Grand Rapids: Eerdmans, 1988.

Winn, Adam, ed. *An Introduction to Empire in the New Testament*. Atlanta: SBL, 2016.

# Part IV

# Self and Other: Moral Visions of Togetherness

# 7

# The "Ethnic Other" as the "Neighbor"

## A *Perichoretic* Imagination of Moral Responsibility

Youdit Tariku Feyessa

"Human-ness" is often conjoined with our "humanity toward others."[1] Being human is associated with being relational, the way one lives with others. The renowned Greek philosopher, Aristotle, seems to affirm this when he said, "humans are social animals."[2] Humanness, then, is tuned with the interconnectedness of life and the responsibility of relating with one another with peace and harmony. In a diversified society like Ethiopia, however, ethnic diversity has been both a blessing and a nuisance to the country. Freedom of language and culture has created a space in the public sphere where ethnic identities and diversities are not only celebrated, but also contested.

In Ethiopia today, inter-ethnic relations are being hardened with elevated ethnic views of the self, and fear, grievance, and resentments towards the other. Consequently, the aesthetics of diversity is more and more tinged with fear and enigma, as the relationship between ethnic communities becomes more tense and violent. Such violent relations are fueled by the discourses of oppression and domination, and of grievance and resentment.[3] This is the case even to the extent that applying the historical background for ethnic relations in Ethiopia is a difficult endeavor.

---

1. Gade, "Historical Development," 303–29.
2. Deslauriers and Destr´ee, *Cambridge Companion*, 178.
3. Bekalu, "Ethnic Federalism."

For that matter, there are various resurgences of revisionist historiography, resulting in competing historical narrations in Ethiopia.[4] Afework Hailu's historiographical discussion about "*Ethio-nationalist* thesis" and "*ethno-nationalist* anti-thesis" in this volume attests to this fact. In their own distinct idioms, all the other chapters in this volume also deal with the contentious reality of ethnic relations in Ethiopia from the historical, legal, sociological, philosophical, and political perspectives. In his book, *The Politics of Metanoia: Towards a Post-Nationalistic Political Theology in Ethiopia*, Theodros A. Teklu discusses "Ethiopia as *homo-ethnicus*"[5] and brings to the fore the role of contesting self-narrations and polarized subjectivities of Ethiopian ethno-politics. According to him, two interrelated notions—self-writing and ethno-national identities—have dominated the political discourse of Ethiopia, resulting in polarized subjectivities. As a result, narratives of domination–oppression and narratives of victimhood have influenced the discourse of the self and (ethnic) otherness intensifying ethnic tensions, and ethnic-based conflicts in the country.[6]

Such kind of identity politics based on self-construction, and historical memories (whether the *Ethio-nationalist* or *ethno-nationalist*), affect the relationship of the ethnic self and the other in Ethiopia through grievance, anger, hatred, and resentment. Collective memories are recollections of past events, occurrences, happenings that impinge to the present and shared by members of a community;[7] and they can influence inter-subjective relationships, the interaction between the self and others.[8] Violence that is made on an individual based on ethnic difference is the denial of the otherness of the other's existence, belongingness, representation, history, memory, and identity. Throughout modern Ethiopian history, the denial of the otherness of the other has been obliterating ethnic relations, which is often marked by lack of recognition, oppression/domination, grievance, resentment, and the extermination of the ethnic other. Such consequences call for a firm moral responsibility in order to challenge the recurrence of violence, and contribute towards the healing of the historical traumas.

For instance, over the last few years, millions of people were internally displaced from their living places based on their ethnic identity and belongingness, according to the 2019 Human Rights Watch Report.[9] The

---

4. Semir, "*What is Driving Ethiopia's ethnic conflicts?*".
5. Theodros, *The Politics of Matanoia*, 114–127.
6. Theodros, *The Politics of Matanoia*, 114–127.
7. Tekalign, *Reconstruction*, 30.
8. Tekalign, *Reconstruction*, 30–37.
9. "Ethiopia: Events of 2018."

ethnic-based conflict between the Guji and the Gedeo ethnic communities that resulted in displacement could be a case in point.[10] The report also mentioned exacerbated conflict in the Somali and Oromia regions, which displaced about 145,000 people in early August and, yet again, about 15,000 people in the peripheries of Addis Ababa in September 2019.[11] Such internal displacement, interethnic violence, and ethnic cleansing are just a few examples. Such ethnic-based polarizations resulted in enmity between neighbors. People identify with their ethnic communities, and seek to annihilate the ethnic other, who is no longer seen as the neighbor (as chapter 4 of this collection explicates).

In light of the historical and contemporary realities, which are rehearsed above, this chapter seeks to critically identify the kind of ethical principle that should guide the relationship between the ethnic self and the ethnic other(s) through the figure of the neighbor. The chapter attempts to critically correlate contemporary thinking with Christian theology to harness a rich notion of moral responsibility by framing the relationship between the ethnic self and the ethnic other in terms of the concept of the neighbor and the great commandment of loving the neighbor as oneself. Such framing, this chapter argues, is instrumental in combating ethnic-based violence, conflict, fear, and resentment. To be more specific, the endeavor of sketching this vision of moral responsibility in the figure of the neighbor will be achieved by consulting with the theological concept called *perichoresis*, an analogy of Trinitarian relationship.

To this end, I will first locate my discussion of the relation between the self and the ethnic other in the discourse of the political theology of the neighbor which bases its argument on the great commandment of loving the neighbor. Next, the chapter will attempt to draw ethical responsibility based on the ethics of neighbor love embedded in perichoretic imagination of the Trinitarian life that could serve not only as a prototype for the neighborly relationship but with potentiality in curbing ethnic-related problems.

---

10. Gedeo and Guji are ethnically different ground found in the border between the Oromo region and the Southern nations and nationalities. Although they often engage in conflicts because of grazing land, the recent conflict is politically motivated and orchestrated by political agents who manipulated ethnic identity.

11. "Ethiopia: Events of 2018." See also Mumbere, Ethiopia Govt Confirms Thousands Killed."

## The Neighbor as a Political-Theological Concept

The introduction highlighted the relationship between the ethnic self and the ethnic other by briefly rehearsing the historical and sociopolitical discourse within the Ethiopian context. It postulates the relationship between the ethnic self and the ethnic other that has been obliterated by many factors resulting in denial of the otherness of the ethnic other through ethnic-based violence, atrocities, fear, and resentment. It also hints toward the need of a guiding principle, a moral responsibility that upholds the enigmatic relationship between the ethnic self and the ethnic other in order to curb the challenge of ethnic-based atrocities, and violence.

This section tries to situate the discussion of ethnic otherness with the concept of the neighbor in political-theological discourse that impinges in the Christian moral imperative *par excellence, to love the neighbor as oneself*, via consulting with Christian theological and philosophical sources.[12] By limiting the discussion on this imperative, this section attempts to furnish the political theology of the neighbor through the investigation of who the neighbor is and demarcating the kind of relationship with the neighbor. In political-theological discourses, the notion of the neighbor is the point of intersection between the ethico-moral and the politico-social. The Judeo-Christian perspective, *love of the neighbor*, "you shall love your neighbor as yourself" (Lev 19:18), is the "*principle par excellence*" in the political theology of the neighbor.[13] The commandment *par excellence* demonstrates the impossibility of loving God without loving the neighbor.[14]

Luke Bretherton argues that the politics of the neighbor in political theology holds three tenets: the encounter with the neighbor that entails response to injustices, poverty, and sufferings; the way one's identity or belonging relates with others—strangers–enemies—that determines one's faith/theology; and the distribution of power relationship among oneself and another that forms the politics of "common life."[15] According to Bretherton "political theology is how power is constructed, circulated, and distributed within patterns of common life," which is based on neighbor love.[16] This is also evident in ancient Greek philosophy where the term "political" connotes a discipline concerned with the common good

---

12. Reinhard et al, *The Neighbor*, 2–7. Also, Bretherton, *Christ and the Common Life*,1–32.

13. Reinhard et al., *The Neighbour*, 5. Cf. Scott and Cavanaugh, eds., *Political Theology*, 1.

14. Davis, *Theology and Political Society*, 58–59.

15. Bretherton, *Christ and the Common Life*, 2.

16. Bretherton, *Christ and the Common Life*, 17–22.

denoting the *polis* that requires one to acquire a virtuous, good relationship with the neighbor.[17]

Within this framework, the next subsection discusses the neighbor and the neighborly relationship to furnish the dynamics between the self and the ethnic other, moving toward locating the ethnic other as the neighbor. Towards this end, the chapter tries to locate the neighbor via discussing the parallax of the neighbor, the view of the neighbor from different perspectives, and it also tries to investigate the notion of loving the neighbor that entails the neighborly relationship, the possibility and impossibility of loving the neighbor as oneself, which calls for Christian moral response towards challenging ethnic-based violence. I will be mainly conversing with Emmanuel Lévinas and Slavoj Žižek to bring to the surface the various, mostly divergent, perspectives in the political theology of the neighbor. In doing so, the subsection investigates and points out the loopholes in ethnic relations and directs to the kind of aspired relations between the ethnic self and the ethnic other.

## Locating the Neighbor

Before diving into the discussion of the notion of the neighbor in political-theological discourse, discussing the semantics of the term reveals the range of meaning and interpretation the term bears and also indicates how interpretation can determine actions and relationships. The etymology of the word has a German origin, *Nächste*, signifying a residential nearness or proximity, which has social and political connotations and responsibility.[18] According to the early Jewish sources, the Hebrew term for the neighbor is *rēa*, which implies some form of closeness, physical or social or ethnical.[19] Understanding of the term is mostly associated with those who are under the covenant, related with the love of fellow Jews or Israelites implying the "the love within a community"[20] as Gupta elaborated. Or, it is the love for a kin.[21] Similarly, Naim Kattan affirms that the neighbor is a "near dweller" and usually a kin.[22] In the same vein, Michael Fagenblat views the neighbor as a "person encountered in a covenantal relationship."[23]

17. Phillips, *Political Theology*, 3–4.
18. Mendes-Flohr, *Love, Accusative and Dative*, 5–15.
19. Painter, "Politics of the Neighbour," 8–10.
20. Painter, "Politics of the Neighbour," 8–10.
21. Gupta, "Neighbor, Neighbor Love," 547–48.
22. Kattan, "Neighbour," 11–19.
23. Fagenblat, "Concept of Neighbor," 541.

However, this particularistic approach never seems to be without critique. Martin Buber and Franz Rosenzweig argue that in the commandment to love the neighbor *rēa* is not only confined to fellow Israelites; instead, it extends to the resident strangers (Lev 19:34).[24] According to Rosenzweig, the neighbor being fellow Jew or near dweller or stranger is the one like the self or similar to the self, the Hebrew term *kamokha*, who is supposed to be loved in same way one loves the self.[25] Furthermore, Hermann Cohen even extends the etymological meaning of *rēa* (to care for the one like us) from the root word meaning "shepherd."[26] In the same vein, the New Testament presents this latter view, the Greek term *plēsion*, connotes nearness or near dwelling. The New Testament has a universalistic approach that even extends to loving the enemy, the neighbor.

Answering the question "Who is my/the neighbor?" is not an easy task and demands further elaboration. Even Jesus himself did not reply instantly, rather preferring to elaborate his answer by telling the parable of the Good Samaritan. Jesus flips the question from "Who is my neighbor?" as stated by the lawyer, to "Who was a neighbor to the person in need?" "thereby shifting the focus on 'neighbour' from an object of obligation to a proactively loving subject."[27] The question shifted from "'who is my neighbour?' to 'to whom am I a neighbour' or even, 'how neighbourly am I?'"[28] In addition, Jesus' parable surpasses ethnic-based neighborly relationship, as he brought ethnically divergent groups into the scene, a Samaritan and a Jew.[29] Therefore, the neighbor could be a fellow Jew or a fellow human being or a stranger or a near dwelling person. From this, it is possible to say that one's view of the neighbor will directly impact and influence the way one relates, treats and lives with the neighbor having a socio-ethical and political implication.

## The Neighbor as the "Face"

Emmanuel Lévinas, who is known as a philosopher of alterity or otherness, in his notable work, *Totality and Infinity: An Essay on Exteriority* and *Otherwise than Being: or Beyond Essence*, discusses issues related to the meaning of life and death, the relationship between the self and others,

24. Rosenzweig, *Star of Redemption*, 239–40.
25. Rosenzweig, *Star of Redemption*, 257–58.
26. Cohen, *Ethics of Maimonides*, 152–54.
27. Mescher, "Doing Likewise."
28. McFarland, "Who Is My Neighbour?," 57–66.
29. Sim, *Postmodernism*, 269–70.

and the vitality of love.³⁰ Dealing with Lévinas's notion of the neighbor and neighborly relationship demands focusing on three important concepts: the "Face," "proximity," and the "Third."³¹

For Lévinas, the "face" is a term used to describe the otherness of the other or the neighbor. He borrows the meaning from the Hebrew word *panim* (root word *panah*) that connotes "a turning towards something and also a kind of personal presence" thus, "facing" means being "confronted with, turned towards, facing up to, being judged and called by the other."³² The encounter with the face calls for automatic response and responsibility.³³ In the appearance of the face there is a commandment that says "thou shall not kill," and an order that says "here I am"; hence, the face is the locus of the word of God in the other.³⁴

Another consideration: Lévinas's ethics of "*alterity*."³⁵ Alterity is the insistence that others always remain irreducible to the representation of one's experience. Otherness is no more located in the self or explained in reference to the self, but rather in the face.³⁶ For Lévinas, otherness is not bounded within knowledge.³⁷ The uniqueness or otherness of the other is not reduced in the name of objective knowledge. According to Lévinas, conflating otherness with human knowledge is problematic as it limits otherness to mere experience, and this reduces or smashes the uniqueness/otherness of the other.³⁸

In simple terms, what Lévinas is saying is that the knowledge that I have about the other person does not adequately define the identity of that person. That person is beyond one's understanding because he/she is the other. In his explanation of otherness, that means whenever one encounters the face, in this case the ethnic other, an instant response and responsibility appears in the relationship even before knowledge of the ethnic identity of that person comes to one's mind. One should care for a person not because he/she is from the same ethnic community, but simply because he/she is the face. And the face says "thou shall not kill" and calls for responsibility for the face. This is a

---

30. Morgan, *Emmanuel Lévinas*, 147–55.
31. Lévinas, *Alterity*, 169; *Otherwise than Being*, 87.
32. Handelman, "Facing the Other," 63–64.
33. Lévinas, *Alterity*, 1.
34. Lévinas, *Alterity*, 104.
35. Lévinas, *Alterity*, 101.
36. Lévinas, *Alterity*, 169–77.
37. Lévinas, *Alterity*, 98–101.
38. Lévinas, *Alterity*, 98–101.

very important concept, especially in a country like Ethiopia where there is a proliferation of ethnic-based atrocities and killings.

One may ask the question: why a facing relationship? According to Emmanuel Lévinas, the facing relationship is infinite as the other is the manifestation of God, the trace of God and the point of intersection with God.[39] On the one hand, the face embodies the trace of God, and, on the other, encountering and knowing of God is impossible without encountering the face. Therefore, the encounter with the face is indispensable for relationship with God.[40] As such, Lévinasian ethics presumes the universality of otherness as well as the responsibility that comes with facing this otherness.[41]

The other terminology that Lévinas frequently uses in the self/other relationship is "proximity." For Lévinas, proximity does not signify the spatiality between the self and the other relationship; instead, it is "the movement of the self towards the neighbour."[42] In proximity there is this perpetual movement towards the other and that movement is responsibility characterized by subjectivity.[43] As Lévinas states, "proximity is to be described as extending the subject in its subjectivity, which is both a relationship and a term of this relationship";[44] as "Proximity, difference which is non-indifference, is responsibility. It is a response without a question, the immediacy of peace that is incumbent on me."[45] An asymmetrical and non-reciprocal relationship is the biding principle as the other always takes priority and the self is endowed with responsibility. The responsibility to the neighbor is without choice and, according to Lévinas, it is only in responsibility that neighbor love is possible.

The other idea Emmanuel Lévinas uses in his self/other relationship is the "third party" which extends to the other neighbors, the society, and the relationship endowed in justice.[46] According to Lévinas, "the third party is other than the neighbor, but also another neighbor, and also a neighbor of the other and not simply his [her] fellow [sic]."[47] The third party "interrupts the asymmetry of responsibility between the self and the neighbour by revealing the existence of other subjects who are neighbours to my neighbour." Justice,

---

39. Morgan, *Emmanuel Lévinas*, 147.
40. Lévinas, *Totality*, 76–78.
41. Hand, *Lévinas Reader*, 294.
42. Lévinas, *Otherwise than Being*, 81–82.
43. Lévinas, *Otherwise than Being*, 81–86.
44. Lévinas, *Otherwise than Being*, 86.
45. Lévinas, *Otherwise than Being*, 139.
46. Lévinas, *Otherwise than Being*, 128.
47. Lévinas, *Otherwise than Being*, 157.

for Lévinas, refers to "community of 'neighbours' and society is founded not on commonality but on community of others"; for him, justice is about "the control of responsibility of the one for the other."[48]

In other words, the vitality of relationship with all others is determined by one's relationship with the other as the neighbor which is endowed in proximity, the responsibility of the one to the other.[49] As Lévinas avers "justice, society, state, and institutions, exchange and work are comprehensible out of proximity."[50] And this is how the three important notions of Lévinas function together: the face is the neighbor who is the bearer of a call of command and an order that says "thou shall not kill" that calls for love. The relationship between the self and the other is a relationship of proximity, asymmetrical and non-reciprocal responsibility towards the neighbor; and the responsible relationship towards the "community of neighbours" not based on commonalities but rather communities.[51] The conception of the neighbor and the neighborly relationship superseding commonalities is paramount for ethnic relations between the ethnic self and the ethnic other as demand for ethnic sameness or commonality would be overridden by respecting diversity of the community of others (neighbors).

## The Ambiguous Neighbor

In his essay titled "Neighbours and Other Monsters: A Plea to Ethical Violence," Slavoj Žižek discusses the politics of the neighbor, the neighborly relationship and the impossibility of loving the neighbor as oneself.[52] Žižek pointed out the error in the contemporary oversensitivity towards harassment by the other and the tolerant attitude that leads to "unconstrained permissiveness" that lacks expurgation.[53] In his writing, Žižek wants to contrast the widespread criticism on the notion of ""ethical violence", in other words, to the tendency to submit to criticism of ethical injunctions that "terrorize" us with brutal imposition of their universality."[54]

According to Žižek, contrasting Levinas, the commandment to love one's neighbor does not adhere to self-knowledge or a mirror image as contemporary thinking presupposes; rather it assumes the neighbor as a

48. Lévinas, *Otherwise than Being*, 159.
49. Lévinas, *Otherwise than Being*, 159.
50. Lévinas, *Otherwise than Being*, 159.
51. Lévinas, *Otherwise than Being*, 145–59.
52. Žižek, "Neighbours and Other Monsters," 134.
53. Žižek, "Neighbours and Other Monsters," 134.
54. Žižek, "Neighbours and Other Monsters," 135.

real thing, not an imagination of sameness. In his discussion, Žižek uses two key features that are also helpful in understanding the ethnic-based atrocities in the Ethiopian context: the monstrosity of the other and the faceless other that elaborates the ambiguity entailed in the neighbor and the neighborly relationship.

According to Žižek, "... an alien traumatic kernel forever persists in my Neighbour—the Neighbour remains an inert, impenetrable, enigmatic, present that hystericises me."[55] The neighbor, when the level of proximity is not maintained, becomes a "traumatic intruder" and their varied way of life disturbs and messes one's way of life.[56] Žižek further elaborates that "the reduction of the radically ambiguous monstrosity of the Neighbor-Thing into an Other as the abyssal point from which the call of ethical responsibility emanates."[57] In the name of maintaining the proximity to the neighbor, one needs to resist "gentrification of the neighbour."[58] Here, what Žižek attempts to assert is the change in the notion of the neighbor to an appealing form of a call for ethical responsibility of loving the neighbor masks the monstrous character of the neighbor. The ethnic-based brutal attack, rape, looting, and displacement of ethnic others in Ethiopia can be taken as a good case in point to demonstrate the enigmatically ambiguous monstrosity of the neighbor—a good application of Žižekian ambiguous neighbor who turned into a traumatic intruder, a monster that kills.[59] For him, the neighbor that terrorizes remains engimatic.[60]

Žižek is not comfortable with the notion of the face, which entails a face-to-face relationship; instead, he opts for another important concept called "the faceless other." He utilizes Giorgio Agamben's figure of the *Muselmann*, who is the faceless other who cannot say "Here I am" in a face-to-face relationship. The *Muselmann* is considered the "zero level" existence or the living dead, who is the neglected figure in the neighbor love discussion, the faceless other.[61] The incident of the lynched person in Shashemene, referred

55. Žižek, "Ethical Violence," 2.
56. Žižek, *Violence*, 59.
57. Žižek, *Parallax View*, 114. Žižek, "Neighbours and Other Monsters," 163.
58. Zukić, "My Neighbor's Face," 1.
59. The ethnic-based brutal attack, rape (including a five year old girl), looting, and displacement of the Gamo, Gurage, and Dorze people who reside in the outskirts of Addis Ababa, Burayu, by ethno-nationalist Oromo youth illustrates the enigmatically ambiguous, monstrosity of the neighbor.
60. Žižek, "Plea to Ethical Violence," 2.
61. Žižek, "Neighbours and Other Monsters," 159–62. Here again Slavoj Žižek is critiquing Emmanuel Lévinas for arguing that the neighbor is the face who says here I am, that calls and commands at the same time. And one have responsibility towards

to in chapter 1 of this volume, can be considered as inhumane, with "zero level" existence as that of the *Muselmann* who has become external to humanity, reduced to inhumanity.[62] Therefore, according to Žižek, the notion of the neighbor needs to be not in the Judeo-Christian sense but rather in the Judeo-Freudian sense as "the bearer of monstrous otherness, inhuman neighbour, who cannot say here I am."[63] In this sense, the lynched person can be regarded as Žižekian faceless other.

The other point Žižek argues is the notion of loving the neighbor. He is against the notion of love that is considered as a moment of cutting into an indifferent multitude, privileging others against others. He rather prefers the notion of justice. Žižek claims that it is justice, not love, which has the capacity to encompass all, since loving all is impossible. Justice has the capacity to encompass "the Third" who is away from the face-to-face relationship, the other face, the monstrous, enigmatic one. For Žižek, "Justice and love are thus structurally incompatible: justice, not love, has to be blind, it has to disregard the privileged One whom I 'really understand.' What this means is that the Third is not secondary: it is always-already here, and the primordial ethical obligation is towards this Third who is NOT here in the face to face relationship, the one in shadow, like the absent child of a love-couple."[64] For Žižek, the neighbor is not displayed through a face, as we have seen in his discussion, but rather in the fundamental dimension a faceless other. Thus, in order to love one's neighbor there is a need to reduce them to a "pure subject."[65]

## The Politics of *Agapic* Solidarity: A *Perichoretic* Imagination

Thus far, I have first rehearsed what obliterates the relationship between the ethnic self and the ethnic other by many factors that resulted in the denial of the otherness of the ethnic other through ethnic-based violence, atrocities, fear, and resentment. Subsequently, I have situated the relation of the

---

that face a responsibility of commandment. But, according to Žižek, Lévinas missed those who have been treated as inhuman are forgotten. Because they cannot say here I am in order to receive what they owe to, responsibility to the other for example the *Muselmann*, in Nazi concentration camp. The only thing they encounter is the huge metal concentration camp.

62. Žižek, "Neighbours and Other Monsters," 160–61.
63. Žižek, "Neighbours and Other Monsters," 162.
64. Žižek, "Neighbours and Other Monsters," 183.
65. Žižek, "Neighbours and Other Monsters," 183–84.

ethnic self with the ethnic other in political theology of the neighbor that embeds in the figure of the neighbor in the Christian imperative, *loving the neighbor*. In doing so, I have sorted out the parallax of the neighbor first by presenting the etymological and theological meaning and significance of the term, neighbor, then, by conversing with Emmanuel Lévinas and Slavoj Žižek with a particular focus on their notion of the neighbor and the neighborly relationship. The former is concerned with responsibility to the face of the other, the neighbor for whom one is responsible without any precedents. The latter is concerned with two notions of the neighbor: the neighbor who is a faceless other whose face does not present itself to the face, and the neighbor who could also be the monster who seeks to destroy and hystericize, the traumatic intruder (cf. chapter 4, in which Sara A. Kedir discusses the depiction of the ethnic other as the "man-eating" *jiboch* [hyenas] and aganintoch [demons]).

This sub-chapter will engage in the task of critically correlating the different notions of the neighbor with Christian theological concepts of agape and perichoretic relations in order to harness a robust notion of moral responsibility that should guide self-other relationship that is instrumental in combating ethnic-based violence, conflicts, fear, and resentments. Even though both notions of the neighbor and neighborly relationships (Lévinasian and Žižekian) have the potentiality of curbing ethnic-based violence in their own regards, they are insufficient as ethnic-based atrocities have multidimensionality especially when embedded in long histories of ethnic atrocities, collective memories, grievance, and resentments, like the Ethiopian case. It needs an all-encompassing approach in order to harness a rich notion of moral responsibility towards framing the relationship between the ethnic self and other and also to halt ethnic-based violence and atrocities.

This comprehensive form of moral responsibility towards the neighbor can be illumined by tilting towards "*agapic* solidarity"[66] that is rooted in a *perichoretic* imagination of the Trinitarian analogy. The term *agapic* solidarity is borrowed from Rene Sanchez's doctoral dissertation and it refers to "a process which seeks to honor particularity without being parochial and seeks to be universal without being hegemonic."[67] To this end, I will first demonstrate the notion of *perichoresis* as a complete embrace, a turn to the face, the faceless other, and the monstrous other, thereby addressing all kinds of neighbors and neighborly relationships in the embrace. Second, I will exhibit the vitality and relevance of the *perichoretic* embraces as a

---

66. Sanchez, "Agapic Solidarity."
67. Sanchez, "Agapic Solidarity," 132.

moral response for the current Ethiopian context, which is characterized by ethnic-based conflicts and tensions.

## *Perichoresis*

Oliver Crisp explains *perichoresis* as a theological "black box" due to its high usage in the history of theology.[68] *Perichoresis* is a Greek term meaning "whirl or rotation" or as "to dance" or "dance around" in noun form and "going from one to another, walking around, encircling, enclosing, or embracing" in its verb form.[69] The initial Latin translation of the term is *circumincessio* and *circuminsessio*; the former comes from the verb *perichoreuo* and *perichoreo*, which implies a meaning of dynamic interpenetration and a movement, "to dance around" and "to encircle" or "encompass"; and the latter implies a lasting and resting mutual indwelling.[70]

In Christian theological history, *perichoresis* is used in two modes: Christological (nature *perichoresis*), which explains the relationship between the two natures of Christ, and Trinitarian (person *perichoresis*) that explains the relationships within the three persons of the Godhead.[71]

In Trinitarian theology, the concept of *perichoresis* is used to explain the relationship within the Godhead, which helps to affirm both the unity and distinctness of the divine persons.[72] *Perichoresis* preserves both the unity and the individuality of the Trinitarian person that avoids dividing God into three and yet maintaining the personal distinctions within God.[73] As Jürgen Moltmann avers,

> The doctrine of the perichoresis links together in a brilliant way the threeness and the unity, without reducing the threeness to unity, or dissolving the unity in threeness. The unity of the tri-unity lies in the eternal *perichoresis* of the Trinitarian persons.[74]

---

68. Crisp, "Problems with Perichoresis," 119.
69. Moltmann, "Perichoresis," 113.
70. Moltmann, "Perichoresis," 113–14.
71. Saint Gregory of Nazianzus (one of the Cappadocian Fathers) initially started the application of the concept of *perichoresis* in Christology in order to explain the relationship between the two natures of Christ in the hypostatic union. Then, Saint Maximus the confessor expounded the concept, and it is only John Damascus that used the term in Trinitarian form (Crisp, *Divinity and Humanity*, 270–78).
72. LaCugna, *God for Us*, 270–78.
73. Grenz, *Social God*, 317.
74. Moltmann, *Trinity*, 175.

Four points can be drawn for this. First, the Trinitarian relationship is a relationship of equality, mutuality, and reciprocity that holds both particularities and unity of the divine persons.[75] Second, in the Trinitarian relationship there is no domination or lordship of one person over the others; rather it is about "the fellowship of the three persons who are related to one another and exist in one another."[76] Third, in the Trinitarian relationship of *perichoretic* embrace there is no subordination; instead, the three persons are co-equal: they live and become visible in one another and through one another.[77] Fourth, *perichoretic* relationship avoids sameness and holds their distinctiveness; this helps us to view others beyond us.

In his book titled *The One, the Three and the many*, Colin Gunton strongly argues the notion of *perichoresis* can provide a valuable and suggestive ways for human beings at different levels. According to Gunton, since the notion of *perichoresis* is applied to relationships constitutive of persons, it will therefore give us a framework of perfect relationship.[78] Important significant considerations can be drawn to the figure of the neighbor and the relationship entailed in it. First, as I have already demonstrated, the Trinitarian relationship explained in *perichoretic* embrace is a relationship based on a dynamic movement towards the other.

This dynamism, *circumincessio*, a movement of going from the one to the other to embrace with love, has affinity to Lévinasian notion of proximity, a movement of the self towards the other, because in proximity there is this perpetual movement towards the other, the face, and that movement is responsibility characterized by subjectivity.[79] But, the Trinitarian dynamism goes a step beyond the Lévinasian notion of proximity that is non-reciprocal and asymmetrical. The *perichoretic* embrace acknowledges reciprocity but not as in a sense of gift exchange that Lévinas feared but rather reciprocity of responsibility. This reciprocity of responsibility started in the creation of humans. In the creation story the triune God created humanity with "the gift of life," being created in the image and likeness of God out of the Triune God goodness with a responsibility of caring and stewarding creation, to give that gift to others. This is the relationship

---

75. LaCugna, *God for Us*, 173–74.
76. Moltmann, *Trinity*, 175.
77. Moltmann, *Trinity*, 176.
78. Gunton, *One, the Three and the Many*, 230.
79. Lévinas, *Otherwise than Being*, 81–86.

human beings are called into.[80] Human responsibility towards the neighbor is embedded in this giveness, the "graced human existence."[81]

Again, the dynamic movement towards the other not only illumines the Lévinasian notion of proximity, but also the notion of the face and the Third. The Trinitarian *perichoretic* relationship is a relationship of equality, mutuality, and respect without domination or subordination while also acknowledging particularities and distinctiveness without reducing the subject to sameness. This acknowledgment celebrates the community of others and avoids commonalities or sameness and treats individuals as a "pure subject," which Lévinas argues about with the Third. Any encounter with the neighbor is an encounter of relationship modeled after the Triune God relationship through which the gift of life is reciprocity of responsibility.

The other point that can be drawn from *perichoresis* is that the immanent Trinity manifests itself as the economic trinity, through the history of salvation.[82] In the history of salvation, humanity is called into a relationship with the creator through the work of Christ in the Christ event, that Christ emptied himself and was crucified in order to save and reconcile us with God. Thus, the Kenotic Love is a model of relationship for humanity to reflect the *perichoresis*. That bears the notion of self-giving love as well as the justice of God. Kenotic love is given to all in spite of status, class, ethnic identity, and wealth.

The demonstration of kenotic love can be seen in two ways. One is on the incarnation when God reduced himself to humanity in order to save humanity from sin that is the self-giving love. The other is on the cross when Christ himself became the "faceless other" who died not his own sin but for the sin of the whole world. It is by these works that humanity gains entrance into the *perichoretic* embrace. Christ's death was as that of the *"Muselmann"*[83] but it also goes beyond the Žižekian notion, due to the vindication of the resurrection. Moreover, Christ's death also bears the deaths of many sinners, the monstrous others who crucified him. Thus, the *perichoretic* embrace welcomes all kind of neighbors, the face, the faceless other, and the monstrous other.

80. Tanner, *Jesus, Humanity and the Trinity*, 90–94.
81. Tanner, *Jesus, Humanity and the Trinity*, 13.
82. Grenz, *Social God*, 79.
83. Žižek and Milbank, *Monstrosity of Christ*, 18–21.

## The Politics of *Agapeic* Solidarity: The Vitality and Relevance of *Perichoresis* for the Ethiopian Context

So far, I have attempted to demonstrate the *perichoretic* embrace as an all-encompassing view of the neighbor and their concerns that even go deeper than the face, the faceless other, and the monstrous neighbor. Now, I will turn into the politics of *agapic* solidarity showing the vitality of *perichoretic* embrace for the Ethiopian context with the aim of drawing a comprehensive moral responsibility towards halting ethnic based atrocities. In order to do so, I will draw some examples of moral principles against ethnic-based atrocities.

*Agapeic* solidarity is only possible through the *perichoretic* embrace. In the *perichoretic* embrace, the immanent Trinity, the relationship among the Godhead, is a loving relationship. As Moltmann declares, such a loving relationship retains the particularity as well as difference and unity of the three persons of the Trinity.[84] The Immanent Trinity overflows, or manifests itself, in the economic trinity, in the economy of salvation; Christ, one person of the Trinity emptied himself in order to save humanity. We, human beings, are drawn into this loving relationship through the work of Christ, whose atonement satisfied the justice of God and we are called to remember this justice of God through the sacrament of the breaking of the bread. Three ethical notions can be drawn from the *perichoretic* embrace, the manifestation of the immanent trinity in the economic trinity, which can provide a prototype for our human-human interaction, which further has a potentiality to avoid and challenge violence and foster peaceful co-existence in a multiethnic context.

First, *perichoretic* embrace challenges sameness via acknowledging identity, particularity, and difference. Some of the ethnic-based violence in Ethiopia emanates from an intolerance of difference; people tend to expel those who are not from the same group. This is evident in the displacement and violent extermination of ethnic others. The analogy of *perichoretic* embrace could bring light to such undesirable relationship between the ethnic self and the ethnic other. The three persons in the Godhead have three distinct but at the same time one person without losing, conflating, dismantling, and obliterating their particularities. Such relationship challenges any sort of domination, oppression, assimilation, and ethnocentrism in the relationship between the ethnic self and the other by enhancing equality, diversity, particularity, and difference. As a result, it encourages the recognition of the ethnic other, belongingness, and representation.

---

84. Moltmann, *Trinity and the Kingdom*, 175–76.

Second, *perichoretic* embrace can challenge grievances and resentment of collective memories. This might not be an easy task as ethnic-based atrocities in Ethiopia have a long complex history of victimhood, domination, and conflation of identities and cultures by many factors like state-formation, religious expansion, and political ideologies. For instance, the current ethnic relations and the politics of identity of the Oromo nationalist movement is characterized by the narratives of domination–oppression and narratives of victimhood which have influenced ethnic relationships in Ethiopia through grievance, anger, hatred, and resentments of collective memories of the past.[85]

In the *perichoretic* embrace, *agapeic solidarity*, the immanent trinity manifests itself in the economic trinity through the kenotic love, the self-giving love on the cross for justice. That love is celebrated via remembrance, and through the breaking of the bread we enter into the memory of our sinfulness and the work of Christ on the cross. Such an imagination can be helpful to remember those who are afflicted and affected by ethnic-based conflicts and so on. In such remembrance, we will give recognition to the evil act, to the victims of their pain, grief, and suffering, while simultaneously recognizing the possibility of forgiveness of the griever and healing of the grieved, and of moving forward.

Third, and finally, in the *perichoretic* embrace of *agapic* solidarity we engage in a hope of a new beginning. Through the economy of salvation, we find the forgiveness of our sins and reconciliation with God, the Trinity, and are given an eschatological hope to be restored and consummated in God's love. Therefore, such an encounter will lead us to forgiveness and reconciliation and starts a new beginning in our neighborly relationship. Through the figure of the neighbor that embeds in *perichoretic* embrace one finds respect, recognition, and diversity in unity, healing of past wounds, recognition of pain and suffering as well as remembrance in order to forgive, heal, reconcile, move forward, and enjoy the hope of new beginning.

## Conclusion

The relationship between the ethnic self and the ethnic other in Ethiopia has a complex history influenced by many factors that are still stirring ethnic-based conflicts and atrocities in the country. Ethnic relations and identity politics in Ethiopia oscillate between the history of oppression-domination, victimizer–victimized, and memory–resentment. Together with many other factors, such history has contributed to the displacement

---

85. Theodros, *Politics of Metanoia*, 114–27.

of millions of people, genocidal ethnic cleansing, rape, and robbery by neighbors against neighbors.

The relationship between the ethnic self and the neighbor needs to be embedded in a well-founded moral responsibility that has the potentiality of halting violence and enhancing peaceful coexistence. This is done through the figure of the neighbor, as a point of intersection between the ethical, political, and theological. The neighbor could be the face, the faceless other, or the traumatic intruder, the monstrous other, or the *perichoretic* embracer. The relationship between the ethnic self and the other is embedded in our being created in the image of the Triune God and has its prototype in the *perichoretic* embrace. Such relatedness is characterized by the capacity to hold difference, appreciate particularities, acknowledge identities, and a gift of life that extends to give to others.

In *perichoresis*, justice and love are conjoined together: whenever there is love there is also justice. Consequently, the ethnic other is the neighbor we are called to love; the enemy is our neighbor; and the intruder is our neighbor, not only our resemblant. Such kenotic love is a love of justice which is only possible via loving the neighbor. Loving the neighbor is exercising *agapeic* solidarity which makes human relatedness and love possible. In *agapeic* solidarity, not only do we encounter God through the other, the neighbor, but it further creates an opportunity of recognition for otherness. It also gives a model of repentance, forgiveness, reconciliation, and directing to a new beginning of hope for peaceful coexistence. Therefore, loving the neighbor, the ethnic other, is participating in the divine *agapeic* solidarity, which is ethical, politico-theological by its essence, and also counters violence.

## Bibliography

Bekalu Atnafu Taye. "Ethnic Federalism and Conflict in Ethiopia." *African Journal on Conflict Resolution* 17.2 (2017) 41–66.

Bretherton, Luke. *Christ and the Common Life: Political Theology and the Case of Democracy*. Grand Rapids: Eerdmans, 2019.

Cohen, Hermann. *The Ethics of Maimonides*. Translated by Almut Sh. Buckstein. Madison, WI: Wisconsin, 2004.

Crisp, Oliver D. *Divinity and Humanity: The Incarnation Reconsidered*. Cambridge: Cambridge University Press, 2007.

———. "Problems with Perichoresis." *Tyndale Bulletin* 56.1 (2005) 119–40.

Davis, Charles. *Theology and Political Society*. Cambridge: Cambridge University Press, 1994.

Deslauriers, Marguerite, and Pierre Destr´ee, eds. *The Cambridge Companion to Aristotle Politics*. Cambridge: Cambridge University Press, 2013.

"Ethiopia: Events of 2018." https://www.hrw.org/world-report/2019/country-chapters/ethiopia.
Fagenblat, Michael. "The Concept of Neighbor in Jewish and Christian Ethics." In *The Jewish Annotated New Testament: New Standard Revised Version*, edited by Amy-Jill Levine and Marc Zvi Brettler, 540–43. Oxford: Oxford University Press, 2011.
Gade, Christian B. N. "The Historical Development of the Written Discourses on Ubuntu." *South African Journal of Philosophy* 30.3 (2011) 303–29.
Grenz, Stanley. *The Social God and The Relational Self: A Trinitarian Theology of the Imago Dei*. London: Westminster, 2001.
Gunton, Colin E. *The One, the Three and the Many: God, Creation, and the Culture of Modernity*. Cambridge: Cambridge University Press, 2004.
Gupta, Nijay K. "Neighbor, Neighbor Love." In *The Dictionary of Scripture and Ethics*, edited by Joel B. Green, 547–48. Grand Rapids: Baker, 2011.
Hand, Seán. *The Levinas Reader*. Blackwell Readers. Oxford: Blackwell, 1989.
Handelman, Susan. "Facing the Other in Levinas, Perelman and Rosenzweig." *Religion & Literature* 22.2/3 (Summer–Autumn, 1990) 61–84.
Kattan, Naim. "The Neighbour." In *The Neighbour and Other Stories*, 9–20. Toronto: McLelland and Stewart, 1982.
LaCugna, Catherine M. *God for Us: The Trinity and Christian Life*. San Francisco: HarperCollins, 1973.
Levin, Donald. *Greater Ethiopia: The Evolution of a Multiethnic Society*. Chicago: University of Chicago Press, 1974.
Lévinas, Emmanuel. *Alterity and Transcendence*. Translated by Michael B. Smith. London: Athlone, 1999.
———. *The Levinas Reader*. Edited by Sean Hand. Oxford: Basil Blackwell, 1989.
———. *Otherwise than Being or Beyond Essence*. Translated by Alphonso Lingis. Pittsburgh: Duquesne University Press, 1974.
———. *Totality and infinity: an Essay on Exteriority*. Translated by Alphonso Lingis. Pittsburgh: Duquesne University Press, 1969.
McFarland, Ian. "Who Is My Neighbour? The Good Samaritan as a Source for Theological Anthropology." *Modern Theology* 17.1 (January 2001) 57–66.
Mendes-Flohr, Paul. *Love, Accusative and Dative: Reflection on Leviticus 19:18*. The B. G. Rudolph Lectures in Judaic Studies New Series, Lecture Four. New York: Syracuse University Press, 2007.
Mescher, Marcus. "Doing Likewise: A Theology of Neighbor and Pedagogy for Neighbor-Formation." PhD diss., Boston College, 2013. https://dlib.bc.edu/islandora/object/bc-ir:104081/datastream/PDF/view.
Moltmann, Jürgen. "Perichoresis: An Old Magic Word for a New Trinitarian Theology." In *Trinity, Community and Power: Mapping Trajectories in Wesleyan Theology*, edited by Douglas Meeks, 111–25. Nashville: Kingswood, 2000.
———. *Trinity and the Kingdom*. Minneapolis: Fortress, 1993.
Morgan, Michael L. *The Cambridge Introduction to Emmanuel Levinas*. Cambridge: Cambridge University Press, 2011.
Mumbere, Daniel. "Ethiopia Govt Confirms Thousands Killed, Millions Displaced by Ethnic Clashes." *Africa News*, September 25, 2019. https://www.africanews.com/2019/09/25/ethiopia-govt-confirms-thousands-killed-millions-displaced-by-ethnic-clashes.

Painter, Joe. "The Politics of the Neighbour." In *Environment and Planning D: Society and Space* 30.3 (2012) 515–33.
Phillips, Elizabeth. *Political Theology: A Guide for the Perplexed*. London: T. & T. Clark, 2012.
Reinhard, Kenneth, et al. "Introduction." In *The Neighbor: Three Inquires in Political Theology*. Chicago: The University of Chicago Press, 2005.
Rosenzweig, Franz. *The Star of Redemption*. Translated by Barbara E. Galli. Madison, WI: University of Wisconsin, 2005.
Sanchez, Rene. "Agapic Solidarity: Practicing the Love Command in a Globalized Reality." PhD diss., Boston University, 2013. http://hdl.handle.net/2345/3294.
Schmitt, Carl. *Political Theology: Four Chapters on the Concept of Sovereignty*. Translated by George Schwab. Cambridge: MIT Press, 1985.
Scott, Peter, and William Cavanaugh, eds. *The Blackwell Companion to Political Theology*. Oxford: Blackwell, 2004.
Semir Yesuf. "What Is Driving Ethiopia's Ethnic Conflicts?" *ISS East Africa Report* 28 (November 2019). https://media.africaportal.org/documents/What_is_driving_Ethiopias_ethnic_conflicts.pdf.
Sim, Stuart, ed. *The Routledge Companion to Postmodernism*. London: Routledge, 2001.
———. *The Routledge Companion to Postmodernism*. 3rd ed. Routledge Companions. London: Routledge, 2011.
Spencer, Stephen. *Race and Ethnicity: Culture, Identity and Representation*. New York: Routledge, 2006.
Tanner Kathryn. *Jesus, Humanity and the Trinity: A Brief Systematic Theology*. Minneapolis: Fortress, 2001.
Tekalign Nega Angore. "Reconstruction of Ethiopia's Collective Memory by Rewriting its History." PhD diss., Tilburg University, Netherland, 2017.
Theodros A. Teklu. *The Politics of Matanoia: Towards a Post Nationalistic Political Theology in Ethiopia*. Frankfurt: Peter Lang, 2014.
Youdit Tariku. "Political Theology of the Neighbour: Reflections from Saint Maximus the Confessor towards Challenging Violence." MTh Thesis, Ethiopian Graduate School of Theology, Addis Ababa, 2016.
Žižek, Slavoj. "Neighbours and Other Monsters: A Plea to Ethical Violence." In *The Neighbour: Three Inquires in Political Theology*, edited by Slavoj Žižek et al., 134–90. Chicago: The University of Chicago Press, 2005.
———. *The Parallax View*. Massachusetts; Cambridge: MIT Press, 2006.
———. "A Plea for Ethical Violence." *The Bible & Critical Theory* 1.1 (2004).
Žižek, Slavoj, and John Milbank. *The Monstrosity of Christ: Paradox and Dialectics*. Massachusetts: MIT Press, 2009.
Zukić, Naida. "My Neighbor's Face and Similar Vulgarities." *Liminalities: A Journal of Performance Studies* 5.5 (2009) 1–15. http://liminalities.net/5-4/neighbor.pdf.

# 8

# After Self Assertion

## On a *Paraclesis* of a Political Theology of *Kenosis*

SAMSON TADELLE DEMO

A THEOLOGY THAT ASPIRES to be relevant needs to raise the fundamental question: "What time is it?" Without this diagnostic "thick description," one cannot proceed to answer, "What do we do *now*?"[1] Such an engagement depends on the realistic analysis of the situation on the ground. Hence, any theological analysis, if it aspires to be valid and relevant, should be founded on such thick description, or be "a kind of ethnography."[2] In this regard, this chapter scrutinizes the current political dynamics of Ethiopia in such a way as to provide a moral input to the political aporia. In this manner it attempts to delineate a way forward on what we can do now.

If one investigates the historical trajectory of politics that has transpired in the history of modern Ethiopia, especially after Emperor Téwodros, it is conspicuous that it is a checkered history driven by a centralist agenda to forge a polity that has depoliticized the variegated people groups. This culminated in the 1974 revolution that sideslipped into a political morass from which we were unable to come out till now. According to Merera Gudina, the way forward from "a zero-sum political game [that] lacked the art of compromise" is "a *behavioural* change on the part of today's political elites" with a

---

1. Smith, "Foreword," 11.
2. Smith, "Foreword," 11.

seriousness of "soul-searching."[3] Such a change of behavior can "mediate and accommodate diversities rather than exacerbate differences."[4]

This chapter argues that such a mediating principle from which we can derive a moral injunction that is capable of effecting a behavioral change can be gleaned from the theology of Hans Urs von Balthasar (1905–88). Balthasar is a Catholic theologian who wrestled with the immanent forces of secularism to forge his sacramental theology. Thus, his theology of kenosis can offer us a way out of our political deadlock, which is the outcome of a full-fledged immanentism. This immanentic process is featured in the over-assertion of ethnic identity, which is taken as the sole marker of political identity. Affirmation of our identity, or self-assertion, in whatever form is a commendable endeavor. But over-asserting ethnic identity is oblivious to transcendental values from which it derives its significance. Thus, it can be easily instrumentalized and idolized when taken as an end by itself. The objective of this chapter is to show that, after self-assertion, we need a kenotic turn to politics to impugn the nihilistic tendencies of the instrumentalization of ethnic identity. This kenotic turn offers us an ethic of mediation that quickens us to move forward from our stagnation.

To execute this task, we need to undertake a hermeneutical scrutiny of the political anthropologies that grounded the politics before and after the revolution. Then, we can proceed to formulate an alternative political theology of kenosis, which can offer the way out of the political vertigo. After deliberating on the nature of the political anthropology of kenosis, we proceed to demonstrate how such a political theology of kenosis can offer the morality is urgently needed now, followed by a conclusion.

## The Political Anthropology of Ethiopia: From Univocity to Equivocity

The focus of this section is to rehearse the politico-anthropological principles that undergird the form of governance from Emperor Téwodros till the post-1991 era. At the risk of generalization, we have traversed from a univocal politics into an equivocal politics in the contemporary form. Univocal politics aspires to forge homogenization by disregarding the inherent diversity, while equivocal politics feasts on the affirmation of difference as its end. The recognition of difference is a worthwhile step, but we need to go beyond that to avert the political stalemate. Such a move creates a feasible

---

3. Merera, "Contradictory Interpretations," 128. Emphasis added.
4. Merera, "Contradictory Interpretations," 129.

political ground that facilitates human flourishing. This task prepares us to formulate an alternative anthropology of kenosis that offers a way forward after the unmediated self-assertive equivocity into an intermediated space offered by theology of kenosis of Balthasar.

## The Univocal Politics up to the Därg Regime

What has transpired predominantly since Emperor Téwodros up to the reign of Emperor Haile Silassie with an accentuating centripetal force is the formation of a homogeneous state. This has created *"Homo Æthiopicus"* in the narrative ideological furnace of "Greater Ethiopia."[5] This homogenization of the diverse people groups in Ethiopia is assimilation into the cultural symbols of Amharic language as *"pax amharica,"* and the adoption of Orthodox Christianity.[6] The production of this image of citizen–subject may be associated with the narrative of "Greater Ethiopia."

In this regard, the mandate for the unification project is grounded in the political theology of *Kəbrä Nägäśt*. In this vein, Donald Levine asserts that *Kəbrä Nägäśt*, as "a societal script," is an embodiment of "symbols that provides specialized cultural legitimation both for the societal enterprise as a whole and for privileged positions within society."[7] More specifically, *Kəbrä Nägäśt* blended the diverse components of an Ethiopian self-image into working synthesis that could define a national mission and legitimate the privileged positions of those responsible for bearing this mission.[8]

Here, one notes the missional thrust of *Kəbrä Nägäśt* for the assimilationist agenda. In the same vein, Bahru notes that the cultural and political legitimacy of the Shawan political preponderancy dictated in *Kəbrä Nägäśt* was evident during the reign of Emperor Haile Silassie. Bahru adds that the only history of Ethiopia is that of the Semitic north that considers "the people of the south as objects rather than subjects of history."[9]

Moreover, according to Mohammed Girma, the notion of "covenantal centralization" is wielded in the pages of this fourteenth-century document. Thus, the ideological bearing of *Kəbrä Nägäśt* is a theological justification of uncontested political power for the kings of the Solomonic line.[10] The "mas-

---

5. Theodros, *Politics of Metanoia*, 87–99.
6. Theodros, *Politics of Metanoia*, 96–97.
7. Levine, *Greater Ethiopia*, 101.
8. Levine, *Greater Ethiopia*, 107.
9. Bahru, "Burden of History," 19.
10. Mohammed, *Religion and Social Change*, 12–16.

ter text"[11] of *Kǝbrä Nägäśt* that has functioned to forge *Homo Æthiopicus* is a kind of univocal principle.

According to William Desmond's metaphysical sense of being, "the univocal sense stresses sameness to the diminution or underplaying of differences."[12] The accentuation on "unmediated unity" fails to consider "the complex differences" with its reductionist account of being.[13] This univocal mode of being grounds immanence in different forms. Desmond mentions "subject creation to the homogeneity of a projected human measure," and revolutionary Marxist totalitarianism as types of univocal immanence among many.[14]

In this regard, one finds correlation of such immanentism in the intensification of univocal politics since Emperor Téwodros. More specifically, the ideological instrument of *Kǝbrä Nägäśt* forged the formation of a homogenized Ethiopian*ness* in the image of *homo Æthiopicus*. Here, the missional and formative impulse of *Kǝbrä Nägäśt* has been deployed to rob Christianity of its "transcendental values" and instill "system–integrative values" in its place, thereby rendering the ecclesial realm an instrument of the state.[15]

Similarly, the full-fledged immanentism that characterize the Därg regime is reflected in its denigration of transcendence underwritten in the ideology of "scientific materialism."[16] Thus, the process towards immanence started by *Kǝbrä Nägäśt* comes to its apogee in the secularization of the state during the Därg regime. The overt denial of theistic worldview at the state level led to the demolition of transcendental values. The eclipse of transcendence gave way to untrammeled immanence. The consummation of the univocal metaphysics that grounds immanence is "tyrannical politics."[17] Such tyranny is expressed in the form of "an organized outrage to the *passio essendi* [passion of being]."[18] This is the final seal of a univocal politics.

---

11. Teshale, *Making of Modern Ethiopia*, 12, as cited in Theodros, *Politics of Metanoia*, 90.
12. Desmond, *God and the Between*, 9.
13. Desmond, *Perplexity and Ultimacy*, 12.
14. Desmond, "Neither Servility nor Sovereignty," 161.
15. Theodros, *Politics of Metanoia*, 103.
16. Mohammed, *Religion and Social Change*, 96.
17. Desmond, "Neither Servility nor Sovereignty," 164.
18. Desmond, "Neither Servility nor Sovereignty," 164.

## The Equivocal Politics of the Post-1991 Era

Bahru Zewde asserts that modern historiography that has dominated the historical research has encountered a "'postmodernist' challenge." As also noted by Afework Hailu in this volume, this challenge questioned the positivistic tone of standard historiography and portrayed history as a type of literature.[19] In this regard, the metanarrative of the societal script in the period preceding 1974 has been rendered illegitimate by the revolution.[20] Similarly, Jon Abbink concurs that, albeit without traversing the modern phase, the post-1991 period of Ethiopia shows post-modern features, like the "casting out of grand narratives, its emphasizing multiple identities, and in its encouraging of relativist commitments."[21]

In this regard, after the demolishing of the metanarrative of *Kəbrä Nägäśt*, the Ethiopian historiography is filled with "contradictory interpretations of Ethiopian history by competing ethnic elites."[22] Now we have "several stories with as many narrators," to put it in postmodern parlance.[23] The unprecedented emphasis given to ethnic identity has given rise to a plethora of dissenting versions of history. Such a "freezing [of] ethnic identity as the prime marker of political allegiance" provided the ground for divergent and counterpoint propositions that curtailed political consensus.[24]

This stalemate is associated with the fact that each interpretation is obsessed with a narcissistic "itching" of its wound by recourse to narrative of victimhood.[25] Via the process of reification of history, "the privileging of victimhood has led to the mobilization of the categories of the figure of the victim—whether Oromo or Tigrean or others."[26] Similarly, the default tone of the micro-narratives is a chanting "in the emotions, nostalgia, and painful experiences of the ethnic past."[27]

This has led to the ossification of the fluid concept of "ethnicity" in such a way as to forge "*homo ethnicus*" that aspires for "the assertion of cultural uniqueness in the struggle for the right to self-determination."[28] Hence, the

---

19. Bahru, "Century of Historiography," 16.
20. Bahru, "Century of Historiography," 19.
21. Abbink, "Ethnicity and Constitutionalism," 173.
22. Merera, "Contradictory Interpretations," 119.
23. Mohammed, *Religion and Social Change*, 108.
24. Yonatan, *Ethnic Diversity and Federalism*, 235–36.
25. Theodros, *Politics of Metanoia*, 126–27.
26. Theodros, *Politics of Metanoia*, 127.
27. Mohammed, *Religion and Social Change*, 108.
28. Theodros, *Politics of Metanoia*, 127.

resultant *homo ethnicus* is driven by the will to "self-determination, including the right to secession."[29] Such a "microhistory" of victimhood by different "ethnic" categories has replaced the "metahistory" or "grand historical narrative" of the pre-Därg era.[30]

The "paradigm of compartmentalization" that recognizes individuals only with the brand of ethnicity marked upon them rings in tune with the ethos of the equivocal metaphysics à la postmodernism.[31] The enthronement of *homo ethnicus* in the political arena after the demise of the univocal politics of the earlier eras birthed ethnic politics founded on equivocal metaphysics. In this regard, Desmond posits that the equivocal sense of being refers to "unmediated difference . . . and zones of tension that resist any simple reduction to univocal unity." In equivocal metaphysics there is "sheer plurality" without "any deeper relatedness." The upshot of equivocity is not community building but "a dispersal of beings that is merely fragmenting."[32]

In this regard, the reaction of the deconstruction of univocity yields the shattering of being into equivocity.[33] However, the immanence inherent in univocity is not deconstructed. Thus, "postmodern immanence [of equivocity] is still immanence" because it is fetched from "the same gene pool" of univocal immanence that exudes the "will to power."[34] On the political horizon, this implies that "the totalitarian form may have mutated into a pluralistic form or anarchist form."[35] Similar to the univocal politics up to the Därg regime, the immanence of the equivocity of *homo ethnicus* merely orbits "around itself," effectively curtailing vestiges of transcendence.[36]

In order for the present aporia of politics to move forward from the self-assertion of the equivocity of *homo ethnicus*, a mediating principle that offers space for relationship among the equivocal politics must be in place. As the loss of transcendence via "the immanent absolutization of the political" ultimately leads to "loss of the wisdom of the immanent," a mediating principle must reinstall transcendence to redeem the sphere of immanence.[37]

---

29. The Constitution of the Federal Democratic Republic of Ethiopia, art. 39.1.
30. Bahru, "Century of Historiography," 16.
31. Mohammed, *Religion and Social Change*, 103.
32. Desmond, *Perplexity and Ultimacy*, 13.
33. Desmond, *Perplexity and Ultimacy*, 13.
34. Desmond, "Neither Servility nor Sovereignty," 161.
35. Desmond, "Neither Servility nor Sovereignty," 161.
36. Desmond, "Neither Servility nor Sovereignty," 161.
37. Desmond, "Neither Servility nor Sovereignty," 156.

This can be located in the kenosis of Jesus Christ, who is both transcendently "beyond" and immanently in our "midst" in a truly "metaxological" sense. For Desmond, metaxological metaphysics emanates from the double sense of "*meta*," meaning both "in the midst" (or "*metaxu*") and "beyond."[38] Unlike the unmediated equivocity, the metaxological sense emphasizes "mediated community" which is "hospitable to the mediation of the other, or transcendent, out of its own otherness."[39] The metaxological goads us beyond the festering of equivocal politics by rectifying the disequilibrated metaphysical matrices of immanence (in the midst) and transcendence (beyond).

In a subtle manner, Desmond locates the acme of metaxology in Jesus Christ by citing a kenotically framed poem of G. M. Hopkin, "As Kingfishers Catch Fire": "for Christ plays in ten thousand places/lovely in limbs, and lovely in eyes not his/To the Father through the features of men's faces."[40] In other words, the nexus of the coordinates of immanence and transcendence zeroes in on Christ, who is the "*Concretum universale*," or concrete universal. This is a double affirmation of particularity in his incarnation; while beyond comparison as being God, which affirms his universality, in the analogical syntax of Balthasar.[41] Similarly, in terms that allude to kenotic act of Christ, Desmond synopsizes by proposing that

> the singular person Jesus is the Incarnation of God—God as singular human being undergoing the time and mortality of the human, and divine even in the death that is the last suffering of our sojourn in the between.[42]

The space of the metaxology or "the between" that Desmond adumbrates here finds robust explication in the theology of kenosis of Balthasar. With this in mind, we will deliberate on the nature of theology of kenosis as depicted by Balthasar in the next sub-chapter.

## Theology of Kenosis in Hans Urs von Balthasar

In the previous section, we looked at an interpretation of the political anthropologies of the Ethiopian government from the time of Emperor

---

38. Desmond, *Being and the Between*, 44.
39. Desmond, *Intimate Strangeness of Being*, 36.
40. Hopkins, *Gerard Manley Hopkins*, 129 as cited in Desmond, *Intimate Strangeness*, 245.
41. Balthasar, *Explorations*, 170.
42. Desmond, *God and the Between*, 194.

Téwodros till the present administration. We deployed the metaphysical lens of William Desmond to show the univocity of totalitarian regimes till the Därg regime and equivocity of the post-1991 government. In this section, we will focus on the theology of kenosis in Balthasar's theology that offers a metaxological milieu from which we can derive morality. This enables us to move forward from the state of stagnation into a new political horizon of consensus. Such a state facilitates intermediation between communities and political entities to construct a stable form of governance that fosters human flourishing.

## Hans Urs von Balthasar: Theological Trajectory from Analogy to Kenosis

Hans Urs von Balthasar (1905–88) is a Catholic theologian who trenchantly exposed the drift of Western culture from the sense of wonder of metaphysics to a materialist enchantment of the "instrumentalist–positivist" ambience of modernity.[43] More particularly, his theology is birthed out of an engagement with the world where totalitarianism and fascism were looming to destroy Europe.[44] The influence of Henri de Lubac, one of the theologians who forged the sensibility of *nouvelle théologie*, was formative in Balthasar's theological imagination. Regarding his encounter with de Lubac, Balthasar says: "He showed us the way beyond the scholastic stuff to the Fathers of Church . . . and Daniélou, Bouillard and I . . . got down to Origen, Gregory of Nyssa, and Maximus."[45]

The *nouvelle* theologians were concerned with "the horizontalizing (the exclusion of vertical relationship with God) or immanentizing (the rejection of any transcendent impact on historical cause and effect)"[46] process in the modern cultural development. Their vision was to "reconnect nature and the supernatural." [47] This "inescapable duality" is the beginning of theological reflection for Balthasar.[48] Thus, bearing the sacramental perspective fermented within the *nouvelle* theologians, Balthasar's theological grammar is "determined by a fundamental commitment to

---

43. Shindler, "Preface," xi–xii.
44. Wigley, *Balthasar's Trilogy*, 16, 18.
45. Balthasar, *Prüfut alles*, 9, as cited in Henrici, "Hans Urs von Balthasar," 12.
46. Boersma, *Nouvelle Théologie*, 11.
47. Boersma, *Nouvelle Théologie*, 5. Balthasar, *Theo-Logic*, 1:637.
48. Balthasar, "Résumé of My Thought," 2.

the analogical knowledge of being" as a consideration on *"identity-in-difference* of the world and God."[49]

In other words, on the transcendent realm of the triune God, there is a difference of persons where one cannot be reduced to the other. But, at the same time, the persons are related in unity grounded by divine essence. This "primal reality" is analogically related, albeit with great dissimilarity, with the finite order of creation. In words reminiscent of Desmond's metaxological senses, individual being is "not something closed in itself," as a univocal being; neither it is something that derives its concept "outside of itself," as an equivocal being. Rather, it is "open to the totality that transcends them," as an analogical being, having a "unity in distinction from the totality of Being" from which it derives its specificity.[50]

In this vein, Balthasar avers that the "insurmountable distance between God and his creature" can only be comprehended from the vantage point of analogy.[51] Here, analogy is understood as "a relationship between two entities allowing for some similarity and equivalence without insisting on either a total identity or a total distinction,"[52] as succinctly defined in the Fourth Lateran Council: "ever-greater dissimilarity however great similarity."[53] Thus, theology, for Balthasar, can be approached from "an analogy not of an abstract Being, but of Being as it is encountered concretely in its attributes."[54]

In this manner, Balthasar set his sails off into the deep theological waters within the matrix of the traditional transcendental attributes of Being: "the One, the Good, the True and the Beautiful" as analogical expressions of God's "plenitude."[55] In this manner, the transcendentals are mapped onto his trilogy: *The Glory of The Lord, Theo-Drama, and Theo-Logic*. Hence, Balthasar correlates "the Beautiful" with God's revelation as a "theological *aesthetique*" that is consummated in Jesus Christ. This is followed by "the Good" which finds its analogy in God's "*dramatique*" entrance "into an alliance with us in Jesus Christ." The last oeuvre of Balthasar's trilogy deals with God's "*logique* (a *theo-logique*)," which is a representation of "The True."[56]

---

49. Gardner and Moss, "Something Like Time; Something Like the Sexes," 76. Emphasis original.
50. Treitler, "Authentic Theology," 175.
51. Balthasar, "Résumé of My Thought," 3.
52. Wigley, *Balthasar's Trilogy*, 16.
53. Wigley, *Balthasar's Trilogy*, 40.
54. Balthasar, "Résumé of My Thought," 3.
55. Balthasar, "Résumé of My Thought," 3.
56. Balthasar, "Résumé of My Thought," 4.

The role of creation in Balthasar is "participat[ion] in the transcendentals only in a partial, fragmentary fashion."[57]

The concept of analogy of being (*analogia entis*) comes into sharp focus in Balthasar via Erich Przywara (another source of inspiration for Balthasar),[58] especially in Przywara's engagement with Karl Barth's analogy of faith (*analogia fidei*).[59] Barth rejected analogy of being interpreting it as a "neutral concept of being" that ascribes "an indissoluble relation" between God and the world, contrary to the "real distinction" propounded in Thomas Aquinas's theology.[60] Thus, Balthasar, while consenting with Barth's "narrowing of everything" to the christological center of divine revelation, avers that the analogy of faith leaves little "breathing room between creation and covenant."[61]

In this regard, Balthasar employs the image of "hourglass" that helps to mediate a way between the emphasis on analogy of being that leads to a univocal understanding of being (Duns Scotus and late Scholastic rationalism) and analogy of faith that tends toward a negation of God and creation, as in an equivocal direction.[62] Thus, Balthasar says that in the analogy of the hourglass

> the two contagious vessels (God and creature) meet only at the narrow passage through the center: where they both encounter each other in Jesus Christ. The purpose of the image is to show that there is no other point of contact between the two chambers of the glass.[63]

Thus, analogy of being and analogy of faith find their acme in Christ, "the concrete *analogia entis*," who transcendentally possesses the "form of God" (*morphē theou*, Phil 2:6) and, immanently, "the form of a servant."[64] In Christ, "the supernatural 'heightening of tension' in man does not inhumanly tear his existence apart."[65] For Balthasar, this occurs because of the nature of God as "essentially Love" that necessarily "supposes the Other" in the triune life of God and "the otherness of creation" which is "an image of

---

57. Balthasar, "Résumé of My Thought," 3.

58. Henrici, "Philosophy of Hans Urs von Balthasar," 165.

59. Boersma, *Nouvelle Théologie*, 131–32.

60. Treitler, "Authentic Theology," 173.

61. Balthasar, *Theology of Karl Barth*, 256.

62. Treitler, "Authentic Theology," 173. Balthasar, *Theo-Drama*, 3:383.8. Also Balthasar, *Glory of the Lord*, 5:36.5.

63. Balthasar, *Theology of Karl Barth*, 220–21.

64. Balthasar, *Theo-Drama*, 2:506.6.

65. Balthasar, *Theo-Drama*, 2:758.9.

God."[66] Hence, the Son of God can assume the image of creation "without contradiction" and "without destroying it."[67]

More emphatically, Balthasar depicts this dynamic in theatrical context in which God has set "the stage" in the grand "theo-drama" where Christ is "the actor" whose kenotic, disponible, obedience marks "the transcendental inauguration of the dramatic acting area."[68] It is in the theatrical "mask" that the "person" both "loses and finds himself," in a kenotic sense.[69] Here, Balthasar employs the notion of "*disponibilité*," as "a principle of active indifference,"[70] to show how Christ has displayed "humility and the exhibitionistic loss of self" to focus on the will of the Father, rather than at himself, or his conscience, for the unique, personal role.[71]

In this regard, the question "who am I?" finds the ultimate answer by the role (*persona*) "I" plays.[72] This implies that a specific role (or mission) that God offers to humanity has a personalizing function (Eph 2:10). Via the "name" that God addresses the "I" as he summons and gives mission, we find the answer to the "who am I?" question that defines the uniqueness of a person.[73] For Balthasar, the "personalizing medium" of "the between" comes from the revelation of "God in the relationship that he has created."[74] This is consummated in Jesus Christ where "the 'I' and the role become uniquely and ineffably one in the reality of his mission."[75] Thus, the dialogical space of "the between" provided by the "normative drama of Christ's life, death, and Resurrection"[76] anticipates and perfects the metaxological principle of William Desmond which is also presented as "*staging the between*."[77] In a subtle manner that echoes the incarnation, Desmond avers that the space of "the between" prevents absolute boundary between the human and the divine, thereby enabling the "passage and communication of the good" by venturing into an "ontological vulnerability" in a kenotic disposition.[78]

66. Balthasar, "Résumé of My Thought," 4.
67. Balthasar, "Résumé of My Thought," 5.
68. Balthasar, *Theo-Drama*, 3:89.9.
69. Balthasar, *Theo-Drama*, 1:220.4. Also, Balthasar, *Theo-Drama*, 3:365.1.
70. Balthasar, *Glory of the Lord*, 5:192.6.
71. Balthasar, *Theo-Drama*, 3:927, 928.4.
72. Balthasar, *Theo-Drama*, 1:231.9.
73. Balthasar, *Theo-Drama*, 1:1111.3, 1127.1.
74. Balthasar, *Theo-Drama*, 1:1122.8.
75. Balthasar, *Theo-Drama*, 1:1141.4.
76. Balthasar, *Theo-Drama*, 2:95.2, 164.
77. Desmond, "Theatre of the *Metaxu*," 113–24.
78. Desmond, "Neither Servility nor Sovereignty," 178.

Balthasar asserts that "the *good* which God does to us can only be experienced as the *truth* if we share in *performing* it."[79] This is because the kenotic act of Christ is the drama *par excellence* that not only illumines "life 'as it is,'" but also indicates "how it ought to be."[80] The kenotic drama is not only an invitation "to play our play in his play,"[81] but it also serves as a "theodramatic hermeneutics" whereby "in revealing himself in Jesus Christ, God interprets himself."[82]

Overall, the concept of analogy enshrined within a sacramental panoptic is crucial for Balthasar. By sacramental panoptic one appreciates the analogical imagination of Balthasar where "all analogy is given a Christocentric determination by Christ." This implies that Christ is "the absolute analogy or the concrete analogy of being."[83] Similar to Desmond's metaxological space where the horizontal and vertical find their zenith, via the sacramental panoptic, "all is suspended from above [or Christologically determined]."[84] Such a sacramental panoptic facilitates the theo-drama between God and creation by opening a space for action. Such "a theology of hiatus, the *diastasis* between God and creation, . . . fosters a theological *kinesis*, which is kenotic."[85] With this, we turn to the specifics of the theology of kenosis of Balthasar, as it is unfolded in Christ and Trinitarian life.

## From Trinitarian Kenosis to Christ as *Homo Kenosus*

Balthasar's theology of kenosis can be considered as the *sine qua non* of his analogical imagination. On the trinitarian plane, Balthasar posits that the primal kenotic act that undergirds all acts of kenosis is that "of the Father, expropriating himself by 'generating' the consubstantial Son,"[86] as the Father "*is* this movement of self-giving that holds nothing back."[87] This comes out of the fountain of the Father's love that effects renunciation because "he will not be God for himself alone."[88] Similarly, "God-given Being is both fullness and poverty at the same time: fullness as Being without limit . . . [and] poverty,

---

79. Balthasar, *Theo-Drama*, 1:35. Emphasis original.
80. Balthasar, *Theo-Drama*, 1:467.5.
81. Balthasar, *Theo-Drama*, 1:35.
82. Balthasar, *Theo-Drama*, 2:179.8.
83. Treitler, "Authentic Theology," 174.
84. Milbank, "Number and the Between," 16.
85. Ward, "Kenosis," 44.
86. Balthasar, *Theo-Drama*, 4:504.9, 594.9.
87. Balthasar, *Theo-Drama*, 4:579.9.
88. Balthasar, *Theo-Drama*, 4:581.3.

because he knows no holding on to himself."[89] The kenosis of the Father into the Son should be understood as a "way of participating in the identical Godhead" within "an absolute, infinite 'distance' that can contain and embrace all the other distances ... including the distance of sin."[90]

In this regard, the kenosis of the incarnation, as a mission (*missio*), is grounded by the primordial kenosis (*processio*) from God.[91] The kenosis of the Son into the world of sin in his incarnation, an act of "represent[ing] the world" does not entail any change of "place" or "*topos*," that is, "absolute distinction within Trinity."[92] The "forsakenness" of Christ on the cross is an expression of "infinite distance" between the Father and Son that has definitively "opened up" the "acting area" between God and man.[93] Thus, Christ can be called *Homo Kenosus par excellence*, as he ecstatically plunges into the abyss of abandonment to reveal the infinite love of God.

In the death and resurrection of Christ, or "the collapse and rebirth," Christ "maintains his identity." This entails that, in order to maintain his identity and be himself, "he must be trinitarian," or "needs the Father and the Spirit."[94] This kenotic space is a realm where we allow ourselves "to be fashioned by it" as a way of discipleship.[95] Christ reveals "that he is wholly other precisely in his abasement, his humility, his service of all." This "inimitable quality" is transcribed as a moral injunction for others "to imitate."[96]

What has begun with the kenotic "self-giving" of Christ unto the cross, as the unfolding of eternal love, finds its triumph and "eternal vindication" in the resurrection.[97] Here, the locus of the drama of the cross culminates in the resurrection, which is "God's overcoming and revaluation of man's dying."[98] This final enactment of the kenotic drama allows "personal discipleship and mission" as we are "'accepted as sons' in his person."[99] The resurrection allows the Son to "impart the Spirit to the players" as it is the Spirit who initially gave Christ "the freedom and the fullness of power" to be the kenotic stage for "the interplay between God and

---

89. Balthasar, *Glory of the Lord*, 5:1085.0.
90. Balthasar, *Theo-Drama*, 4:581.3.
91. Balthasar, *Theo-Drama*, 3:268.5.
92. Balthasar, *Theo-Drama*, 4:600.4.
93. Balthasar, *Theo-Drama*, 3:89.9.
94. Balthasar, *Theo-Drama*, 3:281.5.
95. Balthasar, *Theo-Drama*, 3:219.6.
96. Balthasar, *Theo-Logic*, 2:115.7.
97. Balthasar, *Theo-Drama*, 2:63.6.
98. Balthasar, *Theo-Drama*, 3:94.2.
99. Balthasar, *Theo-Drama*, 3:82.7.

man."[100] Hence, the resurrection becomes "the cradle of ecclesiology,"[101] as it forges the "nerve of Christian practice."[102]

After the ascension, Christ's "once-tortured body" is promised to be "present" to his followers as "it extends far beyond his separate, individual corporeality," in a trans-corporeal sense.[103] Kenosis culminates as Christ "shares himself out eucharistically... and feels himself touched, bodily."[104] For Balthasar, this implies that individual, corporeal difference is not obliterated because "the risen Christ is not only one with the Church... but is distinct from her."[105] The Eucharistic reality allows others to participate analogously in this kenotic existence as they allow themselves to be "a dwelling place for others."[106] This "eucharistic 'permeability'" respects difference and individual freedom because of participation in Trinitarian freedom.[107]

In summary, one can see that the sacramental perspective of Balthasar is the warp and woof of his theology. The analogy of the dynamics of God and creation, transcendence and immanence, infinity and finiteness comes to apotheosis in the kenotic drama of Christ, *Homo Kenosus par excellence*, that opens space for creaturely participation in the triune life of God. From this, one can derive an ethic framed on this sacramental and kenotic cast, a topic of the next section.

## A Morality of *Homo Kenosus*

In the previous section we saw that the kenosis of Hans Urs von Balthasar is not limited to kenotic Christology proper but extends into the trinitarian realm in such a way as to show the dynamics of love shared within the persons of trinity. For Balthasar, Christ is "the Supreme Ethical Norm" upon which ethics must be modeled.[108] In this section we focus on the moral ramifications of the theology of kenosis as adumbrated by the theology of kenosis of Balthasar. Thus, this section offers an ethic of ontological displacement, transcorporeal affirmation of difference, disponibility for service, and sacramental perspective that delineate the morality of *homo kenosus*.

100. Balthasar, *Theo-Drama*, 3:98.5.
101. Balthasar, *Theo-Drama*, 2:155.5.
102. Scott, *Theology, Ideology and Liberation*, 179.
103. Balthasar, *Theo-Drama*, 5:634.1.
104. Balthasar, *Theo-Drama*, 5:634.1.
105. Balthasar, *Theo-Drama*, 5:634.1.
106. Balthasar, *Theo-Drama*, 5:649.4.
107. Balthasar, *Theo-Drama*, 5:650.8.
108. Ouellet, "Christian Ethics," 232.

## Ethic of Ontological Displacement

Christ as a *Homo Kenosus* is the embodiment of love that is revealed on the cross. He does not grab what is essentially his, but shares it with the other. In the "infinite love" of God, one finds no "boundary" or "limit."[109] Because of this love, Christ has ontologically displaced himself out of the gridlock of divinity to plumb into the abyss of death on the cross. He was not fixated in his ontology of divinity to let creation writhe in its darkness and sin. "Love alone," the phrase that aptly summarizes Balthasar's theology, allows ontological displacement.[110] The vector of this displacement is directed not to self-serving glory, neither to a race for honor, but to a state of servility.[111]

Thus, one can propose an ethics of love as an ethic of ontological displacement that can be imitated from the disposition of Christ as *Homo Kenosus*. In this ontological displacement, one begins from the plenitude of the Father that is poured out into Christ. What Christ has received from the Father's fullness, he has given to creation out of love. This is contra the ethos of *homo ethnicus* which is forged on the anvil of the narrative of victimhood. We have seen that the equivocal ossification of *homo ethnicus* is produced by the micro-narratives forwarded to mobilize ethnic identities by accentuating the nostalgia of wounds inflicted by others.

The resultant ossified *homo ethnicus* can be dislodged out of its ontological fixation by injecting a bolus dose of an ethics of love derived out of the ethic of *Homo Kenosus*. This enables an ontological displacement out of narcissistic wound-scratching ideologies. Thus, the "will to power" that grounds an accentuation of "self assertion up to secession" of equivocity can be turned into the "will to divest" by *Homo Kenosus*.

Similarly, the ethic of ontological displacement offers a mediating ground, a metaxological space. This space is the kenotic stage opened by Christ in his death on the cross. The unmediated ground of equivocity finds an intermediatory stage in the bosom of *Homo Kenosus*. The metaxological space can be effectively provided by the "agapeic relation" of *Homo Kenosus*. Thus, in this space, *Homo Kenosus* enables softening of the over-assertion of *homo ethnicus* by installing "finesse for negotiating boundaries" that have been hardened, or "absolutised" by navel-gazing narratives of victimhood.[112] The firm shackles of *homo ethnicus* will be unloosened as the un-instrumentalized fluidity of ethnicity is restored.

---

109. Chapp, "Revelation," 19.
110. Walker, "Love Alone," 1–24.
111. Gorman, *Inhabiting the Cruciform God*, 16.
112. Desmond, "Neither Servility nor Sovereignty," 178.

In this manner, we will be repositioned to our original place as "between-beings, creatures passing and in passage."[113]

## Ethic of Transcorporeality

Balthasar's theology can offer us an ethic of transcorporeality where difference is affirmed. The primal kenotic interplay that establishes this unity-in-distinction is revealed by the kenotic act of Christ in his death on the cross. The kenosis among persons of the Trinity is dramatically played out in the intersubjective dynamics of the fullness and poverty of God. In this manner, "Trinity is the condition for a transcorporeality which is the hallmark of not only Jesus Christ's historical existence but also human existence *tout court*."[114]

For Balthasar, the impartation of the Holy Spirit after the resurrection, the fruit of the cross, links Christology and ecclesiology. The ecclesial body, "the community of resurrection"[115] which is constituted by "individual bodies located in social and political bodies" reveals the resurrection life in all "its truth, its beauty, its goodness" in offering service to the kenotic Servant, the *Homo Kenosus par excellence*.[116] Thus, our serving or "playing our play" in the kenotic space that Christ has opened up as individual bodies, we are continually "opened up" and "endlessly fractured and fed to others" in a Eucharistic sense. Our individual body will be "transduced" or "transfigured" into "the body of Christ broken, given, resurrected and ascended" as it follows "in the wake of the eternal creative Word." In this process of kenotic imitation, "the body does not dissolve or ab-solve." Rather, "it realises its own uniqueness, its own vocation, its own irreplaceability."[117] Similar to the paradoxical interplay of fullness and poverty of the Trinitarian kenosis, the transcorporeal body "expands in its fracturing, it pluralises as it opens itself towards an eternal growth."[118]

In an analogical transcription of Balthasar's kenotic interplay of Trinitarian life, Graham Ward illumines that such "a trinitarian theology of difference" that grounds the interplay of "the giving-in-receiving of the gift" counters the narcissistic and "possessive logic of a debased *eros*."[119] This

---

113. Desmond, "Neither Servility nor Sovereignty," 178.
114. Ward, *Christ and Culture*, 217.
115. Ward, *Christ and Culture*, 189.
116. Ward, *Christ and Culture*, 189.
117. Ward, *Cities of God*, 95.
118. Ward, *Cities of God*, 96.
119. Ward, "Kenosis," 52.

narcissistic form of image-making only yields either a univocal mode of governance till the Därg, that emphasizes sameness in the mold of *Homo Æthiopicus*, or it provides an equivocal anthropology that accentuates difference, as in the simulacra of *homo ethnicus*.

Thus, an ethic of transcorporeality, as an analogy of Trinitarian kenotic interplay, offers "a twofold negation of individual self assertion." The first negation is "a refusal to be for oneself alone, and a refusal to look for the ground of one's being in an individuality divorced from relation."[120] In other words, this ethic impugns "the Promethean identification of man with the Absolute," as in a univocal politics. It also chastens the collectivist ethos of Marxism, and the equivocity of identity politics that instrumentalizes ethnic identity.[121]

In this manner, it serves to demystify an "illusion of self-sufficiency"[122] ingrained in the over-assertion of "self determination up to secession" that marks the ethos of *homo ethnicus*. Affirmation of difference, as in self-assertion, is not an end in itself, as in an equivocal politics. But it needs to be mediated in the transcorporeal matrix of gift exchange where it is neither dissolved into univocal sameness (*homo Æthiopicus*), nor into equivocal difference (*homo ethnicus*). In a eucharistic, transcorporeal service that we render in the kenotic, metaxological stage of Christ, we find affirmation of our difference and uniqueness. More profoundly, our difference will be perfected and restored to us. In other words, as we "lose" our lives in transcorporeal service, we "find" it (Matt 10:39).

## Ethic of Disponibility

The theology of kenosis of Balthasar also offers an ethic of disponibility that denotes "a principle of active indifference"[123] that is ready to perform any role given by God. *Disponibilité* is a theatrical concept that demands "a total dedication—encompassing body, mind, and soul—to the role."[124] Christ has played his role and mission given by the Father perfectly to the extent that his "Person" and "Role" has matched exactly. Christ has displayed disponibility to the Father in his kenotic humility to play the role of a Servant.[125] Thus, the

---

120. Williams, "Balthasar and the Trinity," 42.
121. Ouellet, "Christian Ethics," 239.
122. Williams, "Balthasar and the Trinity," 42.
123. Balthasar, *Glory of the Lord*, 5:192.6.
124. Balthasar, *Theo-Drama*, 1:509.2.
125. Balthasar, *Theo-Drama*, 3:927, 928.4.

disponible character of Christ exhibited in his "nonresistant, surrendering obedience" to the Father grounds "a theodramatic ethics."[126]

In this regard, within the ethic of disponibility, "the element of 'glory' no longer consists in the ascent of eros . . . but in the encounter of the spirit, disponible and humbly ready to serve, as the 'handmaid of the Lord' with the Son who descends."[127] Here, one discerns the tension between the language of ascent and descent. Thus, the thrust of disponibility is oriented not to the ascent of glory that self-serving love aspires to have. Rather, it is a vector that "runs counter to all tendencies toward dis-incarnation," where sinful humanity desires to be "like God."[128] Hence, a disponible attitude is ready to be dispatched to perform a condescending role given by God.

In this manner, disponibility is related to an attentive waiting to the address of God to be given a role. It is a kind of "pure readiness" on the part of "compassion of being" which is enacted in a kenotic effacement to make a way for others.[129] Thus, humanity derives its meaning while awaiting a "Word that he cannot invent for himself, despite the thirst for the Absolute which haunts him."[130] With a disponible readiness to answer God's call, one finds their role that constitutes their person. Similarly, Judith Butler posits that "the divine power of naming structures the theory of interpellation that accounts for the ideological constitution of the subject.[131] Thus, for Balthasar, the constitutive personhood can only be realized in the interpellation of Christ. It is not founded on other markers of identity, or loci of interpellation, such as "dignity, rationality, autonomy, linguistic capability, race, gender, class."[132] This can be presented epigrammatically as: "I am addressed, therefore, I am."[133]

As Butler has noted, the address of God as an authoritative figure in his interpellation of subjects has the "power to diffuse the force of ideology."[134] From the ethic of disponibility, one infers that it is futile to search for mechanisms of attaining glory, honor, or a name outside of the response to God's address. In this vein, Joseph H. Hellerman, professor of New Testament

---

126. Long, *Saving Karl Barth*, 223.
127. Balthasar, *Glory of the Lord*, 5:136.0.
128. Balthasar, *Theo-Drama*, 2:768.8.
129. Desmond, *God and the Between*, 161.
130. Ouellet, "Christian Ethics," 240.
131. Butler, *Psychic Life of Power*, 110–11.
132. Long, *Saving Karl Barth*, 233.
133. Huebner, *Introduction to Christian Ethics*, 282.
134. Butler, *Psychic Life of Power*, 110. I came across this idea in Theodros, *Politics of Metanoia*, 42–43.

Language and Literature, asserts that, *pace* the prevailing honor seeking culture of the Roman colony of Philippi to whom *Carmen Christi* is addressed, Jesus is portrayed as "'descending' a *cursus pudorum* (course of ignominies) that reverses the *cursus honorum* (course of glory) of Roman ideology."[135]

As image-makers, we have made images of *homo Æthiopicus* or *homo ethnicus*, "like the builders of the Tower of Babel" with the aim of establishing "a name for ourselves."[136] Hence, an ethic of disponibility is against any notion of over-self-assertion that aspires to ascend on the ladder of grandiosity to attain glory in an idolatry of *homo ethnicus* or *homo Æthiopicus*. The ethic of disponibility can cut the power grabbing tentacles of ideologies of instrumentalization under the mark of ethnic identity. The eyes of disponibility do not look to themselves, or other sources of interpellation to find any sense of personhood or glory, but are fixated to the role giving God who finally gives "a new name (Rev. 2:17)."[137]

## Ethic of a Sacramental Gaze

The dynamics of the analogy of nature and the supernatural, or the finite and the infinite, and the immanence and the transcendence find their ultimate expression in Balthasar's concrete analogy of being, Christ. Such a sacramental panoptic is critically needed in our setup as our Christologies are not played out on the practical dimension with the dynamics of analogy. At the heart of the Constantinian ideology of *Kəbrä Nägäśt* lies the similitude of *cursus honorum* ideology of the Roman aristocracy that accentuates only the transcendence of God, leaving the realm of immanence to the power plays of the royalty. The emphasis on the divinity of Christ, or "Christ as judge," is not analogically related with his humanity.

This has repercussions as it can effect metaphysical conceptions of reality.[138] One implication of this is the gnostic tendency that denigrates "the material" and promotes "the spiritual."[139] To put it in the literary paradigm of "wax and gold," the anti-sacramental gist is reflected in the aversion of "the wax" (analogy of the material) in favor of "the gold" (analogy of the spiritual). The space that adjoins the "wax *and* gold" is not analogically related to the "Christological narrowing" as in the hourglass metaphor of Balthasar.

135. Hellerman, *Reconstructing Honor*. Also Wright, *Resurrection*, 569.
136. Ward, "Kenosis," 64.
137. Ward, *Christ and Culture*, 188.
138. Mohammed, *Religion and Social Change*, 23.
139. Mohammed, *Religion and Social Change*, 53.

This is correlated with the instrumentalization of transcendental values of religion by the political theology of *Kəbrä Nägäśt*, resulting in an eclipsed transcendence. The decadence of transcendence further ebbed into its loss in the Marxist totalitarian regime of Därg. Such erosion of transcendence is coupled with the loss of "suspension" of the sphere of immanence. This culminated in the idolization of ethnic identity when it is taken as an end in itself. This process depicts the univocal obfuscation of transcendence, and an equivocal positioning of immanence as counterfeit simulacra of transcendence. Therefore, the analogical or sacramental imagination is lost. The upshot of such sacramental indigence is a burgeoning of unbridled immanence.

The need for the restoration of a sacramental mindset is critical, first, to tackle the instrumentalization of ethnic identity. While self-assertion of one's ethnic, linguistic, and cultural background is in line with the sacramental gist, to over assert to the level of instrumentalizing it to political ends is a vivid manifestation of an immanentism that is left unchallenged. The unharnessed immanence has become the breeding ground for endless production of ethnic simulacra. The self-enclosure of ethnic identity only within the realm of immanence needs to be ripped open to the vector of transcendence. We need a "re-suspension" of the immanent sphere with the realm of transcendence. This means that ethnic identity is not an end in itself, but one sign, among many, that expresses the plenitude of God's being.[140]

In Desmond's parlance, ethnic identity escapes "exhaustive immanent determination or self determination" as it is imbued with signs of "over determination" that point towards transcendence.[141] Hence, when viewed through the corrective prism of sacramental gaze, ethnic identity points analogically (sacramentally) to the unity-in-distinction of Being from which it derives its specificity and appraisal. Such vertical suspension of ethnic identity prevents the nihilistic tendency of an autonomous equivocation of accentuated self assertion.

Second, sacramental gaze helps to impugn any impulse of depoliticization that resigns from the political and social sphere. With the help of a sacramental gaze, we affirm the natural order in its analogical relation with the supernatural. If we succumb to the consideration that the immanent sphere, where politics is played out, is altogether evil, we are prey to a gnostic and escapist mentality. Such is not in accord with a sacramental panoptic that perceives all creation, including ethnic identity, as immanent reflections of the transcendence and the goodness of God. Thus, participation in the *Homo*

---

140. Balthasar, "Résumé of My Thought," 3.
141. Desmond, *God and the Between*, 4.

*Kenosus* restores a sacramental panoptic that allows us to serve God in every realm of created order by redeeming the sphere of immanence.

## Conclusion

Many political scientists have noted the enigmatic character of the political history of Ethiopia.[142] The political hangover from previous regimes, especially from the time of Emperor Téwodros, is felt today more than ever. In this chapter we have tried to scrutinize the political theology of Ethiopia from the time of Emperor Téwodros to the present era. The metaphysical lens of William Desmond is deployed to evaluate the underlying political anthropologies.

In this regard, one can note that we have trudged a univocal politics that climaxed up to the Därg regime. Under this univocal umbrella lies the homogenous forging of Ethiopian*ness* using the political theology of Kəbrä Nägäśt. Through this, we have witnessed a robbing of transcendence, which has been subjected to the instrument of the state. The erosion of transcendence is further consolidated by another myth of scientific materialism that ousted the societal script of Kəbrä Nägäśt. Both of these processes have yielded a univocal politics of homogenization, which is characterized by obfuscation of the transcendent realm and magnification of immanence.

After the tyranny of the Därg was dismantled, the different people groups, which had been forced to wear the univocal mask of Ethiopian*ness*, have revealed their real face. This process unveiled the true character of difference via the recognition of our ethnic identities, which had been sublated for long. However, the undue accentuation of ethnic identities spawned instrumentalization, thereby transforming the fluid character of ethnic identities into an ossified state. This process is fueled by the micro-narratives of victimhood that replaced the metanarrative of Kəbrä Nägäśt or scientific materialism. The upshot is the culmination of equivocal politics that borders towards the precipice of nihilism. This is correlated with obsession within the myopic dimension of immanence, which is now blind to the light of transcendence.

The failure to constitute a stable form of administration is because of lack of accommodation of difference. The lack of resolution from the quagmire of equivocal politics demands a mediating principle. The urgent need to find a mediating principle that serves as a milieu of communication can be located in the theology of kenosis of Hans von Balthasar. Balthasar comes

---

142. Messay, *Survival and Modernization: Ethiopia's Enigmatic Present*. The subtitle, "*Enigmatic Present*" attests to this puzzle.

to our aide as his astute diagnosis of the denigration of transcendence and the emergence of immanence in the rise of totalitarian and fascist states is countered by his sacramental theology. Balthasar's analogical theology boils down to the concretion of transcendence and immanence in the kenotic life of Christ. From this, we can derive ethical principles that propel us from equivocity to metaxology. This can restore the loss of transcendence and resuspend immanence back to its place.

Hence, via participation in Christ, the *Homo Kenosus par excellence*, one can configure an ethic of ontological displacement that can transform the ossified *homo ethnicus* by dislodging it from its ontological fixation into the fluid character of ethnic identity. Similarly, an ethic of transcorporeality affirms difference without relinquishing identity, thereby enabling an ecstatic and transcorporeal embrace of others. Moreover, an ethic of disponibility for service interpellates kenotic anthropology grounded with a frame of missional and vocational existence. The thrust of disponible anthropology runs counter to the glory seeking technology of the ethnic self. Finally, a sacramental perspective can redeem the immanent sphere that has become a feasible breeding ground of instrumentalization of ethnic identity and chastens any politics of withdrawal and resignation.

Finally, a concluding remark is in order. From the above discussion the Christological question is critical to the political equation. The response to the question "who do you say that I am?" could determine our metaphysics, which in turn influences the political order. In our setup, the metaphysics of "Wax and Gold," in an analogical sense, has been taken as a hermeneutical lens to interpret reality in a dualistic sense.[143] The accent on the apophatic dimension of God as "*mystery*" and the "lack of transparency" of his will has rendered an immanent sphere where creation is given "independence and self-sufficiency."[144]

Arguably, this has facilitated the operation of immanence to take the upper hand, coupled with a parallel curtailment of transcendence. The wax *and* gold metaphysics has to be transformed into "*between* wax and gold" in such a way as to allow a theodramatic interplay between God and creation. The "between" takes us beyond the "dialectical conception" that interprets dynamics of wax and gold as an endless "recasting of destinies, in the reversal of positions."[145] Such dialectics of wax and gold sanctions war to determine one's destiny or "*idil*" in a Heraclitean sense in order to wield power.[146] The dialectics of wax and gold deploys war to ascertain "will to survival."[147]

---

143. Mohammed, *Religion and Social Change*, 3, 30.
144. Messay, *Survival and Modernization*, 182–183. Emphasis original.
145. Messay, *Survival and Modernization*, 186.
146. Messay, *Survival and Modernization*, 185–86.
147. Messay, *Survival and Modernization*, 193.

*Pace* the agonistic thrust of the upward social mobility undergirded in the dialectics of wax and gold, the metaphysics of "between" wax and gold affirms relationality founded on "plenitude of divine charity," not "scarcity of finitude" that begets vicious cycle of strife.[148]

Hence, we have to review our confessional and practical Christologies (Myaphysitic or Chalcedonian), whether they depict a metaxological and theodramatic space that counters the unabated warrant of war underwritten in the metaphysics of wax and gold. The declaration that "Jesus is Lord" had been politically subversive and revolutionary enough to refute the idolatry of the worship of Caesar in the first three centuries.[149] As such, "theology is political simply by responding to the dynamics of its own proper themes: Christ, salvation, the church, the Trinity."[150] Speaking on such topics has direct ramifications in the context in which we live. Our theological declarations in word or praxis have to be evaluated if they have responded to the prevailing metaphysics of wax and gold, a subject for further inquiry.

# Bibliography

Abbink, Jon. "Ethnicity and Constitutionalism in Ethiopia." *Journal of African Law* 41 (1997) 159–74. http://doi.org/10.1017/S0021855300009372.

Bahru Zewde. "The Burden of History: The Constraints and Challenges of the Democratization Process in Ethiopia" Paper presented at the Wits History Workshop, Johannesburgh, the University of Witwaterstrand, 1994. http://wiredspace.wits.ac.za/handle/10539/8115.

———. "A Century of Ethiopian Historiography." *Journal of Ethiopian Studies* 33.2 (2000) 1–26.

———. *Society, State and History: Selected Essays*. Addis Ababa: Addis Ababa University Press, 2008.

Balthasar, Hans Urs von. *Explorations in Theology*. Vol. 1, *The Word Made Flesh*. Translated by A. V. Littledale with Alexander Dru. San Francisco: Ignatius, 1989.

———. *The Glory of the Lord: A Theological Aesthetics*. Vol. 5, *The Realm of Metaphysics in the Modern Age*. Translated by Oliver Davies et al. Edinburgh: T. & T. Clark, 1991.

———. "A Resume of My Thought." In *Hans Urs Von Balthasar: His Life and Work*, edited by David L. Schindler, 1–6. San Francisco: Ignatius, 1991.

———. *Theo-Drama: Theological Dramatic Theory*. Vol. 1, *Prolegomena*. Translated by Graham Harrison. San Francisco: Ignatius, 1988.

———. *Theo-Drama: Theological Dramatic Theory*. Vol. 2, *Dramatis Personae: Man in God*. Translated by Graham Harrison. San Francisco: Ignatius, 1990.

———. *Theo-Drama: Theological Dramatic Theory*. Vol. 3, *The Dramatis Personae: Persons in Christ*. Translated by Graham Harrison. San Francisco: Ignatius, 1992.

---

148. Bell, "Theological Ontology," 212.

149. Wright, *Resurrection*, 570.

150. O'Donovan, *Desire of the Nations*, 3.

———. *Theo-Drama: Theological Dramatic Theory*. Vol. 4, *The Action*. Translated by Graham Harrison. San Francisco: Ignatius, 1994.

———. *Theo-Logic*. Vol. 1, *Truth of the World*. Translated by Adrian J. Walker, San Francisco: Ignatius, 2000.

———. *Theo-Logic*. Vol. 2, *The Truth of God*. Translated by Adrian J. Walker. San Francisco: Ignatius, 2004.

———. *The Theology of Karl Barth: Exposition and Interpretation*. Translated by Edward T. Oakes. San Francisco: Ignatius, 1951.

Bell, Daniel, Jr. "Only Jesus Saves: Toward a Theopolitical Ontology of Judgment." In *Theology and the Political: The New Debate*, edited by Creston Davis et al., 200–229. SIC 5. Durham: Duke University Press, 2005.

Boersma, Hans. *Nouvelle Théologie and Sacramental Theology: A Return to Mystery*. Oxford: Oxford University Press, 2009.

Butler, Judith. *Psychic Life of Power: Theories in Subjection*. Stanford: Stanford University Press, 1997.

Chapp, Larry. "Revelation." In *The Cambridge Companion to Hans Urs von Balthasar*, edited by Edward T. Oakes and David Moss, 11–24. Cambridge: Cambridge University Press, 2004.

Davis, Creston, et al., eds,. *Theology and the Political: The New Debate Creston*. London: Duke University Press, 2005.

Desmond, William. *Being and the Between*. New York: State University of New York, 1995.

———. *God and the Between*. Oxford: Blackwell, 2008.

———. *The Intimate Strangeness of Being: Metaphysics After Dialectic*. Washington, DC: The Catholic University of America Press, 2012.

———. "Neither Servility nor Sovereignty: Between Metaphysics and Politics." In *Theology and the Political*, edited by Creston Davis et al., 153–82. Durham, NC: Duke University Press, 2020.

———. *Perplexity and Ultimacy: Metaphysical Thoughts From the Middle*. New York: State University of New York Press, 1995.

———. "The Theatre of the *Metaxu*: Staging the Between." *Topoi* 30 (2011) 113–24.

Gardner, Lucy, and David Moss. "Something Like Time; Something Like the Sexes—An Essay in Reception." In *Balthasar at the End of Modernity*, edited by Lucy Gardner et al., 69–138. Edinburg: T. & T. Clark, 1999.

Gardner, Lucy, et al., eds. *Balthasar at the End of Modernity*. Edinburg: T. & T. Clark, 1999.

Gorman, Michael J. *Inhabiting the Cruciform God: Kenosis, Justification, and Theosis in Paul's Narrative Soteriology*. Grand Rapids: Eerdmans, 2009.

Hellerman, Joseph H. *Reconstructing Honor in Roman Philippi: Carmen Christi as Cursus Pudorum*. Cambridge: Cambridge University Press, 2005.

Henrici, Peter. "Hans Urs Von Balthasar: A Sketch of His Life." In *Hans Urs Von Balthasar: His Life and Work*, edited by David L. Schindler, 7–44. San Francisco: Ignatius, 1991.

———. "The Philosophy of Hans Urs Von Balthasar." In *Hans Urs Von Balthasar: His Life and Work*, edited by David L. Schindler, 149–68. San Francisco: Ignatius, 1991.

Huebner, Harry J. *An Introduction to Christian Ethics: History, Movements, People*. Waco, TX: Baylor University Press, 2012.

Messay Kebede. *Survival and Modernization: Ethiopia's Enigmatic Present: A Philosophical Discourse*. Asmara: Red Sea, 1999.

Levine, Donald N. *Greater Ethiopia: The Evolution of a Multiethnic Society*. Chicago: University of Chicago Press, 2000.
Long, D. Stephen. *Saving Karl Barth: Hans Urs von Balthasar's Preoccupation*. Minneapolis: Fortress, 2014.
Merera Gudina. "Contradictory Interpretations of Ethiopian History: The Need for a New Consensus." In *Ethnic Federalism: The Ethiopian Experience in Comparative Perspective*, edited by David Turton, 119–30. Eastern African Studies. Oxford: Currey, 2006.
Milbank, John. "Number and the Between." In *Thinking Metaxologically: William Desmond's Philosophy Between Metaphysics, Religion, Ethics, and Aesthetics*, edited by Dennis Vanden Auweele, 15–44. Cham, Switzerland: Springer Nature, 2018.
Mohammed Girma. *Understanding Religion and Social Change in Ethiopia: Toward a Hermeneutic of Covenant*. New York: Palgrave, 2012.
Oakes, Edward T., and David Moss, eds. *The Cambridge Companion to Hans Urs von Balthasar*. Cambridge: Cambridge University Press, 2004.
O'Donovan, Oliver. *The Desire of the Nations: Rediscovering the Roots of Political Theology*. Cambridge: Cambridge University Press, 1996.
Ouellet, Marc. "The Foundations of Christian Ethics according to Hans Urs von Balthasar." In *Hans Urs Von Balthasar: His Life and Work*, edited by David L. Schindler, 231–50. San Francisco: Ignatius, 1991.
Scott, Peter. *Theology, Ideology and Liberation: Towards a Liberative Theology*. Cambridge: Cambridge University Press, 1994.
Shindler, David L. "Preface." In *Hans Urs von Balthasar: His Life and Work*, edited by David L. Shindler, xi–xiii. San Francisco: Ignatius, 1991.
Shindler, David L., ed. *Hans Urs von Balthasar: His Life and Work*. San Francisco: Ignatius, 1991.
Smith, James K. A. "Foreword." In *The Politics of Discipleship: Becoming Postmaterial Citizens*, by Graham Ward, 11–14. Grand Rapids: Baker, 2009.
Theodros A. Teklu. *The Politics of Metanoia: Towards a Post-Nationalistic Political Theology in Ethiopia*. Frankfurt: Peter Lang, 2014.
Treitler, Wolfgang. "Foundations of Authentic Theology." In *Hans Urs Von Balthasar: His Life and Work*, edited by David L. Schindler, 169–82. San Francisco: Ignatius, 1991.
Turton, David. ed. *Ethnic Federalism*. Oxford: Currey, 2006.
Walker, Adrian J. "Love Alone: Hans Urs von Balthasar as a Master of Theological Renewal." *Communio* 32 (2005) 1–24.
Ward, Graham. *Christ and Culture*. Oxford: Blackwell, 2005.
———. *Cities of God*. London: Routledge, 2000.
———. "Kenosis: Death, Discourse and Resurrection." In *Balthasar at the End of Modernity*, edited by Lucy Gardner, 15–68. Edinburgh: T. & T. Clark, 1999.
———. *The Politics of Discipleship: Becoming Postmaterial Citizens*. Grand Rapids: Baker, 2009.
Wigley, Stephen. *Balthasar's Trilogy*. New York: T. & T. Clark, 2010.
Williams, Rowan. "Balthasar and the Trinity." In *The Cambridge Companion to Hans Urs von Balthasar*, edited by Edward T. Oakes and David Moss, 37–50. Cambridge: Cambridge University Press, 2004.
Wright, N. T. *The Resurrection of the Son of God*. Minneapolis: Fortress, 2003.
Yonatan Tesfaye Fessha. *Ethnic Diversity and Federalism: Constitution Making in South Africa and Ethiopia*. Fernham: Ashgate, 2010.

# 9

# The Rite of "Footwashing" at *Abinet* Schools and Its Ethics of Humility

## Setargew Kenaw

WASHING THE FEET OF elderly people and guests who traveled long distances has been a longstanding cultural practice among many societies around the world. In Ethiopia, too, warm greetings, followed by footwashing, is a generous gesture to demonstrate that the guest must feel at home. In many rural homesteads, it could even be practiced regularly for guests as well as respectable members of the household.

However, footwashing could also be done out of the sense of duty over against the symbolism it carries as a sign of reverence for guests and elderly members of a homestead. Also, young people, housemaids, or any other residents of a household with low-ranking status are expected to do the job out of the sense of duty. Footwashing in this context goes beyond the symbolism of hospitality. The rhetoric that the act is done out of respect and done enthusiastically could still be there but it is also undertaken to signify power relations, differentiate seniors from juniors, masters from slaves, men from women, etc. In domestic environments, slaves and women were forced to do the task as "an uncompromising assertion of the power held by those to be washed."[1]

This chapter concerns the symbolism and meaning that footwashing embodies within the context of Abinet schools in Ethiopia. As we shall see below, in Abinet schools, the tradition acquires a deeper meaning. The cultural practice in fact gets a unique power way beyond its ordinary, routine usage.

---

1. McGowan, "Missing Sacrament? Foot-washing," 108.

Washing the feet of newcomers in these schools signals that the new comer is in principle accepted and embraced without any preconditions.

The chapter consists of five sections. The first draws on and briefly presents the cultural and religious meanings of footwashing, eventually forging the conceptual tools that are used to unpack the meanings of the practice in Abinet schools. An overview of the range of meanings attached to footwashing definitely put the discussion of the ritual in the life of Abinet schools in perspective. The second section presents a few exemplary stories of former Abinet school students and the general social and educational spirit of these schools on the basis of the field observations of the author. The next section contextualizes humility within the Ethiopian Christian literature. The next describes current developments within university campuses, highlighting ethnic tensions and conflicts, and how the ritual of footwashing could serve as exemplary to ameliorate these problems. The last section gives a few concluding remarks.

## Footwashing: Cultural and Religious Meanings

As biblical stories, historical and ethnographic accounts, and biographical notes of travelers show, footwashing used to be a longstanding cultural practice in many societies around the world. In the context of rural and/ or ancient homesteads, washing the feet of the house master, that of the elderly and older relatives, or those of respectable guests has always been a treat many enjoy because of these (and the kindred) status positions.[2] In the Old Testament, especially in a good number of the stories in which people are depicted as receiving guests, the first thing hosts do is to offer water for washing their feet. In the book of Genesis, Abraham (18:4) ordered water (symbolically?[3]) to be available for the messengers who came to his house to break the news that his wife Sarah will give birth to a son, and Joseph (43:24) offered water for his brothers and feed for their animals.[4]

As the sources just cited indicate, accounts in the Old Testament are important sources for how certain cultures embraced footwashing as a gesture of hospitality and respect. Walter L. Fleming[5] (1908) further points out that it has been an old tradition in the East that guests would remove their

---

2. Fleming, "Religions and Hospitable Rite"; Von Duam Tholl, "Life According to the Rule."

3. Abraham ordered water symbolically probably, because the visitors were not humans.

4. Thomas, "Footwashing in John 13"; Keener, *Gospel of John*, 903.

5. Fleming, "Religions and Hospitable Rite."

sandals before entering a house or a tent as a sign of respect for the place, and hosts on their part would offer water for washing the feet and hands. In many "private houses of Christians in Asia, Africa and Europe," Fleming adds, footwashing had been "practiced as a simple act of civility or of hospitality."[6] As the Old Testament accounts show, footwashing has been an age-old and widespread custom of Judaism.[7] This cultural practice therefore expresses various meanings at various levels. As an everyday practice, when, for example, a maid washes the feet of an employer, footwashing might simply be considered as ordinary service that is expected of a person for the payment she receives from the household. Research[8] shows that women in socialist Albania were forced to wash the feet of their husbands.

In the Ethiopian context, young people are encouraged to wash the feet of a very close relative, a parent for example, without the expectation that one would get something in return except blessings. One could also do it in order to relieve a person from exhaustion following a very long and tiresome trip. This could be done by younger members of a household, mostly with the order of parents or any senior member of the household. Thus, a guest or a complete stranger might be well-received and one of the treats for this reception is to get one's feet washed.

However, as already hinted, the act does not always signify hospitality or humility; it could in fact reflect a hierarchical power relation within a homestead. Household heads, mostly men, are privileged to get the service of maids, male servants, and even wives. Craig Keener[9] points out that household heads or people with some status do not actually wash the feet of their guests; they order somebody younger or lower in rank to do the job. This has always been something most Ethiopians grow up witnessing and practicing. Referring to the ancient Greco-Roman culture, Keener states: "For a person of status, particularly a patron host, to wash his guests' feet *as if a servant* would be unthinkable!"[10]

As already pointed out, the Gospel of John has been the principal source elaborating the theological meanings of the act of footwashing. Raymond E. Brown, in his *The Gospel and Epistles of John*, accentuated humility as one of the most principal meanings of footwashing: "The humility and self-abasement of the Son of God is clearly the meaning of the

---

6. Fleming, "Religions and Hospitable Rite," 5.
7. Von Duam Tholl, "Life According to the Rule," 155–56.
8. Vullnetari and King, "Washing Men's Feet," 203.
9. Keener, *Gospel of John*.
10. Keener, *Gospel of John*, 1:907, emphasis added.

foot-washing scene."[11] He adds: "The washing of another's feet, begrimed by travel upon dusty roads in sandals, was a menial task not required even of Jewish slaves. Such utter humiliation on the part of Jesus leads Peter to object."[12] This shows that Christ's act of washing the feet of his disciples must have been embedded with a very special meaning.

John C. Thomas[13] selects passages from major figures in the early development of Christianity to show how the theme of humility has been highlighted. To cite one example, John Chrysostom was said to have stated the following:

> "Let us wash one another's feet" He [Christ] said. "Those of slaves, too?" And what great things is it, even if we do wash the feet of slaves? For He himself was Lord by nature, while we were slaves, yet He did not beg off from doing even this . . . God made us debtors to one another—after He Himself had begun this process—and debtors in regard to a smaller amount.[14]

Keener discusses humility as an expression of love and "self-sacrifice." Drawing on and interpreting John's Gospel, Keener writes:

> By humbly serving his disciples (13:4–6), Jesus takes the role of the Suffering Servant (cf. Isa 52:13—53:12) that John has mentioned (12:38), epitomizing Christological motifs from his Gospel and other early Christian sources. Because biblical and early Jewish customs use foot washing in welcoming guests, some see it as an act of eschatological hospitality.[15]

Jesus's act of footwashing has also been understood as having "sacramental motif."[16] On the other hand, footwashing has been considered by a few as a substitute (a form of "polemic," as Thomas[17] [1990] puts it) for (posed against) baptism and rite of cleansing. As Thomas[18] points out, Jesus's action has been conceived "as a symbol for the eucharist"; as "forgiveness of sin," and as salvation.

In the Ethiopian context, *Tselote Hamus* (Maundy Thursday) is among the most highly celebrated days of the Orthodox Church. The patriarch,

11. Brown, *Gospel and Epistles of John*, 71.
12. Brown, *Gospel and Epistles of John*, 72.
13. Thomas, "Footwashing in John 13," 167–71.
14. Thomas, "Footwashing in John 13," 169.
15. Keener, *Gospel of John*, 1:901–2.
16. Brown, *Gospel and Epistles of John*, 71.
17. Thomas, "Footwashing in John 13."
18. Thomas, "Footwashing in John 13," 3–7.

archbishops, bishops, and ordinary priests engage in washing the feet of the faithful. There is also a longstanding footwashing tradition in monasteries throughout the Christian world in receiving guests. In some monastic orders, footwashing was only, as a rule, for visiting monks and priests. "When people come to the door of the monastery, they are to be received with greater honor if they are clerics or monks. Their feet shall be washed, according to the Gospel precept."[19] In Ethiopian monasteries the service is in fact offered to any ordinary visitors.[20]

However, Jesus's act has also been interpreted a signal for the final moment. According to Keener, the fact that Christ washed the feet of his disciples immediately before he was crucified has invoked the meaning that Jesus was gesturing goodbye to his disciples. Thus, because Christ served his disciples before the passion, Keener seems to tell us that we should not forget the "Farewell Discourse" among the range of connotations that the practice may have.[21]

## Biographical Notes and Current Developments

Abinet schools, as we shall see, are beacons of diversity. The emphasis that the idea of humanity receives in these schools makes these schools exemplary in terms of inclusiveness. The question "Where did you come from?"—according to an interviewee in a school in Bahir Dar (September 2019)—is an unacceptable question and considered disrespectful because where one is coming from does not have anything to do with the ethics of Abinet schools. Instead, the question that is thought to be legitimate for newcomers to answer and would be legitimate in asking is: What kind of lessons are you expecting to get here?

This section focuses on the rite and specific rituals of footwashing in Abinet schools and the meanings attached to them, which is the principal subject of this chapter. The section again is divided into two major subsections. The first subsection draws on the biographical notes of former students of Abinet schools on the basis of books that capture the spirit of humility and

---

19. Quoted in Thomas, "Footwashing in John 13," 172. Some sources indicate that washing guests' feet at the entrance of monasteries might as well be done in order to protect the sacred place from being contaminated by dirty feet (see McGowan, "Missing Sacrament? Foot-washing," 117).

20. Ethiopian Orthodox Tewahdo Church, የኢትዮጵያ ኦርቶዶክስ ተዋህዶ ቤተ ክርስቲያን, 234.

21. Keener, *Gospel of John*, 1:899.

modesty in these schools. The second subsection pivots to a brief excursion into current developments at Abinet schools.

## Biographical Notes

One of the ways to tell the story of Abinet schools is to consult books written by and about scholars who have gone through these schools and, a few of them, have had a career as teachers. *Yeneta* Yitbarek Ghidey is one of these; he organized an autobiography entitled የቅኔ ቤት ባህልና የሕይወቴ ገጠመኝ (*The House of Qenie and My Life's Encounters*). The book includes accounts of the journeys he and fellow students made. He also depicted life at Abinet schools.

*Yeneta* Yitbarek narrated his travel from Temben to Gondar. He left Temben (where he was born and raised) in 1952 and met fellow students (one from Wello and the other from Axum) and depicted their harsh and dangerous journey. Crossing Tekeze River was one of the challenges. After Tekeze, they had to climb up and descend down Mount Ras Dashen, passing by terrifying cliffs, walking on freezing, icy paths barefoot. Despite their plan to travel to Gondar town, the young boys decided (mainly because of exhaustion) to attend a school at a place known as Beyeda. By the time they arrived there, the master teacher was not there; one of the senior students inquired about the purpose of their visit and invited them to take rest. *Yeneta* Yitbarek writes,

> He [one of the students] brought us water immediately but we resisted his offer to wash our feet. He then reacted: "Please do not resist this; it is the custom of the school to do so. Let alone I the ordinary mortal, didn't our Lord Savior Jesus Christ wash the feet of his disciples?" He then washed us [our feet] . . . While washing our feet, he said "I wash your feet so that you could do the same thing to other guests." In saying so, he taught us humility and responsibility.[22]

The reception the young boys received was phenomenal. The very interchange between the host and his guests has a clear import of modesty and humility. The story of Jesus Christ washing the feet of his disciples has come out clearly.

There are similar accounts by other writers. *Abba* Kidane-Mariam Getahun, in his ጥንታዊው የቆሎ ተማሪ, *The Classical Abinet Student*, described well the reception of new students. In a chapter on the "reception" of newly

---

22. Yitbarek, የቅኔ ቤት ባህልና የሕይወቴ ገጠመኝ, 16–17. Original in Amharic. Translation author's; other translations are also mine unless and otherwise indicated

joining students into Abinet schools, he discusses how the students of the receiving school would happily welcome newcomers. He writes:

> As soon as students recognize somebody who is hesitatingly watching their school from around their premises, they would approach the guy and inquire about the purpose of his visit. [Once they learn that he is there for getting admission], the students would scramble to do what they can. One would receive his bag [*akufada*], the other his stick [instrumental to protect oneself from dogs], and still the other his sleeping hide mat. They would then take him to a hut or a place where he could wait and take rest. Then proceeds the act of footwashing, [whereby] one would bring the water and others would sit and wash the feet of the guest student. Mostly, since students involved in the task could be more than two or three, one student would wash one foot and another the other. The rest would roast grain [for the guests].[23]

Concluding the chapter entitled "on reception," *Abba* Kidane-Mariam interjected that "a school is not only there to provide lessons; it is also a marketplace for love and humility."[24]

It is to actively play in this unique "marketplace," to use the writer's own expression, that students, including very young boys aged between eight and ten[25] (after finishing reading and writing in their respective parish churches), would begin their journey. In planning a journey to Abinet schools students or would-be students would definitely expect hardships. At the very least they would start a journey with the knowledge that the distance they are supposed to cover would be tough and testing. On top of harsh weather conditions, difficult terrains, and wild animals—not to mention the starvation and thirst—young boys would face human-made disasters, would find themselves amidst battles, and, something not infrequent, they would be victims of robbers. A 2003 fieldwork report conveyed accounts of teachers and students:

> Students stumble on areas . . . notorious for serving as havens for robbers . . . lose books they have acquired dearly and the small amount of money that they [have] . . . robbed of [even] their

23. Kidane-Mariam, ጥንታዊው የቆሎ ተማሪ, 24. Original in Amharic.
24. Kidane-Mariam, ጥንታዊው የቆሎ ተማሪ, 25. Original in Amharic.
25. Children attending parish schools (to study Ge'ez alphabets, including reading and writing) should be four or five years old. Thus, students in their teens would be considered too old to join an Abinet school. *Aleqa* Lemma Hailu, a renowned Qenie scholar, had almost been turned down when his father took him to school; the teacher thought he was "aged" (Mengistu Lemma).

tattered clothes ... [They could at times be] victims of physical abuses. [Informants reveal] whenever robbers do not find anything they can take, they become very apprehensive and assume that the student has some kind of machination or magic to hide materials beyond an ordinary search ....[26] Robbers are capable of flogging innocent, poor students and sometimes inflict severe injuries [including causing death lest a victim could use a magical charm to harm the perpetrator].[27]

These kinds of troubles are not of course things unexpected but what is important is that the difficulties in question have always been, as the informants in 2003 noted, overcome by the ardent passion they have for the school and the teacher they have always been looking forward to join and meet. This goes well with what *Yeneta* Yitbarek was witnessing in the 1950s at the time of his arrival at his dream destination: "I didn't have any words to express the extent of my happiness once we were in Gondar. I felt as if I already finished *aquaquam* and *qenie* [Abinet school lesson types]."[28] The warm reception and hospitality at the destination—something students would normally assume they would have, added to the thirst and longing for knowledge that they naturally have, would in fact not stop the students from taking steps to travel from home to school, and from school to school.

The responsibility of the students at Abinet schools is not confined to newly admitted students. Any visitor to a school would be welcomed and respectfully seen off at the time he leaves. *Abba* Kidane-Mariam relates:

> During one's stay in an Abinet school, he [the student] takes it to be his duty to welcome any person, be they guests or fellow students. One of the first tasks in this reception is washing the guest's feet. Then, he would offer food [to the guests] whatever is available and then prepare a mat for the guest to rest for the night. In case the guest is resuming his journey by the morrow and has too many stuff to carry, the student would lend the guest a helping hand and see him off, carrying his stuff for considerable length of the travel until the guest insists that the student should no more proceed.[29]

---

26. "People who are not conversant with the methods of church schools believe that students of church schools are equipped with certain maliciously construed magical formulae in order to put things out of sight, or for that matter inflict injuries magically on people who have harmed them" (Setargew, "Studying Traditional Schools," 107–22).

27. Setargew, "Studying Traditional Schools," 113–14.

28. Yitbarek. የቅኔ ቤት ባህልና የሕይወቴ ገጠመኝ, 18.

29. Yitbarek. የቅኔ ቤት ባህልና የሕይወቴ ገጠመኝ, 53.

The other attraction of the schools (other than the education, of course) is the extent of freedom and choice they provide. Yitbarek relates:

> In *Qenie* school ... there was no boundary, restricted zone ... No one could claim that "this is my area ... Don't ever trespass, etc. etc." No one stops anyone. Every student sees schools all over the country as his own house. Those from Tigray would migrate to Gondar and Wello; those from Wello and Gondar would travel to Tigray. Young people would travel from Eritrea to Gojjam and from Gojjam to Eritrea.[30]

The spirit of cooperation and friendship that reigns in Abinet schools is also exemplary. When students stay in the same school, they undertake their study and other tasks (including begging for food, or helping their teacher in activities such as farming, sowing, weeding, etc.) in great comradeship. Describing an ideal friendship between students, *Abba* Kidane-Mariam writes:

> When one student goes out to beg and bring food, the other could either wait at home roasting grains or goes out to fetch drinking water. When the one who goes out returns home, he would be well received by his friend who stayed in the hut, including getting his feet washed ... If one gets ill, the other would take the whole responsibility to take care of him.[31] (Original in Amharic.)

This does not, however, mean that Abinet schools have never witnessed conflicts. Naturally, there are also differences and some clashes among students. Accounts show that the reason behind these conflicts would vary. According to *Likesiltanat* Habte-Mariam Workineh,[32] one possible reason for conflict could be food. Students of one Abinet school would be assigned to different quarters in the surrounding vicinity. It is therefore considered inappropriate if one student is found in the place to which he was not assigned. *Abba* Kidane-Mariam[33] also observed a similar experience: Students from two separate Abinet schools could be dragged into a fight when they trespass each other's assigned places where they are supposed to beg for food. Another recurrent source of conflict is competition among students of different types of schools. One such notorious rivalry that writers discuss is between

---

30. Yitbarek, የቅኔ ቤት ባሀልና የሕይወቴ ጉዞመኝ, 18–19. Original in Amharic.
31. Kidane-Mariam, ጥንታዊው የቆሎ ተማሪ, 51.
32. Habte-Mariam, ጥንታዊ የኢትዮጵያ ትምህርት, 293.
33. Kidane-Mariam, ጥንታዊው የቆሎ ተማሪ, 54.

*Qenie* and *Zema* students. According to *Abba* Kidane-Mariam, *Qenie* students assume that their study is superior to *Zema* lessons.[34]

## Current Developments

As pointed out in the research report I already cited,[35] the tradition of welcoming guests and new students has continued into the new millennium. My experience in Bahir Dar and Gondar in 2003 was (seen in retrospect now) a living witness for the accounts I discussed above. As I mentioned in the research report, I had serious difficulty getting permission from the head office of the Ethiopian Orthodox *Tewahdo* Church—that was supposedly what researchers would or should do as a matter of course before visiting the schools. Frustrated because of the bureaucratic holdup, I had to go to Bahir Dar and Gondar without *the* paper, with all the doubts if I could make it, and yet the kind of reception I got from all the schools I visited (except one at the center of Gondar city—maybe because it was much closer to "power") was overwhelming; I was even allowed to attend the night session lessons at Shimbit Michael Church.

What about now? At the time I am writing this piece, one of my former students who is teaching at Bahir Dar University (Ato Sisay Tamirat) kindly volunteered to support my research by taking a few of my questions to two Abinet schools in the same city in September 2019. One of them was the same *Qenie* school at Shimbit Michael Church (officially designated as Andinet Ghedam, Unity Monastery) I visited sixteen years ago. Almost all of the students responding to the questions surrounding the rite of footwashing answered positively. Samuel, one of the students at Felege Qedus Giorgis *Aquaquam* school, stated:

> We wash the feet of new students and guests after the example of our Lord who prostrated in front of his disciples and washed their feet. The meaning attached [to footwashing] is only religious, not cultural. Since our Lord washed his disciples humbly, we too, learning humility from our Lord, are supposed to carry out this.

When asked what he felt when getting his feet washed in a similar circumstance, the way Samuel (who came from Wellega about a year ago) made his response was in some way couched humbly; he seemed

---

34. Kidane-Mariam, ጥንታዊው የቆሎ ተማሪ, 55.

35. Setargew, "Studying Traditional Schools." For much recent development see Mersha, በአንተ ስማ ለማርያም፡.

transported back to the situation itself and replied to the question with so much humbleness: "Well, I felt bad when I got my feet washed. However, I also realized that when they showed me that humility, it had a purpose, i.e., I should [in turn] serve in humbleness."

Another student underlined that the act is pretty religious and it teaches humility and, in return, when one acts in humbleness he will be blessed in life.

Lisanework, a senior student, provided a rather acerbic answer because he also saw a threat to the very practice itself. He commented:

> Those monasteries that are not contaminated by science do still use it. Those who think that they know science and assume that they are "modern," they look down on this virtue and consider it backward. They behave this way because they are oblivious of the secret behind it. Their [science] education seems to assume [but wrongly] that humans are equal. We still practice the act. It was only yesterday that we [the students] were racing to wash the feet of a guest, an old man who spent the night [in the school compound].

Lisanework's bitterness spotlighted the monasteries because, apparently, he seemed to think that the very source that should have nourished and sustained the ritual (i.e., monastic life) is seemingly deteriorating in its religious ardor, especially owing to its increasing exposure to the "scientific" attitude. But then, there seems to be hope, which students like Lisanework can hang on to: that the rite of footwashing is still around in the Abinet schools.

The moral lessons that Abinet schools teach, and the emphasis on an education system that is characterized by modesty and humility, must have been one of the factors attracting students from diverse places. As was the case several decades (and probably centuries) ago,[36] the youth (diminishing in number, of course) are still joining these schools from various parts of the country, especially from predominantly Orthodox Christian settlements.

Interviewees from the two schools in Bahir Dar have also established that students join these schools from places mentioned above, including from some districts in the Oromia Regional State. Following the peace talk between Ethiopia and Eritrea, a few students began coming from Eritrea and had been attending lessons for some months until, according to the account of one of the interviewees, they left following "the June 2019 bloodshed in Bahir Dar because of a mounting pressure from their relatives in Eritrea."

---

36. See Yitbarek, የቅኔ ቤት ባህልና የሕይወቴ ገጠመኝ , 18–19.

## Humility in Context

The cultural and religious meanings of the footwashing ritual *seem* to be entertained throughout the Christian world, with all kinds of variations and nuances of course. As briefly mentioned, the ritual covers acts of respecting seniors and superior members of a household through signaling hospitality and welcoming guests (including strangers) to the religious symbolism that the act stands for (viz. love, modesty, and humility).

Among these meanings, the Abinet school tradition has, expectedly, singled out the religious meaning compared to the cultural ones. Consistent with the interpretations of Christ's act of washing the feet of his disciples, the act of footwashing in Ethiopia, unlike in many other Christian countries around the world, has not only been an annual ritual observed on Maundy Thursday but also widely practiced in monasteries and Abinet schools.

Consistent with the tradition of Christian ethics, at the helm of the Ethiopian classical education system is the virtue of humility. The Ethiopian Orthodox Church has several religious texts other than the holy books of the Bible, addressing humility as one of the key virtues that the devout must follow and live by. Humility takes center stage in the biographies of religious figures such as Saint Yared, Saint Christos Semra, and Saint Teklehaimanot. Saint Walatta Petros's life and teachings could be taken as an example here.

Walatta Petros, who led a religious resistance movement against the official adoption of Catholicism by Emperor Susenyos during the first few decades of the seventieth century, was notable for her modesty in her life and teachings. On top of the intermittent allusion to the modest life throughout the hagiobiography (*ghedl*), one chapter takes up her humility as a subject. Chapter 80 of the *ghedl* reads thus: "Praise for Our Mother's Humility." The author of the *ghedl* mentions activities such as that Walatta Petros "used to minister in the community"; she used to take care of kitchen chores; "sweep up the ashes and rubbish" in the kitchen.[37] Galawdewos, the author of the text, recalled one memorable event:

> One day—it was the Feast of Our Lady Mary's Assumptions—Walatta Petros held a great banquet and prepared many tables with all kinds of dishes and drinks. She then assembled all the sisters, adults and youths, seating each one at her place. Our holy mother Walatta Petros remained standing and ministered to them, pouring water for [them to wash] their hands, and making them happy.[38]

---

37. Galadewos, *Life and Struggles*, 243.
38. Galadewos, *Life and Struggles*, 244.

Galawdewos matched this with what Christ did to his disciples during the Last Supper:

> On that day she performed every work of humility, just as our Lord did at the Last Supper, when he washed his disciples' feet and said to them, "Do you understand what I have done for you? While you call me 'Our Master' and 'Our Lord'—and you speak rightly because I am indeed your master and your Lord—I have just washed your feet. Therefore, it likewise is right and behooves you, too, to wash your companions' feet. For I have given you my example so that you too will do as I have done to you. Our holy mother Walatta Petros did the same and led the sisters toward the path of humility. As for them, they followed her and emulated her.[39]

The model of humility that Walatta Petros showed was Christ himself. As Christ served his disciples, Walatta Petros "poured" water on the hands of her disciples—pouring water for guests and senior family members when they wash their hands is the job of children and servants in Ethiopia. By serving the nuns that she oversaw (including cooking and cleaning for them occasionally), Walatta Petros was displaying humility after the exemplary deeds of Christ. Detailing the activities of modesty Walatta Petros accomplished, the phrasing the author of the biography employed to extol her was powerful. He said:

> There was no gate of humility through which our holy mother Walatta Petros would not pass; she could be found in every one. While she was a free woman, she became a maidservant. It was just as Paul says, "While I am free of all this, I have subjected myself to everyone."[40]

Acting as if she was a maidservant was supposed to convey the message that humans should lead their life on the basis of the ethics of humility.

One of the recurrent themes of *Ghedle Abune Teklehaimanot* is living in humility. According to the saint, leading a life in reticence, humility, and to be God-fearing are three cardinal virtues humans must observe. "These three [virtues]," the hagiobiography states, "leads to eternal life. I tell you [on the other hand] to be careful of the three paths of disgrace, namely jealousy, arrogance, and bigotry."[41]

---

39. Galadewos, *Life and Struggles*, 244–45.
40. Galadewos, *Life and Struggles*, 244.
41. Debre Libanos, ገድለ ተክለ ሃይማኖት, 42.5. Author's translation.

I have also come across a few *Qenie* poetry verses emphasizing Christ's life of charity and kindness. Saint Yared, the eminent *Degua*[42] scholar, had to say:

ሐዋርያቲሁ ከበበ፤

እግረ አርዳኢሁ ሐጸበ፤

ኮኖሙ አበ ወእመ ወመሐሮሙ ጥበበ፡፡

[ሐዋርያቱን ሾመ የደቀመዛሙርቱንም እግር አጠበ . . . አባትም እናትም ሆናቸው . . . ጥበብንም (ትህትናን/ራስን ዝቅ ማድረግን) አስተማራቸው]

He chose the prophets,

He washed the feet of his followers,

He became father and mother to them and taught them wisdom (humility, self-abnegation).[43]

Another Ge'ez *Qenie* that articulates a similar theme (this time apparently in line with the *Farewell Discourse* mentioned previously) runs as follows:

እደ ሆሣዕና በማይ ፍዳ ዘሃፀበ፤

አርዳኢሁ ኩሎሙ እምቅድመ ሥራ ወድካም፤

ቅንዋተ ሐዊን ሐፀቡ አኢጋሪሁ በደም

ወእብል አንሰ በቢዜሁ፤

ዘንቱ ተሐፅቦ ዘአልቦ ሕማም

ተፍጻሜተ ፍቅር ወሰላም፡፡

Jesus Christ exchanged the act of washing the feet of his disciples with water in exchange for the washing of his own feet with blood (anticipating his own feet washed with blood—note the *Farewell* meaning).[44]

The message is simple: Jesus gave his life for the sake of humanity. The humility that Abinet school students live by and practice is found in this wider Christian ethics of love and living for others while protecting oneself from envy, resentment, and prejudice.

---

42. *Degua* refers to music education.
43. Saint Yared quoted in Habte-Mariam, ጥንታዊ የኢ.ትዮጵያ ትምህርት, 181.
44. Memhir Akalewold quoted in Yohannes "Esidros," 256.

This tradition also works beyond the religious sphere. It takes a secular touch and goes to respecting "others" despite their religious convictions, cultural, and ethnic backgrounds. Even at the secular level, humility helps us see that life is fragile and we should be watchful against sliding into pride and arrogance. Above all, as Charles Whitfield and his associates underline, humility helps one to adopt a flexible hermeneutical attitude so that he or she could in turn help one *see* how others feel, which would in turn help us to become "more inclusive of others and do not compete with their reality."[45]

One of the core lessons that Abinet school students get formally and informally is epistemic humility, which is in fact intertwined with, or an offshoot of,[46] modesty and humbleness at the moral sphere. In Ethiopia, Abinet school students, the laity, and even ordinary people are usually heard quoting the epigrammatic statement that teaches the fear of God as the "beginning" of wisdom from the book of Proverbs. And the utterance is done with the full recognition that having knowledge or wisdom should not be something one should be conceited over since it ultimately belongs to God. This is the model of epistemic humility that the students of Abinet schools follow and adopt in their day to day interactions. Salman Akhtar's characterization of humility seems to be very appropriate for my purpose here. He points out the following key indexes:

> (i) a self-view of being 'nothing special' . . . , (ii) an emotional state of gratitude and tenderness, (iii) a cognitive attitude of openness to earning and considering one's state of knowledge as non-exhaustive, (iv) a behavioural style of interacting with others with attention, respect, and politeness, and (v) an experiential capacity for surrender and awe.[47]

Features (iii) and (iv) seem especially fitting for presenting epistemic humility in the context being discussed now. In other words, as the practice of footwashing and the Ge'ez Qenie verses discussed above showed, these are actually the imperatives that communities of Abinet schools follow and live by.

---

45. Quoted in Akhtar, *Silent Virtues*, 116.
46. Driver, *Uneasy Virtue*; Forsthoefel, "Loving the Ineffable."
47. Akhtar, *Silent Virtues*, 120.

## Concluding Remarks

The chapter aims to explicate the meaning of footwashing as a symbol of epistemic and moral humility among Abinet school students and the lessons other institutions can draw from it. As shown, Abinet schools and their student bodies are always ready to receive and welcome newcomers despite where they come from. Mostly filled with students from diverse backgrounds and places of origin, Abinet schools have always been ready not only to admit new ones but also metaphorically "bow down" and warmly receive them, displaying an exemplary act of humbleness and inclusiveness. In view of the current ethnic tensions and conflicts at "modern"[48] higher education institutions in Ethiopia (now spreading off-campus), the teachings as well as the gestures of humility the Abinet schools display stand exemplary.

Abinet schools do not have any ethnic allegiance or provincial tie to the locality where they are placed. Students who are from Gondar town and its vicinities, for example, do not (or are not expected to) demand a special privilege for attending Ba'eta Mariam Aquaquam School in Gondar. The said educational institution has been and would in principle be open to students from anywhere in the country and these students from other places would be treated equally to those who came from nearby. As indicated in the biographical notes discussed above, Abinet schools do not belong to any one particular group associated with the district where the school is located. Should our measure be "the idea of the university"—an idea that consecrates a university with some kind of cosmopolitanism—the Abinet schools have the preparation to meet that ideal.

In fact, it has been increasingly evident that students and faculty of higher education institutions do usually look down on Abinet schools, for the most part without knowing them. Most Western-educated Ethiopians who wrote about these schools immediately before and after the 1974 Ethiopian Revolution (which abolished the monarchy in the country) tend to evaluate these schools *in toto* as mere tools of indoctrination. In other words, many[49] have assumed that these classical schools were simply busy drilling the minds of students in some theological and ethical precepts, eventually undermining reflective and critical thinking. Although there

---

48. Contrary to the amnesia-like forgetfulness that designates Addis Ababa University as "first higher education institution" (a phrase that the university posted on its webpage for some time) for the country, Ethiopia has centuries-old educational institutions that could legitimately deserve the designation "university." Hence the qualification here "modern" for higher education institutions that we call universities these days.

49. For a thumbnail sketch of the issue, see Setargew, "Studying Traditional Schools," 110–12.

has been significant change since the 1990s in the way Western-educated Ethiopians look at the classical education system,[50] there is still a widespread, partly tacit and partly open, prejudice against it.[51]

Whereas this negative assessment of Abinet schools stands on a shaky ground, students and graduates of these Ethiopian modern higher education institutions do not seem to have the time and willingness to look into their own workings. They rather adopt, to borrow a useful term from the film producer and director Philip Alexander Gibney,[52] a "crushing certainty" that blinds one from critically examining one's own standing and encourage indicting the "other." The on-campus ethnic and related sectarian clashes, which have become almost the norm during the last few years, *partly* emanate from this tendency to live or endorse narrow provincial narratives. On top of this, the competitive spirit that present-day university structures install, directly or indirectly, promote narcissistic behaviors and haughtiness that would in turn preclude people from looking at themselves. As Akhtar[53] rightly puts it: "Being self-absorbed forecloses the ability and desire to know others."

By contrast, Abinet schools, and most probably in many other religious-based educational institutions too, embrace a culture of adopting modesty as a (to employ a phrase that has been used in a similar context) "virtue of ignorance"[54] in the sense that a student is encouraged to shun away from focusing on himself. Akthar's depiction of humility as a "silent" virtue would help us appreciate, to borrow an expression from Thomas A. Forsthoefel,[55] the "axiological value of ineffability" that sways in this tradition. Adopting a reserve has been one of the virtues of knowledge production in classical Ethiopian scholarship. The sixth-century Ethiopian scholar, composer, and author of distinct musical notations, Saint Yared, attributed his music innovations to God's revelation. Traditional paintings and ancient religious manuscripts do not carry authorship signatures. Legend has it that King Lalibela was assisted by angels when carving the world-famous rock-hewn churches.

50. See, for example, Messay, *Survival and Modernization*; Bridges et al., "From 'Deep Knowledge' to 'the Light of Reason'"; Maimire, "Towards a Critical Ethiopian Theory," 67–98.

51. Binns, "Theological Education," 110–11; Aweke, "Foundation of Curriculum in Ethiopia."

52. Julia Driver cited in Forsthoefel, "Loving the Ineffable," 261.

53. Akhtar, *Silent Virtues*, 37.

54. Adopting ignorance as far as the self is concerned does not of course mean self-abnegation.

55. Forsthoefel, "Loving the Ineffable," 261.

The spiritual and religious values that Abinet schools have cultivated in their students have therefore created a culture of cosmopolitanism. As they grow and mature in their moral character, and, educationally, attain enlightenment and excellence, Abinet students would increasingly insulate themselves from provincial identities and adopt an attitude of conviviality and inclusiveness. The ritual of footwashing is a symbolic act of this culture of inclusiveness and, as a practice, just one expression of it. Living frugally, sharing a scanty amount of food, offering the little they have, residing in poorly constructed mini-huts, Abinet students lead a life of austerity and asceticism that enables them to stay calm and sober in the face of any difficulty.

## Bibliography

Akhtar, Salman. *Silent Virtues: Patience, Curiosity, Privacy, Intimacy, Humility, and Dignity*. London: Routledge, 2019.

Aweke Shishigu. "Foundation of Curriculum in Ethiopia: Historical, Philosophical, Psychological and Sociological Perspectives." Paper presented at May Annual International Educational Conference of Bahir Dar University, Bahir Dar, Ethiopia, May 8–9, 2015.

Binns, John. "Theological Education in the Ethiopian Orthodox Church." *Journal of Adult Education Theological Education* 2.2 (October 2005) 103–13.

Bridges, David, et al. "From 'Deep Knowledge' to 'the Light of Reason': Sources for Philosophy of Education in Ethiopia." *Comparative Education* 40.4 (2004) 531–44.

Brown, Raymond E. *The Gospel and Epistles of John: A Concise Commentary*. New York: Union Theological Seminary, 1988.

Debre Libanos Andinet Gedam. ገድለ ተክለ ሃይማኖት [*Ghedle Teklehaimanot*]. Debre-Libanos: Debre-Libanos Andinet Gedam, 2011/12.

Driver, Julia. *Uneasy Virtue*. New York: Cambridge University Press, 2003.

Ethiopian Orthodox Tewahdo Church. የኢትዮጵያ ኦርቶዶክስ ተዋህዶ ቤተ ክርስቲያን ታሪክ ከልደተ ክርስቶስ እስከ ፷፱ ዓ.ም. [*Ye-Itiopia Orthodox Tewahido Bete Kirstian Tarik; Kelidete Kirstos eske Huletshi Amete Mihret*]. Addis Ababa: Ethiopian Orthodox Tewahdo Church, 2007.

Fleming, Walter L. "The Religions and Hospitable Rite of Feet Washing." *The Sewane Review* 16.1 (1908) 1–13.

Forsthoefel, Thomas A. "Loving the Ineffable: Epistemic Humility and Interfaith Solidarity." *Journal of Dharma Studies* 1.2 (2019) 259–68.

Galadewos. *The Life and Struggles of Our Mother Walatta Petros*. Edited and translated by Wendy Laura Belcher and Michael Kleiner. Princeton: Princeton University Press, 2015.

Habte-Mariam Workineh. ጥንታዊ የኢትዮጵያ ትምህርት [*Tintawi Ye-Itiopia Timihrt*]. Addis Ababa: Berhan ena Selam Haile-Selassie I, 1970/71.

Keener, Craig S. *The Gospel of John: A Commentary*. Vol. 1. Michigan: Baker Academic, 2002.

Kidane-Mariam Getahun. ጥንታዊው የቆሎ ተማሪ [*Tintawiw Ye-Qollo Temari*]. Addis Ababa: Tinsa'e Zeguba'e, 1962/63.

Maimire Menasemay. "Towards a Critical Ethiopian Theory of Education." In *Education, Politics and Social Change in Ethiopia*, edited by Paulos Milkias and Messay Kebede, 67–98. Los Angeles: Tsehai, 2010.

McGowan, Andrew. "A Missing Sacrament? Foot-washing, Gender, and Space in Early Christianity." *Archiv für Religionsgeschichte* 18–19.1 (2017) 105–22.

Mengistu Lemma. መጽሐፈ ትዝታ፡ ዘአለቃ ለማ ኃይሉ ወልደ ታሪክ [*Metsehafe Tizita Ze'aleqa Lemma*]. Addis Ababa: Addis Ababa University Press, 2010/11.

Mersha Aleheg. በእንተ ስማ ለማርያም፡ ጥንታዊው የኢትዮጵያ ትምህርት ይዘቱ ሥርአቱ ሕይወቱ [*Bente Sima Lemariam: Tintawiwu Ye-Itiopia Timihirt Yizetu, Sere'atu, Hiywotu*]. Addis Ababa, 2018/19.

Messay Kebede. *Survival and Modernization; Ethiopia's Enigmatic Present: A Philosophical Discourse*. Lawrenceville, NJ: Red Sea, 1999.

Rahmsdorf, Olivia. "'You Shall Not Wash My Feet . . .' (John 13.8): Time and Ethics in Peter's Interactions with Jesus in the Johannine Narrative." *Journal for the Study of the New Testament* 41.4 (2019) 458–77.

Setargew Kenaw. "Studying Traditional Schools of the Ethiopian Orthodox Church: A Quest for Fresh Methodology." *Ethiopian Journal of the Social Sciences and Humanities* 2.1 (2004) 107–22.

Thomas, J. Christopher. "Footwashing in John 13 and the Johannine Community." PhD diss., University of Sheffield, 1990.

Von Duam Tholl, Susan E. "Life According to the Rule: A Monastic Modification of Mandaum Imagery in the Peterborough Psalter." *Gesta* 33.2 (1994) 151–58.

Vullnetari, Julie, and Russell King. "'Washing Men's Feet': Gender, Care and Migration in Albania during and After Communism." *A Journal of Feminist Geography* 23.2 (1990) 198–215.

Yitbarek Ghidey. የቅኔ ቤት ባህልና የሕይወቴ ገጠመኝ [*Ye-Qenie Bet Bahil ena Ye-Hiwotie Getemegn*]. N.d.

Yohannes Afework. "Esidros". የመምህር አካለ ወልድ የሕይወት ታሪክ እና ቅኔዎቻቸው. [*Ye-Memhir Akalewold Ye-Hiwot Tarik ena Qeniewochachew*]. N.d.

# 10

# The Christian Moral Responsibility of Embracing the Ethnic Other

#### Nishan Cheru Degaga

Amid the contemporary challenges of Christianity, ethnic division is becoming the most rampant and threatening social phenomenon. As noted by the African theologian Emmanuel Katongole, the Rwandan genocide was a case of atrocities committed in the most Christianized country of Africa. Rwanda had experienced revival and was regarded as a model of evangelism. That such a horror took place there in 1994 was shocking.[1]

To better engage with the reality of African struggle on ethnic conflicts, it would be of great significance to look into the actual reality of the ethnic exclusion in the context of Ethiopia, an African country through which the concern and initiation of this chapter was born. As mentioned in the previous chapters, the case of the current significant Ethiopian internal displacement and the churches' division arising from ethnic conflicts affirm the gravity of the Ethiopian ethnic exclusion. According to the Directorate General for European Civil Protection and Humanitarian Aid Operations (DG ECHO) report on Ethiopia for 2018, interethnic conflict and violence has increased the number of internally displaced people to 2.35 million[2] and many deaths, according to various media outlets.

The worst consequence of this conflict is that even Christians who claim to be part of the same body of Christ are victims and participants of this phenomenon and churches are divided based on their ethnic affiliation. Even though all who claim to adhere to the Christian faith proclaim their unity in

---

1. Katongole and Wilson-Hartgrove, *Mirror to the Church*, 19.
2. "Ethiopia Internal Displacement," para. 1.

Christ, they are becoming more and more hostile to one another and unwilling to participate in the corporate worship of God as they used to.

Among other churches, the Ethiopian Evangelical Church Mekane Yesus, in which I am a member and witness of the incident, was a victim of ethnic conflict and divided in the year of 1999 until the reconciliation of 2010.[3] Even if the church has officially declared unity after a decade, she is still struggling with ethnic conflicts and is one of the religious institutions most affected by ethnic divisions.

The problem of ethnic division has become the feature of everyday life, encountered globally in different parts of the world including Africa and becoming the source of hatred, separation, and cruel conflicts aggravated unto the death of many. It is indisputable that this problem needs a serious theological engagement. The aim of this chapter is not to develop a full-fledged theology of ethnicity but is an endeavor to add theologically constructive fragments to generate moral resources on Christian ethics of responsibility for embracing the ethnic other. To this end, I will first explicate Volf's theological engagement with ethnic exclusion, deploying the metaphor of "embrace." Subsequently, I will engage with Katongole's pragmatic approach that addresses ethnic exclusion. Finally, integrating the insights of both Volf and Kantongole, I will propose the moral responsibility of embracing the ethnic other that encompasses all levels of relationships, especially at interpersonal and institutional levels as a remedy to ethnic exclusion, surpassing one's ethnicity.

## Miroslav Volf on Identity, Exclusion, and Embrace

### On Identity

In relation to ethnic exclusion, the most significant issue to be addressed is the question of identity as it is the source of disagreement commonly aggravated into severe conflict and division. It is therefore necessary to examine the most significant factors that determine identity in order to counter human relational problems such as ethnic exclusion.

My primary dialogue partner Miroslav Volf knows firsthand what it is like to have a mixed ethnic identity as he was born from a half-German father and Czech mother.[4] He is one of the contemporary leading Protestant theologians who is well engaged in the theological discourse of the problem of identity, noting that, "the problem of ethnic and cultural conflicts is part of a

3. Tsegaye, "Formal Letter of Instruction."
4. Oppenheimer, "Miroslav Volf."

larger problem of identity and otherness."[5] Addressing the problem of identity is therefore part of the solution in countering ethnic exclusion.

Volf also claims that the way we deal with identity and difference decides the future of our world.[6] Currently, the major worldwide contemporary conflicts are related to disagreements on identity between different social groups that end up in division and war. There cannot be a better future for our society unless we properly engage into the problems of identity.

As a solution towards the problems of identity and otherness and the resulting conflicts, Volf suggests that our reflection should not be on the kind of society we should create but rather on what we should be. First, the agent itself, holding the cross at its center, needs to be transformed so that it can transform social arrangements.[7]

## The Model of the Cross

Volf claims that it is the model of divine self-donation that enables us to receive others into communion, "whoever our enemies and whoever we may be."[8] It is the cross through which God's love for his enemies is revealed that we take as the base for our communion with others even when they stand as our enemies.

The cross not only reveals Christ's sacrificial love towards his enemies but also calls all his followers to take their own cross and walk in his footsteps, imitating his inclusive personality that unconditionally embraced his enemies despite the possibility of rejection or violence. The way of the cross is the way to the transformed identity that can counter exclusion, including ethnic exclusion.

## Distance and Belonging

As noted by Volf, the church is capable of playing her role of reconciliation only when proper relation between distance from culture and belonging to it is maintained. In order to explicate this relation, Volf uses the biblical story of the call of Abraham and how it is appropriated by the Christian faith.[9]

---

5. Volf, *Exclusion & Embrace*, 16.
6. Volf, *Exclusion & Embrace*, 20.
7. Volf, *Exclusion & Embrace*, 20–22.
8. Volf, *Exclusion & Embrace*, 20–22.
9. Volf, *Exclusion & Embrace*, 37–38.

The story of Abraham as narrated in Genesis 12 indicates God calling him to leave his country as well as his family towards an unknown destiny. To be a blessing, he needed to depart, "cutting the ties that so profoundly defined him."[10] Abraham had the courage to cut off all his cultural and familial ties as well as leave his ancestors' gods to follow "a God of all families and all cultures."[11] The first step which Abraham was required to take was to leave behind the things that determined his identity. Without this first step of departing, he could have not embraced God's promise of being the father of all families of the earth.

Volf then argues that to be a child of Abraham and Sarah and to respond to the call of their God or to be a Christian means, "to make an exodus, to start a voyage, become a stranger (Gen 23:4; 24:1–9)."[12] Moving away from the old and keeping distance from it is mandatory to get into the new. In relation to the nature of the new Christian identity, Volf writes:

> Much like Jews and Muslims, Christians can never be first of all Asians or Americans, Croatians, Russians, or Tutsis, and then Christians. At the very core of Christian identity lies an all-encompassing change of loyalty, from a given culture with its gods to the God of all cultures. A response to a call from that God entails rearrangement of a whole network of allegiances.[13]

Christianity is not therefore an addition to one's national identity but is itself a new identity under the lordship of a God that rules all humanity and above every culture. As noted by Volf, the other characteristic of Abraham's departure is its foundation for a multiethnic community.[14] This is possible as "all people can have access to the one God of Abraham and Sarah on equal terms none by right, and all by grace"[15] and this was asserted by Paul who mentions in Galatians 3:8 the blessing of all nations through Abraham.[16] The story of Abraham is not about God's favor to one ethnic group but his invitation of all nations through him for the formation of a multiethnic community. It is by the formation of such communal identity that we can fight exclusive ethnicity.

In addition to Abraham's role in the formation of a multiethnic community, Volf argues that we need to consider the cross as the foundation

10. Volf, *Exclusion & Embrace*, 37–38.
11. Volf, *Exclusion & Embrace*, 39.
12. Volf, *Exclusion & Embrace*, 39.
13. Volf, *Exclusion & Embrace*, 40.
14. Volf, *Exclusion & Embrace*, 43.
15. Volf, *Exclusion & Embrace*, 45.
16. Volf, *Exclusion & Embrace*, 45.

of the Christian community which is "the self-giving of the one to the many."[17] The unity that is brought through the cross does not destroy particularity of "bodies" but rather breaks down their enmity. Christianity is not about creating unity by eliminating particular identities but it is the overcoming of their enmity. The role of the Spirit is not to remove differences but to create equality by disregarding them.[18]

Volf's argument on distance and belonging is that even though Christians do not have to lose their cultural identity as Jew or gentile and become new humanity, "no culture can retain its own tribal deities; religion must be de-ethnicized so that ethnicity can be de-sacralized."[19] Christians do not go out from their culture to join a new Christian culture but they hold one foot outside their culture and the other inside, distant and at the same time belonging to it.[20] Both belonging and distance should be maintained as "belonging without distance destroys" and "distance without belonging isolates."[21] The right option is not between the two extremes of particular identity or absolute unity but an equal embrace of both.

According to Volf, distance has two important functions: the first is to create "space in us to receive the other" through the Spirit who recreates us into "a catholic personality."[22] This personality is "enriched by otherness" through which "multiple others have been reflected in it in a particular way." The identity of each local church, which is a catholic community, is formed by the other which means, "each needs all to be properly itself."[23]

Andrew Shepherd agrees with Volf's argument on the "catholic personality" enriched by otherness and refers to Paul's description of the human body in 1 Corinthians 12:12–31. The body which is composed of particular parts (hands, eyes, ears, noses) is still the same body.[24] Supporting Volf's claim, he states that, "[r]ather than difference being dissolved and dissipated into a totalitarian *Same* it is the Christian claim that in *communion* the particularity and uniqueness of each self is honored and celebrated."[25]

The enriching by otherness comes as a result of being part of the body of Christ and his community. In this regard, Volf notes that the self cannot

17. Volf, *Exclusion & Embrace*, 47.
18. Volf, *Exclusion & Embrace*, 47–48.
19. Volf, *Exclusion & Embrace*, 49.
20. Volf, *Exclusion & Embrace*, 50.
21. Volf, *Exclusion & Embrace*, 50.
22. Volf, *Exclusion & Embrace*, 50.
23. Volf, *Exclusion & Embrace*, 51.
24. Shepherd, *Gift of the Other*, 190.
25. Shepherd, *Gift of the Other*, 190.

exist as a self-enclosed personality but, "Communion with this God is at once also communion with those others who have entrusted themselves in faith to the same God."[26] With the new faith comes new relationship with God as well as all others who are in communion with him.[27] Volf states that, "as a person, and as a Christian, one is indeed an independent, and yet simultaneously a socially conditioned entity."[28]

The second function of distance noted by Volf is "the judgment against evil in every culture."[29] Even if a catholic personality is enriched by otherness that does not mean all otherness and everything in every culture is to be integrated. But the judgment of evil should begin from the self and from one's own culture.[30]

## Exclusion

With the aim of explicating differentiation versus exclusion, Volf refers to Cornelius Plantinga's argument on Genesis 1. For Plantinga, the act of creation depicted through that passage shows "a pattern of "separating" and "binding together." God separates things such as light from darkness, day from night, and binds together human beings to other creatures, to himself as well as to each other.[31]

As elaborated by Volf, this separation and binding of creation "suggests that 'identity' includes connection, difference, and heterogeneity."[32] Humanity is not therefore formed by "simple rejection of the other" but "through a complex process of 'taking in' and 'keeping out.'"[33] We are separated and connected and at the same time distinct and related. Volf then argues that "Identity is the result of the distinction from the other *and* the internalization of the relationship to the other."[34] Creation itself affirms that the self cannot exist separately from the other as each is dependent on the other.

For Volf, exclusion is then the sin of reconfiguring creation's pattern of interdependence.[35] This exclusion has two aspects: first, one becomes

---

26. Volf, *After Our Likeness*, 173.
27. Volf, *After Our Likeness*, 173.
28. Volf, *After Our Likeness*, 185.
29. Volf, *Exclusion & Embrace*, 52.
30. Volf, *Exclusion & Embrace*, 52.
31. Volf, *Exclusion & Embrace*, 65.
32. Volf, *Exclusion & Embrace*, 66.
33. Volf, *Exclusion & Embrace*, 66.
34. Volf, *Exclusion & Embrace*, 66.
35. Volf, *Exclusion & Embrace*, 66.

outside the pattern of interdependence as it cuts off the bonds and is placed in a sovereign independence. In the second case, separation is elimination and the other is not recognized "as someone who in his or her otherness belongs to the pattern of interdependence."[36] Volf notes also the necessity of boundaries as it is impossible to have discrete identities without boundaries and there is no relation with the other without discrete identities.[37] The openness towards the other is well explained and illustrated by Volf through the metaphor of embrace, which is a major act in the formation of identity and the struggle against exclusion.

## Embrace

In a world seriously threatened by enmity, Volf argues that it is possible to make and sustain peace between the self and the other.[38] His central thesis in this regard is that "God's reception of hostile humanity into divine communion is a model for how human beings should relate to the other."[39]

As a reflection on both personal and communal identity in relation to the other in the midst of enmity, Volf uses "the phenomenology of embrace" that contains four elements. The four essential movements of embrace are: opening the arms, waiting, closing the arms, and opening them again.[40] The first movement of opening the arms is a sign of the willing to include the other rather than to remain with a self-enclosed identity. For Volf this movement means that, "I do not want to be myself only; I want the other to be part of who I am and I want to be part of the other."[41]

Regarding the second moment of embrace, Volf states that there is a time for waiting where the self, after initiating the first movement, stops and waits for the other to open. There should be a desire and opening of the other. The other cannot be forced or manipulated to accept the embrace.[42] Volf notes also that, "If embrace takes place, it will always be because the other has desired the self just as the self has desired the other"[43] which shows that embrace can never be accomplished without reciprocity.[44]

36. Volf, *Exclusion & Embrace*, 67.
37. Volf, *Exclusion & Embrace*, 67.
38. Volf, *Exclusion & Embrace*, 100.
39. Volf, *Exclusion & Embrace*, 100.
40. Volf, *Exclusion & Embrace*, 140.
41. Volf, *Exclusion & Embrace*, 141.
42. Volf, *Exclusion & Embrace*, 142–43.
43. Volf, *Exclusion & Embrace*, 142–43.
44. Volf, *Exclusion & Embrace*, 142–43.

According to Volf, the third step of embrace is the closing of the arms. Here, a host becomes a guest and the guest becomes a host. For a proper embrace, besides reciprocity, there should be a soft touch. If the touch is too strong, that may imply a hidden power of exclusion.[45]

The fourth and final act of embrace is the opening of the arms again. Regarding this stage, Volf argues that, "The other must be let go so that her alterity—her genuine dynamic identity—may be preserved."[46] As a result of the embrace, the identity of the self is preserved but at the same time enriched by the other.[47]

On this preservation of the self, Volf argues that "the one" according to Galatians 3:28 does not entail a "unified person" beyond any differentiation but rather a "differentiated unity" as a communion.[48] Embrace is not the elimination of the self or the other for the purpose of unity but the enrichment of both in consideration with the will and freedom of the other.

So far, the central claim of this chapter, which is the need for the Christian moral responsibility in countering ethnic exclusion, was derived from the arguments forwarded by Volf. The focus of the following section will be on the pragmatic aspect of the ethics of moral responsibility of embrace as implied by my second dialogue partner, Emmanuel Katongole.

## Emmanuel Katongole's Pragmatic Approach

Emmanuel Katongole has well engaged in the real scenario of the African ethnic exclusion, which he analyzes through the history of the Rwandan genocide, looking into its cause and the way Christianity could have reacted against it. Katongole does not only address the problems of exclusive identity of individuals but also of the society at large. He argues for a Christian social ethics that is capable of challenging this contemporary social phenomenon.

Katongole was born in Uganda from Rwandan immigrants. His father was a poor Tutsi while his mother was from a wealthy Hutu family. He became a Catholic priest and currently teaches at the University of Notre Dame in the United States.[49] Katongole's introduction of his own identity illustrates the mixed or confused identity which he claims to be a better expression of

---

45. Volf, *Exclusion & Embrace*, 142–43.
46. Volf, *Exclusion & Embrace*, 144.
47. Volf, *Exclusion & Embrace*, 145.
48. Volf, *After Our Likeness*, 145.
49. Katongole and Wilson-Hartgrove, *Mirror to the Church*, 14.

an identity composed of different identity markers, such as ethnicity, gender, religion, or others that cannot be claimed separately.

In his book titled *Mirror to the Church: Resurrecting Faith after Genocide in Rwanda*, Katongole thoroughly addresses the case of the Rwandan genocide that took place in 1994, killing around eight hundred thousand people. In order to identify the problem of tribal exclusion that motivated the genocide, he first looks into the background story of the tribalism of Rwanda. Subsequently, he examines the role and response of the church towards the genocide and forwards his reflection in order to present a better alternative in cases of such severe challenges by raising some relevant practical questions.

It is therefore necessary to examine Katongole's evaluation of the Rwandan genocide in relation to its background story and challenges to determine its real cause in order to draw a lesson from such a history and for the prevention of such future occurrence. We will also look into Katongole's evaluation of the types of social engagements that failed to challenge and prevent the genocide together with his proposal of a better alternative. The pragmatic aspect of Katongole's approach to exclusion speaks on how to fight exclusion practically through whatever kind of small or big opportunities at hand.

## The Rwandan Genocide

Katongole first speaks about the different contradictions that Rwanda was living in just before the genocide. It was a country of over 85 percent Christian, which was regarded as a model of evangelization in Africa and where Christianity was well embraced, with a history of revival and church growth.[50] Unfortunately, "The most Christianized country in Africa became the site of its worst genocide."[51] The slaughter began on the Thursday of Easter week, after a week that Rwandans celebrated Maundy Thursday, conducted in remembrance of Jesus' "new command" of loving one another. For Katongole all these contradictions were possible due to the blood of tribalism that was allowed to flow deeper than the waters of baptism.[52]

Upon exploring the story of the genocide, Katongole noted that after the Rwandan broadcaster clearly called for the killing of Tutsis, around eight hundred thousand Tutsis and moderate Hutus were killed in their homes, at roadblocks, and in churches, mostly by their neighbors and fellow church

50. Katongole and Wilson-Hartgrove, *Mirror to the Church*, 18–19.
51. Katongole and Wilson-Hartgrove, *Mirror to the Church*, 19.
52. Katongole and Wilson-Hartgrove, *Mirror to the Church*, 19–22.

members.⁵³ As noted by Katongole, Rwandans faced different kinds of betrayals: by the church, by their own priests, and also by Western Christians who left the country during the genocide, except for few individuals.⁵⁴

## The Story Behind the Genocide

Katongole states that there is a long history of politics behind the formation of tribal identities such as Hutu and Tutsi.⁵⁵ Rwanda was the most homogeneous country in Africa where "for many years Hutu and Tutsi lived on the same hills, spoke the same language, shared the same culture, intermarried, and transacted with one another in a variety of complex modalities."⁵⁶

Katongole observes that the story behind the Rwandan genocide is not just a story about Rwanda. "It is a story rooted in the imagination of Europe, told by European colonialists, retold and deepened over centuries by the church's missionaries, and accepted by converts to the Christian faith."⁵⁷ What is assumed as "natural" identity is none other than the effect of the social and political institutions' stories.⁵⁸ Even if it is necessary to acknowledge the effort of a few faithful servants of the church, the history of the genocide indicates that the church was responsible for actively participating in the violence or for being complacent.

Katongole noted that, although there was "a social hierarchy in the pre-colonial kingdom of Rwanda,"⁵⁹ there were no tribal or ethnic hierarchies between Tutsi and Hutu, and no violence was recorded concerning them in pre-colonial history. To the contrary, Europeans came with their own assumption of a primitive Africa, justifying the enslavement of black Africans through the biblical story of Noah who cursed his own son Ham.⁶⁰

After such a separation, the Belgians started to build Rwanda's modern nation state marking the Tutsis as "natural born leaders" and the Hutus as inferior descendants of Ham.⁶¹ Following this divisive approach, "the church in Rwanda amplified, intensified, and radiated them."⁶² The church

---

53. Katongole and Wilson-Hartgrove, *Mirror to the Church*, 30.
54. Katongole and Wilson-Hartgrove, *Mirror to the Church*, 41–45.
55. Katongole and Wilson-Hartgrove, *Mirror to the Church*, 47.
56. Katongole and Wilson-Hartgrove, *Mirror to the Church*, 47.
57. Katongole and Wilson-Hartgrove, *Mirror to the Church*, 52.
58. Katongole and Wilson-Hartgrove, *Mirror to the Church*, 53.
59. Katongole and Wilson-Hartgrove, *Mirror to the Church*, 55.
60. Katongole and Wilson-Hartgrove, *Mirror to the Church*, 55–57.
61. Katongole and Wilson-Hartgrove, *Mirror to the Church*, 59.
62. Katongole and Wilson-Hartgrove, *Mirror to the Church*, 61.

was also responsible for the reversal of the Tutsi–Hutu situation via the Flemish priests who sympathized with the oppressed Hutu. Afterwards, Rwanda got into a "Social Revolution" that brought the independence of Rwanda from Belgian rule and the power shift to the Hutus while many Tutsis run away to save their lives.[63]

Katongole argues that, after the formation of the so-called natural identity of Tutsi and Hutu tribes, there is nothing that Christianity can do to alter the situation of enmity between them and the resulting genocide. Instead of their preconceived "categories of race and tribe, primitive and advanced," the church should have offered Rwandans possibilities beyond their Hutu and Tutsi labels.[64]

## The Need for Christian Social Engagement

For Katongole, what we need is not "incredible and magnificent promises of salvation for Africa to be achieved through civilization, modernization, nation-building, globalization, privatization, a new world order, and the like."[65] However, what we need is "Christian social engagement that, having learned to suspect these old formulas, ground their praxis in the local, concrete, and particular communities of neglected villages."[66]

On Katongole's emphasis on the value of the local and particular practice, Isabel Apawo Phiri comments that his writing motivates us "to action knowing that whatever bit that each one of us does to create a new future for Africa can actually make a difference."[67] It is not, therefore, necessarily through large-scale visions and strategies that transformation takes place but even better through particular involvement of members of the community.

In spite of his appreciation to Katongole's emphasis on concrete and particular issues of the community and of individuals' impact of the social transformation, Elias K. Bongmba argues that "it is still necessary to engage in a political theology that offers broad critiques of systems and institutions as a necessary condition for creating political reforms and projects that are sustainable."[68] Bongmba's suggestion for broader critiques of

---

63. Katongole and Wilson-Hartgrove, *Mirror to the Church*, 64–65.
64. Katongole and Wilson-Hartgrove, *Mirror to the Church*, 68–71.
65. Katongole, *Sacrifice of Africa*, 137.
66. Katongole, *Sacrifice of Africa*, 137.
67. Phiri, Review of *The Sacrifice of Africa*, 604.
68. Phiri, Review of *Lament and Narrative*, 407.

systems and institutions is to be appreciated as it complements Katongole's vision of social engagement.

## The Insufficiency of Pious, Political, and Pastoral Postures

Among the reasons for the failure of the church in Rwanda, Katongole mentions the insufficiency of Christian social engagement and the way Christians relate to politics and economics.[69] He uses three New Testament stories to indicate how our pious, political, and pastoral postures may be insufficient for proper social engagement.

In Mark 15:21, Simon, a man from Cyrene was forced to carry the cross of Christ. He obeyed and carried the cross without any objection or question, which was a model of pious obedience. He did not stand against the injustice or resist authorities. Similar to this man, Rwandans obeyed the Hutus who ordered them to kill their neighbors without any question. Katongole argues that the church encouraged and even shaped such kind of obedience.[70]

The second posture mentioned by Katongole is the political. In John 18:19–22, we read that an official of the temple guard struck Jesus in the face for his disrespect towards the high priest. He was defending the power of the high priest and showing his loyalty. Katongole connects this story with the loyalty of church leaders to government authorities during the genocide.[71]

The third posture that Katongole speaks about is the pastoral posture. John 19:39–42 narrates that Joseph of Arimathea asked for the body of Jesus and buried him properly. Joseph as well as Nicodemus, who came with him, cared enough for the body of Jesus but did everything without questioning who killed him or why he was killed. As major social players, churches were places of "compassionate care" but at the same time "sites of killing."[72]

On these three types of postures, Katongole's argument is not to discard them as irrelevant for the Christian social responsibility. Phiri's following critique towards Katongole seems to reveal such a misinterpretation as he states,

> The three paradigms of Christian involvement cannot be excluded from finding a solution to the problems of Africa because

---

69. Katongole and Wilson-Hartgrove, *Mirror to the Church*, 96.
70. Katongole and Wilson-Hartgrove, *Mirror to the Church*, 96–99.
71. Katongole and Wilson-Hartgrove, *Mirror to the Church*, 96–99.
72. Katongole and Wilson-Hartgrove, *Mirror to the Church*, 105–6.

each one of them has a legitimate place in the solving of Africa's problems . . . the other three paradigms, which he [Katongole] dismisses, are also making small attempts to contribute to the solving the problems of Africa. It is a holistic approach informed by faith in the God of creation that can work for Africa. The work cannot be done by Christians alone as shown from the stories. It also requires an inter-religious dimension, which cannot be underplayed in the context of Africa.[73]

But Katongole was not dismissing the three paradigms of Christians' social involvement. Rather, he was questioning the nation states' political imagination that was the obstacle for real transformation. For Katongole, influencing government policy (political paradigm), "motivating or infusing Christian action in the world through love (spiritual paradigm) . . . or relief services (pastoral paradigm)"[74] was not enough as what is needed crucially is "a mythological adjustment that addresses the underlying stories that shape the imagination."[75] Katongole was therefore suggesting a new mindset that corrects the corrupted political imagination rather than insignificant political or spiritual mini-involvements.

## The Prophetic Posture

After evaluating the insufficiency of the three postures of the Rwandan church during the genocide, Katongole suggests the alternative prophetic posture that could be possible through the help of the power of the Holy Spirit by way of different interruptions of existing norms. As an example of interruptions, Katongole refers to a biblical story and different people's actual experience during the Rwandan genocide.[76]

Katongole's biblical example is the woman from Bethany mentioned in Matthew 26:6–7. Mary's act of anointing Jesus with a very expensive perfume was an interruption through which she "dares to question the social, economic, and political assumptions of her day with a single act."[77] Similarly, the gospel forces us to question social norms and interrupt them, as we should.

Among the people who prophetically interrupted Rwanda's genocide, Katongole refers to Sister Felicitee Niyitegeta. This Hutu woman, against the

73. Phiri, Review of *The Sacrifice of Africa*, 603.
74. Katongole, *Sacrifice of Africa*, 58–9.
75. Katongole, *Sacrifice of Africa*, 58–9.
76. Katongole, *Sacrifice of Africa*, 111–15.
77. Katongole, *Sacrifice of Africa*, 115–16.

rule of the genocide, was brave enough to shelter Tutsi children and sacrifice her life due to the interruption she dared to make. Father Sibomana was another example who helped and encouraged many to resist the Hutu power. He had a prophetic posture that enabled him to interrupt the norm using any possible means to rescue people and fight for resistance.[78]

Another case Katongole mentions is the interruption of the manager of the Hôtel des Mille Collines. This international hotel was providing shelter and offering good news better than the nearby church. The other story of interruption is of a Muslim community called *Nyamirambo* that refused to be divided as Hutu and Tutsi and where Tutsis were protected.[79]

The story of an Italian social worker that was killed and buried in a place called Nyamata for alerting the international media on the killing of Tutsis is also a good example of interruption. Katongole states that "her story announces the power of Christ's resurrection to create a new community beyond black and white."[80] On these stories Katongole remarks, "these examples reveal a certain kind of confused identity," and which is the right one.[81]

Katongole has been very resourceful in helping us to understand how exclusive identities were formed in Rwanda through a political imagination that created rivalry between two tribes that ended up in a violent conflict and death of many. According to him, it is possible to counter this social challenge through the agency of the church and its social reimagination. He uses different stories to demonstrate the possibility of a reimagination of a new future for Africa. He adequately addressed the historical root causes of ethnic conflicts, the theological explanations related to the problem of exclusion including practical examples of interruptions.

Following the dialogue made with my partners, Volf and Katongole, the final task of this chapter will be to integrate the theological insights of both theologians in order to explore the implied Christian moral responsibility in the embrace of the other beyond one's ethnic identity. The resultant moral responsibility not only addresses the interpersonal level of human relationship but also the institutional levels.

## Towards a Moral Responsibility of Embrace

So far, we have separately examined Volf's view of identity, his suggestion of embrace as a challenge to exclusion, and Katongole's proposal of

78. Katongole, *Sacrifice of Africa*, 117–20.
79. Katongole, *Sacrifice of Africa*, 121–22.
80. Katongole, *Sacrifice of Africa*, 128.
81. Katongole, *Sacrifice of Africa*, 129.

prophetic interruption in the midst of conflicts and violence fundamentally based upon the claims of the Christian faith. Both of them have been very resourceful in providing considerable theological perceptions, suggesting practical approaches in overcoming ethnic exclusion. Both Volf and Katongole had complimentary views on major issues such as identity and exclusion which they thoroughly addressed to forward their proposal in countering exclusion. They have made a remarkable contribution for the development of an integrated approach of a moral responsibility of embrace and which was implied by both of them in different ways.

## Moral Responsibility: The Inter-personal Level

As we examined, Volf mentions the need for a transformed agent, a self, capable of transforming its social arrangement that could counter exclusion, which indicates that moral responsibility should begin with a transformed self at the inter-personal level. Volf has also referred to the model of the cross and its call to all Christians for a mutual embrace similar to Christ's open arms on the cross for the embrace of all humanity. Volf's notification on Christ's model of unconditional embrace is a call for the realization of the moral responsibility in the life of his followers as a challenge to ethnic exclusion.

Volf has also argued that the Spirit does not eliminate the difference between people but aims to create their equality. The fact that the cross does not eliminate particular "bodies" but destroys the enmity between them affirms the interpersonal moral responsibility characterized by peace and equality between members of the body of Christ despite ethnic difference. Volf speaks also of creating space for the other as an opportunity of enrichment for both without shattering their particularity. This implies that the self has a moral responsibility of intentionally looking for the good of the other.

Volf speaks of the interdependence of the self and the other which relates to the nature of God's creation itself. The self cannot be without the other, which implies that the self is by its nature morally responsible for the well-being and completeness of the other. On the relationship between the self and the other, Volf's use of the metaphor of embrace is very essential as it entails a morally responsible movement of the self towards the other which should be the quality of relationships at interpersonal level.

From what Theodros A. Teklu noted on the relation between the self and the other, it is also possible to better understand the kind of moral responsibility required at the interpersonal level. He states that we are called for "solidarity beyond the ethnos."[82] According to him, "the relation of the self to the other should not be simply because the self (the 'I') needs the not-'I' (the other) for its fulfillment but rather because the self should respond to the call, which the other (not-I) poses on the self."[83] The broader perspective of responsibility is the one that reaches the other out of its ethnic boundary and that is the unconditional embrace that could combat ethnic exclusion.

As argued by Volf, essential elements that are required for the realization of embrace are repentance, forgiveness, and creating space for the other, as well as healing of memory. All these elements of embrace are also elements of moral responsibility at the interpersonal level as responsibility towards the other cannot be fulfilled before relationships are healed. Volf's proposed elements of embrace can also be taken as components of the moral responsibility.

On the other hand, we have examined Katongole's approach to identity and exclusion and his practical as well as biblical illustrations on interrupting social conflicts such as the Rwandan genocide. From his approach, just as we saw with Volf, it is possible to identify significant elements for the moral responsibility of embrace.

Among the illustrations given by Katongole, the story of the woman from Bethany mentioned in Matthew 26:6–7 is a model of the moral responsibility of a person towards another. Mary dared to interrupt the social norm to fulfill her responsibility towards Christ. From this story, we observe a moral responsibility at the interpersonal level where a woman goes for embrace and meets the need of the other despite the existing cultural challenge.

To build upon Volf's and Katongole's implied moral responsibility, it is useful to look into Paul Ricoeur's concept of solicitude in relation to the interpersonal level of responsibility. As noted by Henry Venema, "Ricoeur extracts from Aristotle an 'inclusive concept of solicitude, based principally on giving and receiving.'"[84] This giving and receiving between the self and the other is not a reciprocal exchange in terms of an economy of power, but as quoted by Venema, Ricoeur speaks of a mutuality that corresponds to a "non-oppositional difference—an economy of love . . . [where] the desire of each evokes the desire of the other: mutual recognition, mutual yielding/receiving, mutual delighting, mutual empowering."[85] This is therefore the kind of relationship based upon mutual love and responsibility between the self and

---

82. Theodros, *Politics of Metanoia*, 215.
83. Theodros, *Politics of Metanoia*, 215.
84. Venema, "Oneself," 417.
85. Venema, "Oneself," 418.

the other that should exist at the interpersonal level of moral responsibility of embrace and that would counter ethnic exclusion.

As noted by Gary Watson, Stephen Darwall's view of morality is that, in the second-personal standpoint, morality is understood as equal accountability, which is a form of one's respect to the other and a "possibility of mutual recognition."[86] For Darwall, morality is first accountability to God. Secondly, it is a mutual accountability. And, thirdly, it is equal mutual accountability among free and rational beings. Accordingly, "as we freely and rationally cooperate with Him [God] in our obedience,"[87] we are "being in a kind of moral community with God."[88] This is, therefore, the kind of moral responsibility required at the interpersonal level that will prevent ethnic exclusion as relationship between the self and his creator as well as with the other is characterized by mutual respect and accountability.

## Moral Responsibility: The Institutional Level

The institutional level moral responsibility begins with and is built upon interpersonal togetherness. The ethnic conflict and violence encountered in different institutions are, therefore, the resulting effect of interpersonal level conflicts. We will therefore examine, through the moral implication of both Volf and Katongole, the moral responsibility that corrects ethnic exclusion at the institutional level.

As we have seen, Volf has noted that the church is capable of playing her role of reconciliation only when proper relation between distance from and belonging to culture is maintained. He has also described the church as a catholic community where everyone needs the other to be properly itself. This implies, therefore, that the church as an institution cannot entertain ethnic exclusion but correct it through the practice of moral responsibility.

Volf has also argued that the church as a new community is an institution that is in communion with others who also have faith in the same God. Therefore, the communion is not with one's own ethnic group but equally with all the family of faith. Volf implicitly affirms therefore a moral responsibility of embrace beyond ethnicity. In fact, Volf makes embrace the precondition of justice as he argues that, "The will to embrace precedes any 'truth' about 'others' and any construction about their 'justice.'"[89] Justice is then possible when the moral responsibility of embrace takes place.

86. Watson, "Morality as Equal Accountability," 38.
87. Watson, "Morality as Equal Accountability," 41–42.
88. Watson, "Morality as Equal Accountability," 42.
89. Volf, *Exclusion & Embrace*, 18.

Katongole has also argued the insufficiency of pious, political, or pastoral engagement of Christians and underlined the need for questioning and even resisting unjust authorities. When Katongole critiques obedience without a challenge to injustice, or the church's loyalty to the political power, or even the church's role in aggravating social evils such as in the case of Rwanda, he was calling for the church to be a morally responsible agent that could question and challenge injustice at the institutional level.

Katongole also refers to Sister Felicitee Niyitegeta, a Hutu woman that dared to shelter Tutsi children against the rule of the Rwandan Genocide. She was a model of prophetic interruption that stood as a morally responsible agent and a founder of a morally responsible institution that embraced the children of Rwanda without any ethnic boundary. When Katongole talked about the Hôtel des Mille Collines that provided shelter to both Tutsi and Hutu people, he was giving us an example of the moral responsibility that any institution should exhibit.

On the institutional level of moral responsibility, and as quoted by Edi Pucci, Paul Ricoeur states that "living well is not limited to interpersonal relations but extends to the life of institutions."[90] Justice, which calls for the need of reciprocity and equality, is indispensible for the organized communal life.[91] Institutions should therefore be morally responsible agents where justice is for all members and where ethnic exclusion is prevented through equal right and privilege of all.

According to Mathias Nebel, people should acknowledge the reality of institutions' "unjust structure" but also strive for liberation. He noted that "[T]here will have to be a *metanoia*, a change of heart, going beyond what is possible to us, human creatures . . . if Christ's death and resurrection really overcame the sin of the world, then we should also expect and hope for a grace which overcomes these wicked realities."[92] We should therefore anticipate the moral responsibility at the institutional level that transforms their unjust structures so that they would not permit ethnic exclusions.

## Conclusion

Beginning with a proposal of a Christian moral responsibility that could embrace the other in order to counter the challenges of ethnic exclusions, we have examined and evaluated Volf's approach to identity and exclusion and his proposal of embrace. His view on identity and his proposal of embrace

---

90. Pucci, "Review of Paul Ricoeur's Oneself as Another," 198.
91. Pucci, "Review of Paul Ricoeur's Oneself as Another," 198.
92. Nebel, "Transforming Unjust Structures," 124.

was informative on the possibility of a moral responsibility that could challenge ethnic exclusion. We have then moved to the work of Katongole that especially related to the Rwandan genocide, where we have observed that he has been very resourceful in providing us important insights through which we drew significant implications for the moral responsibility of embrace in overcoming ethnic exclusion.

Finally, through the analysis of the works of both theologians and an integration of their approaches, a comprehensive moral responsibility of embrace was proposed, encompassing the inter-personal as well as institutional levels of relationships.

This study, as I had indicated at the beginning of the chapter, was guided by the central question of whether or not the Christian faith generates theological resources that inform the moral responsibility of embracing the ethnic other. With the help of my dialogue partners, I affirm that Christianity has adequate and sufficient provisions that allow the fulfillment of this responsibility at the interpersonal and institutional level relationships.

The climax of the study was to assert that ethnic exclusion can be countered with this understanding of Christian ethics. This chapter has repositioned Christian values on the platform of identity discourse to contribute constructive theological elements to further ethnic-related research in response to the contemporary challenge of ethnic exclusion.

## Bibliography

Bongmba, Elias K. "Lament and Narrative: A Review of Emmanuel Katongole's *The Sacrifice of Africa*." *Modern Theology* 30 (2014) 403–7.

"Ethiopia: Internal Displacement." https://reliefweb.int/map/ethiopia/ethiopia-internal-displacement-december-2018-dg-echo-daily-map-22012019.

Genet Zewde. *No One Left Behind: Redesigning the Ethiopian Education System*. Addis Ababa: Mega, 2018.

Katongole, Emmanuel. *The Sacrifice of Africa: A Political Theology for Africa*. Grand Rapids: Eerdmans, 2011.

Katongole, Emmanuel, and Jonathan Wilson-Hartgrove. *Mirror to the Church: Resurrecting Faith after Genocide in Rwanda*. Grand Rapids: Zondervan, 2009.

Nebel, Mathias. "Transforming Unjust Structures: A Philosophical and Theological Perspective." *Political Theology* 12.1 (2011) 118–43.

Oppenheimer, Mark. "Miroslav Volf Spans Conflicting Worlds." https://www.religion-online.org/article/miroslav-volf-spans-conflicting-worlds/.

Phiri, Isabel Apawo. Review of *The Sacrifice of Africa: A Political Theology for Africa*, by Emmanuel Katongole. *The Ecumenical Review* 64.4 (2012) 600–604.

Pucci, Edi. "Review of Paul Ricoeur's Oneself as Another: Personal Identity, Narrative Identity and 'Selfhood' in the Thought of Paul Ricoeur." *Philosophy and Social Criticism* 18.2 (July 2015) 185–209.

Shepherd, Andrew. *The Gift of the Other: Levinas, Derrida, and a Theology of Hospitality*. United Kingdom: Clark, 2014.

Theodros A. Teklu. *The Politics of Metanoia: Towards a Post-Nationalistic Political Theology in Ethiopia*. Frankfurt: Peter Lang, 2014.

Tsegaye Emana. "Formal Letter of Instruction of Procedures towards Reconciliation." Entoto Evangelical Church Mekane Yesus Congregation. Ref. no. አማም ስ/782/10/02.

Venema, Henry. "Oneself as Another or Another as Oneself?" *Literature and Theology* 16.4 (December 2002) 410–26.

Volf, Miroslav. *After Our Likeness: The Church as the Image of the Trinity*. Grand Rapids: Eerdmans, 1998.

———. *Exclusion & Embrace: A Theological Exploration of Identity, Otherness, and Reconciliation*. Nashville: Abingdon, 1996.

Watson, Gary. "Morality as Equal Accountability: Comments on Stephen Darwall's *The Second-Person Standpoint*." *Ethics* 118 (October 2007) 37–51.

# Contributors

**Theodros A. Teklu** (PhD, Manchester University, UK) is a lecturer in theology and ethics at the Ethiopian Graduate School of Theology (EGST), and Research Associate in the department of Systematic Theology and Ecclesiology at the University of Stellenbosch, South Africa. He is also Founding Director of EGST's Centre for Christianity and Society. Theodros is the author of *The Politics of Metanoia: Towards a Post-Nationalistic Political Theology in Ethiopia* (Peter Lang, 2014) and numerous other articles and book chapters.

**Afework Hailu** (PhD, University of London) is the author of *Jewish Elements in the Ethiopian Church* (Gorgias Press, 2020). Currently, he is a lecturer in church history at the Ethiopian Graduate School of Theology. His academic interests include history of Christianity, African and Ethiopian church history, culture and culture formation, and religion and development/environment.

**Fasil Nahum**, LLB (AAU, 1968), LL M (Yale, 1971), JSD (Yale, 1975), served as Special Advisor of Ethiopian Prime Minster 1991–2017. He was founding President of Ethiopian Civil Service University (1995–98) and Director of Justice and Legal System Institute (1999–2007). He started his long career by teaching and being Dean of the Law School at Addis Ababa University. He has actively participated in drafting the various constitutions of Ethiopia since 1974. He has contributed numerous professional articles and book chapters on human rights and international humanitarian law, constitutional and administrative law, family, and criminal law. Two books he has authored are *Constitution for a Nation of Nations: The Ethiopian Prospect* (1997) and *Visions of Transforming Africa: the Challenge of Leadership* (2002).

**Sara Abdella Kedir** is a graduate of the Logos Institute in the School of Divinity at the University of St Andrews, UK. She has also earned postgraduate degrees from Ethiopian Graduate School of Theology in biblical and theological studies and a BS in electrical and computer engineering from Addis Ababa University. Her research areas and interests include "the Christian self," philosophy of education, ethics, social hermeneutics, media, and communication.

**Daniel Assefa Kassaye (*Abba*)** is a Bible scholar, researcher, and writer from Addis Ababa, Ethiopia. He obtained his MA in biblical sciences from the Pontifical Biblical Institute in Rome and his PhD in biblical theology from the Catholic Institute of Paris. His area of research includes apocalyptic literature, philology and biblical hermeneutics, with special focus on Ethiopian biblical commentaries.

**Nebeyou Alemu** holds a PhD in philology from Addis Ababa University and is currently studying theology (New Testament) at the University of South Africa. He works with Wycliffe Ethiopia as bible translation consultant.

**Youdit Tariku Feyessa** is a PhD candidate at the Vrije Universiteit Amsterdam faculty of religion and theology. She has earned her postgraduate degrees from Ethiopian Graduate School of Theology (EGST) in theology and development studies. Currently, she is a part-time instructor at EGST in systematic theology and Christian ethics.

**Samson Tadelle Demo** has earned postgraduate degrees in theology from Ethiopian Graduate School of Theology, an MD from Gondar University in medicine and a BA from Addis Ababa University in finance and developmental economics. Currently, he is a medical Director at Mercy Care Ethiopia Health Center. His interest lies in interdisciplinary research.

**Setargew Kenaw** (PhD, University of Bayreuth, Germany) is Associate Professor in the Department of Philosophy at Addis Ababa University (AAU), and serves as Editor-in-Chief of the *Ethiopian Journal of the Social Sciences and Humanities*, College of Social Sciences, AAU.

**Nishan Cheru Degaga** has earned a postgraduate degree from Ethiopian Graduate School of Theology in biblical and theological studies and is currently serving at Ethiopian Evangelical Church Mekane Yesus-Entoto Congregation.

www.ingramcontent.com/pod-product-compliance
Lightning Source LLC
Chambersburg PA
CBHW071228170426
43191CB00032B/1136